Re-storying Mediterranean Worlds

Re-storying Mediterranean Worlds

New Narratives from Italian Cultures to Global Citizenship

*Edited by Angela Biancofiore
and Clément Barniaudy*

Translations from French by Joel Duverne, Raffaella Fiorini,
Valentina Gambioli and Thémis Facon, with Kirsty Snaith

BLOOMSBURY ACADEMIC
NEW YORK · LONDON · OXFORD · NEW DELHI · SYDNEY

BLOOMSBURY ACADEMIC
Bloomsbury Publishing Inc
1385 Broadway, New York, NY 10018, USA
50 Bedford Square, London, WC1B 3DP, UK
29 Earlsfort Terrace, Dublin 2, Ireland

BLOOMSBURY, BLOOMSBURY ACADEMIC and the Diana logo
are trademarks of Bloomsbury Publishing Plc

First published in the United States of America 2022
This paperback edition published 2023

Copyright © Angela Biancofiore and Clément Barniaudy, 2022
Each chapter © of Contributors

For legal purposes the Acknowledgements on p. xiii–xv constitute
an extension of this copyright page.

Cover design: Namkwan Cho
Cover image © Angela Biancofiore, *Clear light*, 2020

All rights reserved. No part of this publication may be reproduced or
transmitted in any form or by any means, electronic or mechanical,
including photocopying, recording, or any information storage or
retrieval system, without prior permission in writing from the publishers.

Bloomsbury Publishing Inc does not have any control over, or responsibility for,
any third-party websites referred to or in this book. All internet addresses given
in this book were correct at the time of going to press. The author and publisher
regret any inconvenience caused if addresses have changed or sites have
ceased to exist, but can accept no responsibility for any such changes.

Library of Congress Cataloging-in-Publication Data
Names: Biancofiore, Angela, editor. | Barniaudy, Clément, editor. | Duverne,
Joel, translator. | Fiorini, Raffaella, translator. | Gambioli, Valentina, translator. |
Facon, Thémis, translator. | Snaith, Kirsty, translator.
Title: Re-storying Mediterranean worlds : new narratives from Italian cultures to global citizenship /
edited by Angela Biancofiore and Clément Barniaudy ; translations from French by Joel Duverne,
Raffaella Fiorini, Valentina Gambioli and Thémis Facon, with Kirsty Snaith.
Description: New York : Bloomsbury Academic, 2021. | Includes bibliographical references and index. |
Summary: "An investigation of Mediterranean worlds (history, literature, geography, arts)
between past, present and future, in relation to the interaction among archaic cultures,
sustainability and ongoing globalization"– Provided by publisher.
Identifiers: LCCN 2021007685 (print) | LCCN 2021007686 (ebook) | ISBN 9781501378935
(hardback) | ISBN 9781501378942 (eBook) | ISBN 9781501378959 (ePDF)
Subjects: LCSH: Mediterranean Region–Literatures–History and criticism. |
Literature and globalization–Mediterranean Region. | Mediterranean
Region–Intellectual life. | Postcolonialism in literature. | Postmodernism
(Literature) | LCGFT: Literary criticism. | Essays.
Classification: LCC PN849.M42 R47 2021 (print) | LCC PN849.M42 (ebook) |
DDC 809/.93358209822–dc23
LC record available at https://lccn.loc.gov/2021007685
LC ebook record available at https://lccn.loc.gov/2021007686

ISBN:	HB:	978-1-5013-7893-5
	PB:	978-1-5013-7897-3
	ePDF:	978-1-5013-7895-9
	eBook:	978-1-5013-7894-2

Typeset by Integra Software Services Pvt. Ltd.

To find out more about our authors and books visit www.bloomsbury.com
and sign up for our newsletters.

To the Drowned and the Saved of the Mediterranean Sea

CONTENTS

List of Figures ix
Notes on Contributors x
Acknowledgements xiii

   Introduction: Thinking interconnected worlds 1
   Angela Biancofiore and Clément Barniaudy

1 Mediterranean worlds: Towards an ecology of creation 7
   Angela Biancofiore

2 An impossible abode: The world and modernity 21
   Myriam Carminati

3 Literary Sardness: Between colonialism and postcolonialism, Creoleness and Creolization 35
   Margherita Marras

4 From house to archipelago: Ways of inhabiting Mediterranean worlds 59
   Clément Barniaudy

5 Pasolini and the Mediterranean: Lost cultural worlds and the reappearance of archaic worlds 81
   Matthias Quemener

6 The Mediterranean panorama through migrant writers 97
   Vittorio Valentino

7 The other Mediterranean: Italian migration poetry 111
   Flaviano Pisanelli

8 Naples and Europe, past and future: The *Sud* review – a link between the Mediterranean and Europe 129
   Cathryn Baril

9 The Mediterranean town in question 149
   Raffaele Cattedra

10 Testimony: Where is Tunisia going? 175
   Fethi Nagga

11 Trilingualism in Tunisia: A disturbing topic 179
   Alfonso Campisi

12 The Charter of Palermo: The future of a utopia 183
   Jean Duflot

Appendix: The Charter of Palermo 191
Subject Index 202
Names Index 208

FIGURES

4.1 Sketch of a primitive house under Mount Ida (Crete) 63

4.2 External and internal views of the Cabanon in Cap Martin (France) 64

4.3 Marseilles' Cité Radieuse (France) 66

4.4 Architecture and landscape on the island of Santorini (Greece) 69

4.5 Human beings between inside and outside, at one with their environment source 71

4.6 The wind towers of Yazd (Iran) 74

CONTRIBUTORS

Cathryn Baril is an independent researcher in Italian Studies who collaborates with Paul Valéry University of Montpellier, France. She has worked within the Premio Napoli foundation where she met some Italian authors such as the Neapolitan writer Raffaele La Capria. Trained in digital communication, she is also a consultant for companies and works with students at the PPA School of Business and Communication (Paris).

Clément Barniaudy is Associate Professor of Geography at the University of Montpellier, France, and a member of the research centre LIRDEF (Laboratoire Interdisciplinaire de Recherche en Didactique, Education et Formation). His teaching and research interests lie in ecocultural studies, the environmental humanities and geographical education. His PhD (titled 'To live with the wind in the North-Western Mediterranean area') led him to explore how our practices can be embodied in a living and inhabited environment. More recently, he continues his research by focusing on the theories and practices of *care* in relation to land use planning and with transformative education. On this subject he has published several articles and the book *Aménager au gré des vents: La géographie au service de l'action* (2018).

Angela Biancofiore is Professor of Italian Studies at Paul Valéry University in Montpellier, France, and a member of the research centre ReSO (Recherches sur les Suds et les Orients). Her current research explores the relationship between ecology and artistic creation (arts and literature). She has published several books and articles on Italian studies and Mediterranean literature and the arts, among others *Benvenuto Cellini artiste-écrivain* (1998) and *Pasolini* (Italian edition 2003; French edition 2012). She is a co-founder of the Theory and Practice of Care international centre of studies (https://tepcare.hypotheses.org), linking the ethics of care to the ecological humanities. Since 2011, she has been the editor of the online review *Notos. Espaces de la création: arts, écritures, utopies* (http://notos.numerev.com). Her recent publications include 'Land Ethics and the Appropriation of Living Beings' (in R. Pérez, ed., *Agorapoetics*, 2016) and 'Care et éducation: pour une transformation de l'esprit', *Notos*, 5 (2020).

Alfonso Campisi is Professor of Romance and Italian Philology at the Faculty of Letters, Arts and Humanities of Manouba University, Tunisia. He is interested in the languages and cultures of the Mediterranean and the dialogue between cultures and civilizations. His recent research focuses on the identity, language, culture and history of Tunisia, and Sicilians who emigrated to France, Tunisia and the United States. He holds the chair for Sicilian Language and Culture. Among his publications are *Trilinguisme en Tunisie* (2013), *Mparamu lu sicilianu* (2019) and *I meticci italo-africani nel Corno d'Africa* (2020).

Myriam Carminati is Emeritus Professor of Italian Studies at the Paul Valéry University of Montpellier, France. Her research focuses on Italian literature and poetry, art history, aesthetics and interculturality, exploring the relations between tradition and modernity. She is the author of a book on the poet Umberto Saba, *Le chemin et la voix* (1999), and she is the editor of *Umberto Saba au carrefour des mondes* (2008) and *Parcours et rencontres: La traversée infinie* (2017). She has also published several articles on Italian writers (Ludovico Ariosto, Carducci, Campana, Rebora, Caproni) and painters (Parmigianino, Caravaggio, De Chirico, Morandi).

Raffaele Cattedra is Professor of Geography at the Department of Letters, Languages and Cultural Heritage at the University of Cagliari, Italy, and teaches the geography of the Mediterranean area and the geography of cultural heritage. He works on urban and territorial issues using a comparative approach (Mediterranean region, Europe, Arab world, Africa). His research in the field of geographical theories focuses on sacred and public spaces, cultural heritage and the processes of migration and globalization. Among his latest publications (with other editors) is *Cagliari: Geografie e visioni di una città* (2021).

Jean Duflot is a French writer and reporter working for the *Forum civique européen*. He has published many papers and books on human rights and social justice. He is the author of a book interview with Pier Paolo Pasolini (1981). In 2020, he was distinguished with the major prize *Prix Montluc Résistance et liberté* for his book *Palerme ville ouverte* (2019), an award given to authors who promote freedom and respect for human rights and human dignity. His recent publications include *De la migration comme souffrance à la mobilité comme droit de l'homme inaliénable: Palerme une charte de la dissidence* (2019) and *Roms: voyage chez les autres* (2016).

Margherita Marras is Associate Professor of Foreign Languages at the University of Avignon, France, and a member of the research centre in Italian Studies (CRIX: Centre de Recherches Italiennes de Paris X) at the University of Paris-Nanterre. Her research focuses on insular literatures and identities

(Italy and France), postcolonialism and globalization, gender studies and North–South dialogue. She has published many essays and articles and has edited several volumes, including *Femminismi: teoria, critica e letteratura nell'Italia degli anni 2000* (2015), *Una vita due volte vissuta. Giulio Angioni scrittore e antropologo* (2020) and *Inventions du Sud* (2020).

Fethi Nagga is Assistant Professor of Italian Language and Literature at Tunis El Manar University, Tunisia, in the Translation Department. His teaching and research interests are in the fields of translation and comparative literature. He is a member of the CISDID (Centro Internazionale per lo Studio e la Didattica dell'Italiano e dei Dialetti) at the Gabriele d'Annunzio Chieti-Pescara University, Italy. He has translated several books from French to Italian, including Ahmed Abdessalem, *Ibn Khaldun e i suoi lettori* (2008) and Jalel Abdelkefi, *Medina di Tunisi: Spazio storico* (2010), and from Arabic to Italian, *Antologia di Poeti Tunisini* (2019).

Flaviano Pisanelli is Professor of Italian Language and Literature at Paul Valéry University in Montpellier, France, and a member of the ReSO (Recherches sur les Suds et les Orients) research centre. He is a poet and a translator. He has published several critical studies on the literary and cinematographic works of Pier Paolo Pasolini as well as on twentieth- and twenty-first-century Italian poetry (Ungaretti, Montale, Scalesi, Quasimodo, Bufalino and Merini). Lately, his scientific research has focused on italophone poetry of migration and on the intercultural exchanges of the Mediterranean area. Among the latest publications is *Confini di-versi: Frontiere, orizzonti e prospettive della poesia italofona contemporanea* (with Laura Toppan, 2019).

Matthias Quemener is a former French foreign language teacher and current head of French studies at HRSK (Helsingin Ranskalais-Suomalainen Koulu), the French-Finnish school of Helsinki. During his master's degree in Cultural Studies, he focused his research on the question of the sacred, especially through the work of Pasolini, Bataille and Caillois. He then turned to French teaching to a non-native public. He worked in different bilingual schools, in Eastern Europe and has now reached Finland – new culture, new myths – pursuing his journey and discoveries.

Vittorio Valentino is Assistant Professor at the Tunis University of Manouba, Tunisia. In 2013, he obtained a PhD in Romance Studies working on the link between engaged French and Italian literature and migration in the Mediterranean between 1950 and 2003. His research fields include migrant literature, postcolonialism, feminist writing, ecocriticism and ethics of care. He has published several papers focusing on authors such as De Luca, Lakhous, Scego, Abate, Santangelo, Camilleri and Iovino, as well as the book *Le panorama littéraire méditerraneen entre migrations et engagement* (2018).

ACKNOWLEDGEMENTS

The story of this book started in 2008, at Paul Valéry University in Montpellier, France. At that time, we organized a monthly seminar entitled *Habiter la terre* ('Inhabiting the Earth') attended by many scholars, teachers and students; it was really a precious opportunity for all of us to nourish an intellectual and human dialogue focused on Mediterranean cultures, within different fields such as poetry, ecology, geopolitics, philosophy, arts and more.

In the years thereafter, thanks to the support of our research centre LLACS (Langues, Littératures Arts et Cultures des Suds, which was renamed in 2021 ReSO, Recherches sur les Suds et les Orients), we were able to invite numerous authors in order to gain a direct understanding of their work, in particular migrant writers of the northern and southern Mediterranean basin.

The meetings and seminars we organized at the University of Montpellier marked the key phases in the elaboration of the present volume, in particular, among others, the three annual conferences *Pour une poésie de l'utopie: écriture, frontière, migration* (2011–13), the seminar *Poétiques de l'altérité: littératures, arts, sociétés d'Italie et d'ailleurs* (2012), the international symposium *Pour une écologie de la création: un engagement pour la terre* (2013) and the annual seminar *Éthique de la terre: art, littérature environnement* (2014–15).

In a sense, we can perceive our collective path as a *journey* and this book as a *ship* navigating the waters of the Mediterranean Sea: every stage of this volume is for us like a port of call on the coasts of the *mare nostrum*. Then we set sail from Montpellier with our *crew* constituted by the contributors of the book that we would like to acknowledge with gratitude for their generosity since they offered their research, words and patience during the long gestation of this collection.

Continuing the metaphor, our ship arrived at the Mediterranean port of Cagliari, Sardinia, where an international conference was held in 2010 entitled *Frontiere in-visibili: culture, letterature, paesaggi fra Sardegna e Mediterraneo* (University of Cagliari).

In 2011, the intense continuous debate on Mediterranean studies encouraged us to found the online review *Notos. Espaces de la création: arts, écritures, utopies* (https://notos.numerev.com) in order to publish the papers and interviews that emerged from our common theoretical work over time. In this regard, we would particularly like to thank Julien Mary, Lise Verlaet, Frédéric Rousseau and all the team of *Numerev* (the digital platform of the Maison des Sciences de l'Homme, Paul Valéry University, Montpellier) for their support of *Notos*, which published in French most of the studies gathered in our book. Moreover, the essays were entirely revised and amended for the present publication.

The idea of a collective book took form thanks to Peter Carravetta, Professor at Stony Brook University, who invited us in 2009 to the symposium *Migrations and Transnational Identities: Crossing Borders, Bridging Disciplines* (Stony Brook University). His attentive listening and enthusiasm have nourished our willingness and determination over the years in realizing the volume. His vision of the Mediterranean – both mythical and historical – has inspired us on the path, resonating implicitly in numerous pages of the book.

Our collective reflection on Mediterranean worlds has been enriched by the contribution of Jean Duflot, who has been working closely with Pier Paolo Pasolini and, more recently, with Leoluca Orlando, the mayor of Palermo. Since his essay 'Palermo Open City' represented a source of inspiration for us, we would like to express our gratitude for his courageous work as an investigative journalist highlighting the harsh living conditions of migrants in the Mediterranean area.

During the process of gestation of the book, we were also accompanied by the translators that we want to thank for their crucial role: Joel Duverne, Raffaella Fiorini, Thémis Faucon, Valentina Gambioli, Kirsty Snaith. The translation was made possible through the financial support of our research centre LLACS and the Scientific Advisory Board of Paul Valéry University; our deep thanks go to Jean-Michel Ganteau, Anita Gonzalez, Fabrice Quero and Madeleine Voga who believed in our editorial project.

It is meaningful for us to express our gratitude to Amy Martin from Bloomsbury for her constant support for our project at the different stages of the submission of the manuscript, and our heartfelt thanks to Linsey Hague for her careful editing of the final manuscript. Furthermore, we would like to thank the reviewers of the volume for their time and their valuable advice.

We achieved our editorial work in the time of Covid-19, during the pandemic and lockdown, at the core of a historical sanitary crisis which calls us to engender a new insight into ecology and caring. We are convinced that our theoretical work as teachers and researchers is fundamentally linked to our practices; therefore, we need to embody our values if we want to enhance coherence in each research activity. In other words, a hyper-specialized knowledge accumulating over time does not match our rapidly changing world.

In fact, we affirm the necessity of building new forms of individual and collective narratives in order to root ourselves in a common project considering the vital role of the ecological issue and social justice. However, new narratives would not be disconnected from old forms of narrative related to a place, a native culture and a living ecosystem: in re-storying Mediterranean worlds, we engaged on a path starting from Italian culture and leading to global citizenship.

In conclusion, through the pandemic we have learnt that now more than ever we are interwoven in a web of entangled destinies; therefore, it is urgent for us that we build a *situated* knowledge, harmonizing global and local dimensions, considering the individual within the ecosystem he or she lives in. This new narrative will give a sense to our being on Earth from the wider perspective of a global ethics.

Introduction: Thinking interconnected worlds

Angela Biancofiore and Clément Barniaudy

The chapters gathered in this book invite the reader to *think of Mediterranean worlds* as *interconnected worlds*, seen in the light of how they evolve, disappear, are reborn and perpetually transform. For a number of years, our research centre at Paul Valéry University in Montpellier (Langues, Littératures, Arts et Cultures des Suds, LLACS) has organized several meetings and seminars on Mediterranean worlds, creating bridges between the northern and southern coasts of our sea. Many Mediterranean researchers, writers and artists have been invited to meet a varied public, including the students and teachers from our university, in order to broaden and deepen our understanding of current evolution in Mediterranean worlds, at the cultural, literary, artistic and geopolitical levels. This collective work invites us to *reflect on the Mediterranean worlds* of today, despite the *deep rifts* between the Northern and Southern Mediterranean, as well as between the Eastern and Western worlds.

As Paul Valéry ([1933] 1960: 1135) suggested, we can consider this plural space from the perspective of the intense cultural, economic and human exchanges that have always characterized the *mare nostrum*. A vital space, a heart beating with life and exchanges, the *Mediterranean city* has always been a meeting place for people from cultures of different origins. These people have learned, down through the millennia, to *live together* despite the conflicts, by creating profound links between civilizations and different languages, between past and present.

Seen from the outside, today the Mediterranean seems more divided than ever. '*La mer aux deux rives*' ('the sea with two coasts') dear to Jacques Berque is being fragmented into a multitude of territories that are increasingly distant from each other. Visible and invisible walls strengthen the divergent trajectories between North and South, Orient and Occident, Europe, North Africa and the Middle East. On television, the images of shipwrecked migrants arriving from the other coast alternate with those of their rescue by the military patrols or by non-governmental organizations (NGOs) such as SOS Méditerranée. The press rarely shows us what happens next in their journey, the detention camps which have become the symbol of the distant and ambiguous relationships between political entities with different interests.

However, this outside view of the Mediterranean is too approximate a translation of what people are really living and thinking, how they are perceiving it from the inside. To avoid the temptation to substitute those experienced realities with incorrect images, it has become urgent to *reflect on Mediterranean worlds*, starting with focusing on what they are not.

The Mediterranean is not 'multiple'; it is not composed of a juxtaposition of worlds which ignore and oppose one another. Raffaele Cattedra shows in his chapter (Chapter 9) that the categories of Western, Eastern or Arab-Muslim cities do not resist a precise analysis of their urban forms. The invention of these categories is merely a way of reducing Southern and Eastern Mediterranean cities to an idea of *disorder* and *archaism*, leading to a single horizon: the adoption of a European city model. The complexity of Mediterranean cities is, on the contrary, the fruit of centuries of exchanges and interactions among the Mediterranean worlds.

Likewise, Vittorio Valentino (Chapter 6) reminds us that the Mediterranean area constructed itself over the centuries thanks to migration, a phenomenon that played a crucial role as the *engine for the development of Mediterranean history*, creating relationships of conflict and hospitality simultaneously for the migrants.

For all these reasons, the Mediterranean is not *one*. In fact, Mediterranean worlds cannot be reduced to a cultural or political universal truth. Flaviano Pisanelli (Chapter 7) highlights the reactualization, throughout history, of a Euro-Mediterranean universal truth with Graeco-Roman roots that is opposed to all forms of reciprocity and openness. The supposed homogeneous identity of the Romans' *Mare Nostrum*, reconsidered in the Middle Ages and reinforced in the modern era, is in fact the support for political domination and acculturation of the *other people* residing by the sea. The idea of the Mediterranean as a cradle and a 'melting pot' of civilizations does not leave enough space for the plurality of Mediterranean worlds.

Margherita Marras (Chapter 3) uses a postcolonial approach to show how the Sardinian identity has been frozen by the writers from the continental centre's elite. Overcoming universal values imposed on insular minorities thus consists of embracing the diversity, without, however, withdrawing into an exclusive cultural particularism.

Neither is re-storying Mediterranean worlds today about conceiving worlds that come together under the influence of macroeconomic and technoscientific powers. Angela Biancofiore (Chapter 1) invites us to measure the violence exercised by the supporters of a neoliberal utopia on Mediterranean cultural and living ecosystems. Behind the images propagated by the omnipresent media colonizing our imagination, a slow violence disenchants our relationship with the Earth and standardizes our ways of being in the world. It is precisely this same standardization of cultural worlds that Pasolini denounced in his works. The reinterpretation of Pasolinian thought by Matthias Quemener (Chapter 5) leads us to see the need to rethink the central role of *myth*: we need *a new collective narrative* in order to transform old habits and cultural models that are clearly threatening the life of ecosystems. He states: 'The Mediterranean is this *summary of natural poetry*, whose aesthetic resonances awaken in Pasolini a kind of wonder which is at the basis of the opening to *otherness*'.

Without reducing them to *One* or to *Multiple*, we can consider Mediterranean worlds within an open enactive process, deeply exploring their evolution between nature and culture. We can see that a new attention has emerged regarding the natural environment and all sentient beings which can deeply transform the relationships between humans and non-humans. Clément Barniaudy (Chapter 4) thus presents a number of ways of inhabiting that make the space on the inside and outside porous: appropriate territory and endless environment, inner refuge and external action. It is therefore possible to think about an immanent and rhythmic relationship to the world, which may release human beings from their exclusive affiliations and integrate them into a vast, *biotic community* (see on this topic Callicott 2013).

Mediterranean spaces can become the simple basis for a sensible and creative experience, which reverses the uni-dimensionality of the techno-economical world and allows the sense of the *sacred* to rise again. Moreover, Myriam Carminati (Chapter 2) addresses the issue of the *habitability of the world* through the artistic and literary creation of certain Mediterranean authors. Her reflection underlines the *anti-humanism* of some contemporary artists, whose performances are based on the 'scandal effect' more than on a genuine creative thought. Re-storying Mediterranean worlds means somehow creating a dialogue between those worlds, in order to understand the inherent links connecting their becomings.

Cathryn Baril (Chapter 8) shows how the city of Naples lost its attractiveness and wealth in the Mediterranean and in Europe as soon as it withdrew into the cult of an identity fed by a populist and self-referenced discourse. Likewise, Alfonso Campisi (Chapter 11) denounces the aporia of an imposed Arabic language, which ignores the rich and complex interbreeding of the Tunisian language, use of which furthermore makes it possible for the various Mediterranean worlds to meet. In addition, Fethi Nagga (Chapter 10) reflects on the consequences of the Tunisian revolution of 2011; it is a precious account, written during the events, about an unprecedented historical phenomenon seen from the inside during its difficult evolution.

It appears that nowadays writers and researchers deeply express the need to find a dialogue between the two coasts in order to connect what has been broken. By following their voices, it is possible to encounter the *Poetics of Relation*, which allows us to highlight an intercultural and creolized conscience, traversing the Mediterranean worlds and transcending any idea of communitarian withdrawal. Currently, more than ever, Mediterranean worlds are facing the interaction between *archaic cultures* and *globalization*. In today's literary creation, the strong presence of *archaic myths* and *regional languages* reveals a Mediterranean that is deeply connected to the knowledge of its own cultural origins, without, moreover, being attached to a bygone past.

From regional cultures, contemporary writers draw the energy they need to open themselves up to the world on a planetary scale: they are the *antibodies* facing a globalization that progressively tends to erase the differences (on this topic, see the literary works of Erri De Luca, Marcello Fois, Michela Murgia, Carmine Abate, Cosimo Argentina, Anselmo Botte among others).

Today, Mediterranean worlds are going through two major crises: a *political-humanitarian crisis* and an *ecological crisis*. Regarding the political and humanitarian crisis, Europe is in fact building barriers, a quarter of a century after the fall of the Berlin Wall, to limit the arrival of refugees escaping war and famine.

Since 1988, we have witnessed the landing of thousands of people but also a high number of shipwrecks. The Mediterranean is also one of the most dangerous borders in the world, *a front* where hundreds of thousands of migrants risk their lives every day. In order to deeply understand the history of the Mediterranean and the geopolitical context of an area in which the destinies of three continents (Asia, Africa and Europe) come together, it is essential that we abandon the term 'victim' when referring to those shipwrecked, and also give a detailed overview of the vast political and strategic context in which the departures are multiplying. The Italian writer Alessandro Leogrande, in his book *La frontiera* (2015), helps us to penetrate the extremely complex and always changing universe of migration in today's Mediterranean. In order to transform our insight on the question of migration, Jean Duflot (Chapter 12), an investigative journalist, introduces a radically innovative policy document, the *Charter of Palermo*, written during an international conference organized in 2015 by Leoluca Orlando, Mayor of Palermo: if we understand that there is a urgent need to shift 'From migration as suffering to mobility as an unalienable human right', we can build the foundation of a new idea of global citizenship.

On a different level, though one that is not separate from the geopolitical aspect, the *ecological crisis* questions authors and artists, to such an extent that it constitutes a significant axis of a great number of books.[1]

Many writers have highlighted the *relationship with the natural world*: far from being a step backwards, it is a reflection on *ways of inhabiting the Earth, our world*, this 'wonderful oasis in a sidereal desert' (Rabhi 2008). It is also a way of reaffirming the importance of biological and cultural diversity in order to build *a world where there would be enough space for a plurality of worlds* (see Merchant 1983; Shiva 2015; Iovino 2016; Morin 2020).

Nowadays, if we want to understand *Mediterranean worlds* it is absolutely essential that we *restore the idea of 'limit' or 'measure'*, while recognizing our inherent fragility (see in this regard Miguel Benasayag's (2004) essay, *La Fragilité* and Franco Cassano (2012), *Il pensiero meridiano*). Only *by transforming our inner vision* might it be possible to explore the ancient and modern forms of inhabiting, bearing in mind that we are *guests* and not the *masters* of our planet; in a sense, 'the way out is in' (Thich Nhat Hanh 2008).

Some of the authors featured in this book invite us to revisit the past of Mediterranean worlds, with the purpose of *rewriting history*, because it is vital to *re-found the values from another perspective*. The role of Mediterranean writers, scientists, scholars and artists is crucial for rebuilding relationships, forging another vision of the past and connecting *culture and politics, writing and action*.

If we consider the perspective of the great Mediterranean authors of the twentieth century, Valéry and Camus, Elytis and Pasolini, it is possible to *re-enchant Mediterranean worlds*; this is the answer to a civilization of the artificial, which increasingly deprives human beings of their relationship with Nature. In this regard, the critical thought of Edgar Morin, Franco Cassano, Armando Gnisci and Miguel Benasayag open up theoretical and practical perspectives on the way to *decolonize our Western and European imaginary*, in a vast process of *reconstructing our relationship to the sacred* (see Pasolini 1975; Castoriadis 2010; Dupuy 2013).

To conclude, re-storying Mediterranean worlds is opening up a shared horizon, affirming the need for *another utopia* that gives new substance to the values elaborated down through centuries within those cultural worlds: hospitality, solidarity, sobriety, slowness, contemplation, openness. A utopia that spreads out via the interstices of the cultural worlds, meeting what

---

[1] See the section 'Literature and Ecology' in Biancofiore, Summa and Ben Abdallah 2016: 125–98.

emerges from the Mediterranean – etymologically, the 'sea in the middle of lands'. Therefore, realizing a utopian leap is to create *a new possible horizon* that resists nihilism and the utilitarian rationality of the neoliberal utopia, a *global ethics* beyond any difference in cultures and religions. In addition, a *Mediterranean utopia* is already nourished by several voices that narrate, experience, translate, inform and dialogue with the plurality of interwoven worlds, in order to give a sense of being and dwelling together.

For all these reasons, it is vital today that we *rethink Mediterranean worlds, re-storying our present, past and future,* focusing on new forms of narrative, from Italian cultures to global citizenship. This is the common goal of the studies gathered in this work of many voices.

References

Benasayag, M. (2004), *La fragilité*, Paris: La Découverte.
Biancofiore, A., Summa R. and Ben Abdallah S. (eds) (2016), *Soyons le changement … Nouvelles tendances dans la littérature italienne contemporaine*, Montpellier: Euromedia & Levant.
Callicott, J. B. (2013), *Thinking Like a Planet: The Land Ethic and the Earth Ethic*, New York: Oxford University Press.
Cassano, F. (2012), *Southern Thought and Other Essays on the Mediterranean*, trans. Norma Bouchard and Valerio Ferme, New York: Fordham University Press.
Castoriadis, C. (2010), *A Society Adrift: Interviews and Debates, 1974–1997*, New York: Fordham University Press.
Dupuy, J. P. (2013), *The Mark of the Sacred*, Palo Alto, CA: Stanford University Press.
Iovino, S. (2016), *Ecocriticism in Italy: Ecology, Resistance, and Liberation*, London: Bloomsbury.
Merchant, C. (1983), *The Death of Nature: Women, Ecology and the Scientific Revolution*, New York: Harper & Row.
Morin, E. (2020), *L'entrée dans l'ère écologique*, Paris: L'Aube.
Pasolini, P. P. (1975), *Scritti Corsari*, Milan: Garzanti.
Rabhi, P. (2008), *Manifeste pour la Terre et l'humanisme*, Arles: Actes Sud.
Shiva, V. (2015), *Earth Democracy: Justice, Sustainability and Peace*, Berkeley, CA: North Atlantic Books.
Thich Nhat Hanh (2008), *The World We Have*, Berkeley, CA: Parallax Press.
Valéry, P. ([1933] 1960), *Œuvres*, vol. 2, Paris: Gallimard.

1

Mediterranean worlds: Towards an ecology of creation

Angela Biancofiore

> *The long tradition that can be called solar thought, in which, since the time of the Greeks, nature has always been balanced with becoming.*
>
> ALBERT CAMUS (1965: 701)

The front of olive trees

There is a region in the south of France where olives are no longer picked: the olive trees are full of olives; the trees stand proud on the hills, but no one harvests the fruit anymore. The farmers interviewed say that it is too expensive and that it is better to purchase Spanish oil because it is cheaper than picking olives.

The forgotten tree, *the olive tree, the symbol par excellence of the Mediterranean*, is no longer a source of life or food; it is becoming a decoration for roundabouts and gardens. A *front* is forming, a border that separates the countries where olives are still harvested from countries that have forgotten how important the tree, the earth and its fruits are.

Mediterranean worlds seem to waver between a programmed modernity that distances them from their past and the renewal of certain archaic values. A double movement is appearing in literature and arts: the disappearance of ancient cultural worlds sometimes leaves a worrying void, where ancient values are not replaced by new ones or new collective projects (Biancofiore

2010). Moreover, in recent years the uprising of the people from the southern shores of the Mediterranean demonstrates their willingness to access democracy and a different management of the State. The Tunisians who sacrificed themselves in the 2011 movements were asking for more justice in the distribution of wealth and more transparency in the exercise of power, among other things. The Mediterranean people in Egypt, Syria and Libya also want to write another page in their history, regardless of the cost.

The ravages of a world without measure

Mediterranean worlds are also victims of *excess*: at the end of a tragedy, the Greek hero realizes that he dwells in *hubris*, but it is already too late. Mediterranean cultures can rediscover *phronesis*, the ancient measure that establishes harmony in relationships with the world. On this topic, it is interesting to quote the Mediterranean author Albert Camus, who denounced the abandonment of the cult of beauty through a process that he defined as 'Helen's Exile': Greek culture knew how to fight in the name of beauty and it cultivated the contemplation of nature; yet our world has removed beauty and sees nature as nothing more than a reservoir of exploitable materials. Camus thus continued:

> The Mediterranean sun has something tragic about it, quite different from the tragedy of fogs. Certain evenings at the base of the seaside mountains, night falls over the flawless curve of a little bay, and there rises from the silent waters a sense of anguished fulfillment. In such spots one can understand that if the Greeks knew despair, they always did so through beauty and its stifling quality. In that gilded calamity, tragedy reaches its highest point. Our time, on the other hand, has fed its despair on ugliness and convulsions. [...] We have exiled beauty; the Greeks took up arms for her. First difference, but one that has a history. Greek thought always took refuge behind the conception of limits. It never carried anything to extremes, neither the sacred nor reason. ('Helen's Exile', in Camus 1965: 853)

Camus clearly felt that there was a threat weighing down on our society ever since *contemplating nature* was replaced by the *unlimited exploitation of natural resources*. This action is only possible in a universe dominated by the worship of money and its *abstract symbols*. Camus precisely evaluated the nature of this danger, one that is growing within a society that is mainly founded on abstraction; this is what he proclaimed loud and clear during the speech he made after being awarded the Nobel Prize:

For about a century we have been living in a society that is not even the society of money (gold can arouse carnal passions) but that of the abstract symbols of money. The society of merchants can be defined as a society in which things disappear in favor of signs. When a ruling class measures its fortunes, not by the acre of land or the lingot of gold, but by the number of figures corresponding ideally to a certain number of exchange operations, it thereby condemns itself to setting a certain kind of humbug at the center of its experience and its universe. A society founded on signs is, in its essence, an artificial society in which man's carnal truth is handled as something artificial. There is no reason for being surprised that such a society chose as its religion a moral code of formal principles and that it inscribes the words 'liberty' and 'equality' on its prisons as well as on its temples of finance. However, words cannot be prostituted with impunity. ('Discours de Suède', in Camus 1965: 1082)

The liberal utopia, which imagines a limitless expansion of development, is heading towards catastrophe; this is why, today, economists and sociologists are developing alternative models, in order to initiate a process of *decolonizing the imagination based on an ethic of decrease* (see Latouche 2010 on this point).

We should start by decolonizing our Western minds with regard to our relationship with nature. Nature has become denatured and deprived of its 'bewitching' power; we are, to a certain extent, responsible for a process of *disenchantment of the world* that has taken place within an artificial universe built by humans and increasingly separated from the natural world. On this matter, Hannah Arendt's voice helps us to better understand the condition of modern human being:

The human artifice of the world separates human existence from all mere animal environment, but life itself is outside this artificial world, and through life man remains related to all other living organisms. For some time now, a great many scientific endeavors have been directed toward making life also 'artificial,' toward cutting the last tie through which even man belongs among the children of nature. [...] This future man, whom the scientists tell us they will produce in no more than a hundred years, seems to be possessed by a rebellion against human existence as it has been given, a free gift from nowhere (secularly speaking), which he wishes to exchange, as it were, for something he has made himself. (1958: 2–3)

Similarly, Carolyn Merchant (1983), in her book *The Death of Nature*, condemns today's mechanisms that have progressively consolidated the power of techno-science in the living sphere, starting with the philosophical theories of Bacon. To counteract this dominant trend that aims to appropriate living beings, Serge Latouche (2010), an economist who runs counter to official thought, suggested a *Mediterranean utopia* that is in harmony with the ideas of Franco Cassano (2005, 2012): the countries of Southern Europe, such as Greece, Italy, Spain and France, would be much more open to the idea of degrowth, maybe because of their relationship to an archaic, pre-Christian, pre-capitalist culture, as if the genes embedded in a culture are always able to resurface one day. The *Southern thought*, as formulated by Cassano (2005), focuses on a vision of the South that differs from the one that the North tries to transfer on it: it is the image of the *South through its own eyes*, based on its own standards, rhythms, ways of life and desire to meet others. Today, the south of Italy wants to rewrite its history; in fact, many historians and journalists consider it to be a colony that has been the overexploited by the North, starting with the process of political unification of the peninsula (see, among others, Aprile 2010). If we focus our vision on the ensemble of 'Southern' worlds, we are not only forced to consider the southern shore of the Mediterranean but also Africa, Latin America and India, regions that are now keen to assert their cultural and political presence in the world. New ways of thinking are being developed by the 'Southern worlds', with new analysis tools and a new imagination that opposes the rational, pragmatic vision of the Western world.

A message of considerable significance has recently been broadcast by Vandana Shiva, an Indian epistemologist who is drawing attention to the disappearance of rural agriculture. She denounces the deportation of the people of her country (and the rest of the world) generated by the exploitation of land resources. One of her books is *The Seeds of Suicide*; the title refers to hybrid cotton seeds which are distributed by multinationals. These seeds require large quantities of chemical products, pushing farmers into debt. As a result, the seeds have provoked an unprecedented wave of suicides in India. Shiva is convinced that we need to believe in the fertility of the Earth and that we need to upgrade the ancient terms of our relationship with the ground that the 'green revolution' (meaning the negative revolution that is the result of introducing chemical products into agriculture) has erased by imposing industrial agriculture (for more on this topic, see the film by Coline Serreau, *Local Solutions for Global Disorder* (2010) and the essay *Ecofeminism* by V. Shiva and M. Mies (1993)).

Believing in both nature and the possibility of harmony with its laws is the issue behind the fight for seed banks, a means of avoiding the expropriation of traditional knowledge by agri-food multinationals. Shiva's theoretical and political commitment is a fight for life, a combat against the violence of technology and modern science that often carry out their activities at the expense of both nature and the body (for more on this topic, see also Illich 1973). One of the paradoxical outcomes of thought focused on the negation of nature is '*off-ground cultivation*': we are now eating products that are no longer the fruits of the earth, products whose roots are no longer nourished by the soil but instead 'artificially fed', a sort of *artificial nature under infusion*.

Authors and the Earth: New ways of committing

Since the earliest days of Mediterranean culture, people have invented sacred places – *sanctuaries* – such as those near the tombs of Greek heroes, or later, of Christian martyrs. Many Mediterranean authors have *lived* and celebrated the fertility of *their* earth; one of these authors is Cesare Pavese, who, in the 1940s, clearly depicted the emergence of sacred and mythical places:

> In the clearings, feasts, flowers, and sacrifices, on the edge of mystery that shows signs and threatens among the sylvan shadows. There on the border between the sky and the trunk, God could have emerged. Now, the character, – I'm not talking about poetry –, of mythical fable is the consecration of unique places, tied to a fact to a deed to an event. To a place, among everything, an absolute meaning is given, isolating it in the world. This way, places of childhood come back to memory to everyone; in these places happened things that made them unique, and distinguish them from the rest of the world with this mythical seal. ('Myth, symbols, and more', in Pavese [1940–5] 2002: 126)

Through the relationship with the earth that is built up within his pages, Pavese closely resembles Camus, who celebrates the *nuptials* of humans with the earth:

> the season trembles and the summer slips away. The carob trees breathe the scent of love over all Algeria. In the evening or after the rain, the whole earth, its belly wet with seed that smells of bitter almonds, rests after having given itself, all summer long, to the sun. And once again, this fragrance consecrates the nuptials of man and earth, and arouses in us the only true compelling love in this world: a love both generous and perishable. (Camus 1965: 76)

Somehow, the authors are trying to recreate the *sacred space* that has been progressively marginalized – if not exiled – from our society. The reasons behind development and growth are radically opposed to the sacred because it represents a limitation to the programme for exploiting natural resources. The Italian writer and filmmaker Pier Paolo Pasolini perfectly analysed the destruction of sacred elements planned by capitalist society, openly denouncing this ongoing process in his articles and allegorically in his movies (Biancofiore 2012).

The image of Medea, interpreted by Maria Callas in Pasolini's movie, solemnly pronounces the ritual formula during a sacrifice: 'Dai vita al seme e rinasci con il seme' ('Give life to the seed and be reborn with the seed'). In the movie, the figure of the woman is intimately linked to the earth's fertility: Medea is opposed to Jason, the archaic culture resurfaces against the pragmatism of the new world. By the rewriting of the Euripides' tragedy, the filmmaker denounced the destruction of cultural worlds by neocapitalism. The persistence of the *sacred link* would prevent *exploitation* structures and the *appropriation of living beings* (Biancofiore 2016); this is why the imposition of new cultural models leads to banalization, secularization and disenchantment of the world through propaganda tools, namely schools, radio, newspapers, television and the cultural industry.

The *westernization of the world* – as described by Serge Latouche – derives from the perfect continuity between the imposition of a different culture through *colonialism* and the new methods of *economic development*, which result in the annihilation of local cultures. The concrete forms of this annihilation can range from de-culturation to genocide.

An ecology of creation

With her movie *Biutiful cauntri* (released in 2008, produced in 2007), the filmmaker Esmeralda Calabria had the courage to denounce the ravages of pollution in Campania: in practice, the mafia monopolizes the toxic waste treatment system, creating abusive landfills everywhere in populated areas. As a result, plants and animals are dying, humans too, with one of the highest cancer rates in Europe. The disappearance of natural species, determined by pollution, inevitably induces the destruction of cultural worlds; this will be the price to pay if we continue blindly down the path of unlimited development.

An engaged author, Roberto Saviano, is committed to the battle against organized crime in Campania. His writings are now inseparable from his political action, just like Pasolini in the 1960s and 1970s. In his inquiry novel *Gomorrah*, he described his native region, Campania, where the earth is concealed with cement: a land of waste, a land of violence, where the roads are obviously meant for trucks, devastated land, shaped by the new global economy that governs the activities in the port of Naples and its region (Saviano 2006). Saviano brings to light how the organized crime system functions, acting as a vast network of entrepreneurs at the international level: its action is harmful for both the citizens who live in the region and for the global ecosystem. In an interview published by *Le Figaro*, the author talks openly about the problems created by exercising his job as a committed writer:

> Now I only think about the present. The idea of the future makes me anxious. What was planned could never be realized. There have always been contraindications. So, I live from day to day and I prefer not to think

about the future. The truth is, I am very tired, because I have to fight two battles: one that concerns my lifestyle, which weighs on me more and more. The other one, even harder, is a moral battle. Because the ruling class of Southern Italy can't stand me; they can't stand my work. Even some Italian intellectuals try to make me look like some kind of antimafia 'clown'. [...] Yes, basically, my success embarrasses them and shows them their own contradictions. *Gomorrah* reveals that literature still has a role to play; that it can help to make things, or at least mentalities, change as in the times of Zola or Dickens. However, some have the tendency to marginalize and confine literature and then complain that no one reads. (Saviano 2008)

Through Saviano's work of investigation, literary creation and diffusion of knowledge, *literature meets life*; more than ever before, it is able to fight against an absurd system founded on the idea of *unlimited expansion in a limited world*, our planet.

Contemporary society no longer knows any boundaries because the blank space left by the sacred is now filled with the *economy*. It is thus profit that guides actions against the earth and violence against bodies, and which is the origin of complex international networks (for more on this topic, see Castoriadis 1996, 2005). Mediterranean worlds are currently evolving as a result of globalization and in direct relationship with the world as a whole. In the 1970s, Pasolini had already understood the scope of this phenomenon at the international level and had the intention of showing this through his allegorical novel *Petrolio*, which remained unfinished; long before the judges, he had seen the obscure links connecting *energy management* (ENI) to the Italian and international political and economic world. With *Petrolio*, he wanted to write about the Mattei case.

Enrico Mattei, the president of the energy company ENI, was murdered in 1962. At the time, the Italian energy commission was on the point of naming new countries for Italy's oil and methane supply; however, Italian and American political circles did not see this search for Italian energy autonomy in a positive light. The death of Mattei marked a new trend in Italian politics in the Mediterranean and stressed economic dependence on the United States. Part of Pasolini's manuscript probably disappeared a month after his death. The shadows that had covered much of Italy's political history for forty years were starting to disperse, here and there, when a stubborn judge wanted to get to the truth (Calia), or when an author (Pasolini), a journalist (De Mauro) or a filmmaker (Rosi) wanted to show the real face of power. The consequences were serious for the writers: De Mauro was killed in 1970, and Pasolini was murdered in 1975. In the essay *Profondo nero*, the journalists Giuseppe Lo Bianco and Sandra Rizza (2009) reconstructed the successive phases of the investigative work of De Mauro and Pasolini on the Mattei case. This effort to understand reality clearly demonstrates how great a presence Pasolini had in history, how much he was able to feel the anthropological and political changes. Who better than Pasolini could understand the changes in Italian society within a geopolitical and Mediterranean context during the 1960s and 1970s?

His prophetic words and lucid views drove him to live in the line of fire, 'there where the world renews itself'. According to Pasolini, part of the job of a writer is to experience changes as they occurred, be receptive to the transformations in society and understand new cultural worlds.

Writing is surviving: The literature of emergency

Today in Italy, migrant writers help us view ourselves in a new way. For many of these writers, culture is not separate from survival, and this leads to another approach to existence; existential fragility necessarily has an incidence on forms of writing. We could talk about the writing of emergency, *writing that means a presence in history, a literature which lives between worlds*, and that often talks about the loss of culture and the acquisition – or refusal – of a different culture.

Between two worlds: it is precisely this existential condition that Laila Wadia lets us see through her story 'Curry di pollo': on the one hand, in Italy, the immigrant parents of the protagonist embody the traditional culture of India, representing the archaic world, with its rituals, its food, its way of dressing, its language; and on the other, the young woman in the story decides to be a part of Italian society (Wadia 2005). The immigrant's daughter chooses integration because she wants to erase the differences; she feels the abyss between two worlds that barely communicate, and yet, something happens, a fragile thread is established between two universes, a concrete hypothesis about the coming culture. Through this story, we can see the nature of the phenomenon brought to light by the Caribbean author Edouard Glissant: *Creolization*. Nobody can predict evolution in the complex dialogue between different cultures. *Creolization* is born out of the collision between them, producing new forms of cultural identities (Carravetta 2017).

Christiana de Caldas Brito, born in 1939 in Rio de Janeiro, is a Brazilian author who lives in Italy and writes in Italian. Through her books and stories, she implements a re-enchantment of the world, a process necessary for revalorizing the forces hidden inside nature and in the heart of human beings. She has published several books in Italian. Her writings, at times, are similar to the expressionism of Kafka, the irony of Pirandello and the soberness of Camus. She is able to sink into the most intimate folds of her characters' consciousness, and her writing explores apparently unimportant situations, filling the insignificant details of daily life with new meaning.

In one of her writings published in the collection *Qui e là*, thumbs detach themselves from the bodies they belong to. Millions of immigrant thumbs thus go to the prefecture to give their fingerprints. This story denounces abuse by law enforcement that demands that immigrants record their fingerprints as if they were criminals. De Caldas Brito (2006) denounces a society of standardization, and most importantly a highly monitored society; the irony and lightness of her writing seeps into reality: the art of short story becomes a form of narration which stresses the plurality of worlds, a choral breath goes through the pages of another work, *500 temporali*. In a way, her writings contribute to building a world in which several worlds find their place; the Brazilian author is able to describe this plurality via a dialogism which opens up to the diversity of individual spheres.

The short stories by Christiana de Caldas Brito (2004) initiate a process of *re-enchantment of the world*: nature has taken back its rights over the artificial universe built by humans. In *I due falò*, a mighty oak plants its seeds in the belly of a young girl who loves trees: the seed develops and grows. But the plant which grows in the girl's belly is surgically uprooted; in reality, techno-science takes back its rights over natural forces, by imposing its violence and law on the relationship between humans and nature:

> La dottoressa mi incitava a confessare cose che non erano successe. Mi fece un'ecografia. La vidi a disagio mentre guardava lo schermo. 'Devo parlare con i tuoi', mi disse, molto seria. Cercava le parole per rivelare ai miei genitori chi ero io, sì, incinta, ma ... esitava nel dire quello che aveva visto. Ai miei genitori domandò se avevo l'abitudine di salire sugli alberi. Al loro assenso, lei chiarì che la vita che stava crescendo dentro di me, il seme che si era annidato nella mia parte più intima, era ... era ... il seme di un albero. Mia madre abbassò la testa e disse: 'Di una quercia'. La dottoressa continuò: 'il seme di un albero ha trovato in vostra figlia l'umidità e il calore necessari alla sua crescita'.
>
> Fu fissato l'intervento. La dottoressa tolse la vita che si era avventurata dentro di me. Mise dentro ad un vetro con la formalina una pianta piccola piccola. (De Caldas Brito 2011)

(The doctor encouraged me to confess things that had not happened. She did an ultrasound on me. She was queasy when she was looking at the screen. 'I have to talk to your parents', she told me, very seriously. She was searching for the words to reveal to my parents that I was pregnant, but ... she was reluctant to say what she had seen. She asked my parents if I had a habit of climbing trees. When they said yes, the doctor explained that the life that was growing inside of me, the seed that had nested in the most intimate part of my body was ... was ... the seed of a tree. My mother lowered her head and said: 'An oak tree'. The doctor continued: 'the seed of a tree found the moisture and the heat needed for its growth inside your daughter'.

The surgery date was fixed. The doctor removed the life that had ventured inside me. She put the tiny little plant in a glass jar filled with formaldehyde.)

The issue of *ecological emergency* associated with a desire for a concrete utopia permeates the writing of Caldas Brito who now appears to be a leading figure in the panorama of immigrant writers living in Italy (see Biancofiore, Summa and Ben Abdallah 2016).

The limits of westernization

At a time that Jean-Pierre Dupuy (2013: 184) defines as the *era of reprieve* because it is heading towards self-destruction, critical thinkers clearly express the need for new theoretical models. It is urgent that thought responds to the questions of the new world and, most importantly, that critical thought does not stay confined inside the walls of institutes or universities. The relationships between theory and practice need to become closer in order to fight against an *academization of knowledge*. According to Maria Mies, knowledge acquired by a contemplative, uninvolved 'spectator' must be replaced by *active participation in actions* (see Mies and Shiva 1993). Castoriadis and Dupuy, who denounce the phenomenon of the disappearance of the sacred, express in their writings the concrete demand to adapt critical theory to new practices. Dupuy states:

> The hold of the economy on modern societies is now removing the sacred of which they were constituted [...] Previously, economists used the expression 'perfect competition' as an oxymoron [...]. This formula meant that people did not actually need to meet and exchange anything other than merchandise, even less love each other, in order to form an efficient and peaceful society. This utopia in the form of a nightmare may be the price to pay for a society that is no longer protected by the sacred. The economy, both reality and thought, occupies the hollow space left by the sacred. It is its supreme mark. (2008: 226–7)

Castoriadis affirms several times the need for ecological thought regarding the annihilation of different human environments:

> Ecology is subversive, for it calls into question the capitalist imaginary that dominates the planet. It objects to that imaginary's central motive, that our destiny is to increase continually both production and consumption. There is not only the irreversible waste of one's surroundings of irreplaceable resources. There is also the anthropological destruction

of human beings who are transformed into producing and consuming beasts, dazed channel surfers. There is the destruction of their living environments. For example, cities, [...] are being destroyed at the same pace as the Amazon forest. (Castoriadis 2005: 248)

The *cultural offensive* of the West, its fundamental aggressiveness, does not spare the Mediterranean regions; consequently, there must now be radical changes to our way of thinking, currently built on the cultural model of ultraliberalism. Only once *our imagination has been decolonized* will we be able to invent the future, return to *another* conception of nature and begin a process of re-enchantment with the natural world, in order to become more aware of its richness. *Richness* is one of nature's qualities, one that distinguishes it from *overabundance*. The realization that the offensive being exercised on living beings would allow us to *rewrite history* and create new values, could open up the path to reconsideration of the idea of 'life', the laws of nature, the autonomy of communities, making possible a different movement of common goods and living beings (Traoré 2002). Following Latouche, the fight against genetically modified organisms (GMOs) is meaningful on this matter:

GMOs are the last depiction of the phenomenon of the farmers' dispossession of the natural fecundity of plants in favor of the agri-food firms. The privatization of the living could have precisely been analyzed as a new form of enclosure or appropriation excluding common goods. (Latouche 2010: 101)

One of the *common goods* is *knowledge*, conceived as a *relational good*: schools and universities should be a place for exchange and cultural dialogue between generations. Knowledge is not a piece of merchandise; we cannot negotiate it like all other goods on the market. The defence of knowledge and of forgotten wisdom is one of the objectives of the defenders of degrowth who are inspired, among others, by the thoughts of Ivan Illich. For example, here is what he wrote in *Tools for Conviviality*:

At an advanced stage of mass production, a society generates its own destruction. Nature is denatured. Rootless man, deprived of his creativity, is locked in his own individual shell. Community is ruled by a combined game of social polarization and excessive specialization [...] To formulate a theory about a future world, to draw the theoretical outlines of a society yet to come which is not hyper-industrialized, it will be necessary to recognize the existence of natural scales and limits. (Illich [1973] 2003: 455–6)

Illich, just like Castoriadis, insists on the idea of 'limits' and self-limitation. But what are the limits that should not be crossed? This is the question that

Castoriadis asks himself when he talks about the development of scientific studies; their empowerment in relation to other spheres of humanity may generate a logic of self-destruction:

> How to draw the boundary? For the first time in a non-religious society, we have to face the question: Do we need to control the expansion of knowledge itself?
> 1) We do not want an unlimited expansion of production
> 2) We want a free expansion of knowledge, but we can no longer pretend to ignore that such expansion contains, within itself, dangers that cannot be defined in advance [...] Boundaries exist, and when they are crossed it will be, by definition, too late – as with the heroes of ancient tragedy, who learn that they are in hubris, excess, only once the catastrophe has occurred. (2005: 249)

The Greek philosopher believes that ecology based on a political project of autonomy would have the function of tracking the boundaries of the unlimited expansion of techno-science, as, for the first time in history, religion no longer plays a central role in the society that we live in.

Creation, whether it is artistic, political or philosophical, can give meaning to the Being; it has the possibility of fighting against this immense power machine that is destroying all creativity through pure 'management' of living beings and things, in a continuous process of the bureaucratization of life (Virilio 2009). Serge Latouche, on the path indicated by Franco Cassano (2002), affirms the importance of the cultural roots of the Mediterranean identity shared with Southern Europe because the ancient Mediterranean values could counteract homogenization and cultural standardization:

> This Europe would no longer be the Europe of globalized stock markets, of Frankfurt and the euro, of frenzied Americanization [...] It would be the Europe of a more convivial civilization, more humane, more social, more tolerant [...] more cultural, based on the Mediterranean values that are nowadays being violated and repressed: solidarity, the sense of family, an art of living, a conception of time and death [...] The myth of a Mediterranean path proves that pre-industrial, pre-capitalist, premodern, and even pre-Christian roots do exist at the very heart of the Western world. (Latouche 2010: 163–4)

Nevertheless, a real cultural project needs to be distinguished from sheer political lies. The 'Euro-Mediterranean partnership' proposed by the French and European political class could turn into a process of deculturalization for the people of the Mediterranean basin, as the idea of the Union would mostly be based on economic free trade and not on common cultural values. Based on the theories of Latouche, Castoriadis and Cassano, we would like to ask the following question: Is another Mediterranean possible? Our answer is yes, but only if Europe questions its development model and engages in the slow and difficult process of *de-westernizing* the world.

References

Aprile, P. (2010), *Terroni. Tutto quello che è stato fatto perché gli Italiani del Sud diventassero meridionali*, Milan: Piemme.
Arendt, H. (1958), *The Human Condition*, Chicago: University of Chicago Press.
Biancofiore, A. (2010), 'L'apocalypse selon Ernesto De Martino: autour de la notion de fin du monde', in P. Gabellone (ed.), *Résurgences du mythe*, 173–82, Montpellier: PULM.
Biancofiore, A. (2012), *Pasolini, devenir d'une création*, Paris: L'Harmattan.
Biancofiore A. (2016), 'Land Ethics and the Appropriation of Living Beings', in R. Pérez (ed.), *Agorapoetics*, 199–224, Aurora, CO: The Davies Group Publishers.
Biancofiore, A., Summa, R. and Ben Abdallah, S. (eds) (2016), *Soyons le changement … Nouvelles tendances dans la littérature italienne contemporaine*, Montpellier: Euromedia & Levant.
Calabria, E. (2007), [film] *Biutiful cauntri*, Italy: Lumière & Co.
Camus, A. (1965), *Essais*, Paris: Gallimard.
Carravetta, P. (2017), *After Identity: Migration, Critique, Italian American Culture*, New York: Bordighera Press.
Cassano, F. (2002), *Modernizzare stanca: Perdere tempo, guadagnare tempo*, Bologna: Il Mulino.
Cassano, F. (2005), *Il pensiero meridiano*, Rome: Laterza.
Cassano, F. (2012), *Southern Thought and Other Essays on the Mediterranean*, trans. Norma Bouchard and Valerio Ferme, New York: Fordham University Press.
Castoriadis, C. (1996), *La montée de l'insignifiance: Les carrefours du labyrinthe 4*, Paris: Seuil.
Castoriadis, C. (2005), *Une société à la dérive. Entretiens et débats 1974–1997*, Paris: Seuil.
De Caldas Brito, C. (2004), *Qui e là*, Isernia: Cosmo Iannone.
De Caldas Brito, C. (2006), *500 temporali*, Isernia: Cosmo Iannone.
De Caldas Brito, C. (2011), 'I due falò', in *Notos*, 'Narrations', available online: http://notos.numerev.com/varia-2-65/306-i-due-falo (accessed 2 July 2020).
Dupuy, J. P. (2013), *The mark of the sacred*, Palo Alto, CA: Stanford University Press.
Illich, I. ([1973] 2003), *La convivialité*, in *Œuvres complètes*, vol. I, Paris: Fayard.
Latouche, S. (2010), *Sortir de la société de consommation*, Paris: Les liens qui libèrent.
Lo Bianco, G. and Rizza, S. (2009), *Profondo nero*, Milan: Chiarelettere.
Merchant, C. (1983), *The Death of Nature: Women, Ecology and the Scientific Revolution*, New York: Harper & Row.
Mies, M. and Shiva, V. (1993), *Ecofeminism*, London: Zed Books.

Pavese, C. ([1940–5] 2002), *Del mito, del simbolo e d'altro, Feria d'agosto. Tutti i racconti*, Torino: Einaudi.
Saviano, R. (2006), *Gomorra: Viaggio nell'impero economico e nel sogno di dominio della camorra*, Milan: Mondadori.
Saviano, R. (2008), 'Entretien', *Le Figaro*, 25 November.
Traoré, A. (2002), *Le viol de l'imaginaire*, Paris: Fayard / Actes Sud.
Virilio, P. (2009), *Le futurisme de l'instant*, Paris: Galilée.
Wadia, L. (2005), 'Curry di pollo', in F. Capitani and E. Coen (eds), *Pecore nere: Racconti*, 39–52, Rome: Laterza.

2

An impossible abode: The world and modernity

Myriam Carminati

Can man still live in this world in the age of modernity? This question implies investigation into the representation of the city, which is inevitably a place of modernity and a sort of metonymy of the world. We will also examine perceptions of the human body in this changing world. In order to do so, we will analyse various poetic and pictorial works, from the end of the nineteenth century to the First World War. We will refer to Camillo Sbarbaro, T. S. Eliot, Mario Sironi, Giorgio de Chirico and some of the Futurists, including Filippo Tommaso Marinetti, Antonio Sant'Elia, Giacomo Balla and Umberto Boccioni. Next, we will try to point out the current outcomes of this new view of Man and the world which was created around the 'essential break in our history' (Bensoussan 1998: 87) that was the First World War, a break that was, from our point of view, both anthropological and historical.

This modern world was a strong presence in Baudelaire's city, which he defined in 'La Modernité' as 'grand désert d'hommes' ('a great desert of men'; Baudelaire 1976: vol. 2, 694). Here, the city has a negative connotation. New Babylon, the modern city, challenges the sky with its towers and audacious architecture, but the gods have deserted the sky, just as a certain art of living has been lost at the periphery of the Mediterranean area.

Made of cement, glass and concrete, the modern city does not invite idleness or hedonism; instead, it evokes American cities with their vertiginous towers and architecture which, to an early twentieth-century European, seemed to challenge common sense and refer to another world, totally unfamiliar to humans. In his *Studi per edifici monumentali*

(1912–13), the Italian futurist architect Sant'Elia took his inspiration from America to design buildings which evoked Manhattan, industrial progress, the desire for rupture, the denial of tradition and the rise of modernity all at the same time. In this regard, one should reread the passage from *Voyage au bout de la nuit* by Louis-Ferdinand Céline, where the narrator, amazed by what he sees, describes his arrival in New York, by ship, at the very beginning of the 1930s:

> Pour une surprise, c'en fut une. À travers la brume, c'était tellement étonnant ce qu'on découvrait soudain que nous nous refusâmes d'abord à y croire et puis tout de même quand nous fûmes en plein devant les choses, tout galérien qu'on était on s'est mis à bien rigoler, en voyant ça, droit devant nous ...
> Figurez-vous qu'elle était debout leur ville, absolument droite. New York c'est une ville debout. On en avait déjà vu nous des villes bien sûr, et des belles encore, et des ports et des fameux même. Mais chez nous, n'est-ce pas, elles sont couchées les villes, au bord de la mer ou sur les fleuves, elles s'allongent sur le paysage, elles attendent le voyageur, tandis que celle-là l'Américaine, elle ne se pâmait pas, non elle se tenait bien raide, là, pas baisante du tout, raide à faire peur. (Céline [1932] 1952: 186)

> (Talk of surprises! What we suddenly discovered through the fog was so amazing that at first we refused to believe it, but then, when we were face to face with it, galley slaves or not, we couldn't help laughing, seeing it right there in front of us ...
> Just imagine, that city was standing absolutely erect. New York was a standing city. Of course we'd seen cities, fine ones too, and magnificent seaports. But in our part of the world cities lie along the seacoast or on rivers, they recline on the landscape, awaiting the traveler, while this American city had nothing languid about her, she stood there as stiff as a board, not seductive at all, terrifyingly stiff.) (Céline [1932] 1983: 83)

In this 'absolutely erect' and 'terrifyingly stiff' city, people can only be a crowd, a multitude, an aggregation of individuals who fill the desert of stone. This leads to the notions of spleen, *ennui*, melancholy or nostalgia. In short, this is the early twentieth century's permanent catastrophe, with its works characterized by irreversibility and the irremediable. We purposefully use these two Baudelairean adjectives as, very often, the most disillusioned feature of the poet's thought has been privileged, associating it with another genius with this view of the world in the age of modernity, Nietzsche. Very often, Nietzsche's cry of the death of God and of the end of values results – in literature and the arts – in a degraded and desperate image of the modern city. The city is shown as being an impossible abode. Thus, in the age of modernity, the city becomes the place of anonymity, wandering and *uninhabitability* where vagabonds, prostitutes, drunkards, automatons, employees in a hurry and sleepwalkers can be encountered. As a result, the problem of the relationship between the crowd and the individual will be analysed.

Let us now start with an analysis of the representation of the city in Giorgio de Chirico's metaphysical paintings, where he strongly reconsidered perspective in the pictorial space.[1] In the works of this painter, born in Volos, Greece, perspective is disconcerting. All harmony in the world is lost. The linear classical perspective is in fact completely distorted and corrupted; it is extended, stretched and unusually deep. Very often, the stability of the ground is jeopardized by excessive inclination of the planes, giving an unpleasant impression of instability. Moreover, one can see disruption in the sense of scale and proportion: abnormal objects and ridiculously tiny silhouettes occupy the space, without inhabiting it. Incidentally, how can one live in a space that lacks depth, stable foundations and atmospheric perspective? A slight effect of relief and a reduced model create an impracticable, inhospitable space, deprived of foundation. Things are held together there as if by some kind of miracle, ignoring gravity. As for the light, it neither shines nor vibrates, as if there were no air. Incidentally, air rarefaction is very often associated with a greenish, threatening light of unknown origin. This illumination creates a mysterious, dreamlike atmosphere which the shade, in strong opposition to light, reinforces. In de Chirico, shadow, in its different epiphanies, has its own existence. Most of the time powerful, hard and thick, 'it cuts its black triangles and trapeziums on the ground of squares and streets' (Dagen 1997). Hostile, it is unwelcoming and not regenerating. It makes the view still more mysterious and disharmonic, mainly when its opaque presence imposes itself with a strength greater than that of the objects it derives from. Sometimes it does not appear to refer to any solid object, or it makes us suspect hidden presences. Other times, as in *Mistero e malinconia di una strada* (1914), the young girl's silhouette is no more consistent than the shadow. In short, the shadow, which should testify the reality and solidity of things, does not give any certitude or confirmation of this reality, hence the resulting feeling of strangeness and melancholic anxiety.

Mario Sironi's urban landscapes, painted in the 1920s, are no more welcoming. Sironi liked painting lifeless suburbs, empty and sad outskirts with their sad and lonely backpackers, beggars and drinkers. In these paintings, desolation and tragic everyday life refer to a disturbing modernity and the disenchantment of a world abandoned by the gods and where a

---

[1] See, for instance, some of the works painted between 1912 and 1917: *Melancholy*, *The Silent Statue*, *Ariana's Afternoon*, *The Great Tower*, *The Nostalgia of the Poet*, *The Conquest of the Philosopher*, *The Anxious Journey*, *The Nostalgia of the Infinite*, *Gare Montparnasse (The melancholy of departure)*, *The Sailor's Barracks*, *Mystery and Melancholy*, *The Great Metaphysician*.

new god has yet to come.² In this space, there is no harmony, fulfilment, serenity or happiness. In a time of distress,³ Man is akin to the modern city, like the *Bevitore* (1929) locked up in himself, alone and anonymous, like the industrial suburbs that he symbolizes. Looking at this painting, it is no surprise that Sironi, despite being considered a painter of the Fascist regime, was not always admired by the regime itself which above all appreciated blustering and heroic gestures.

It is in this dehumanized and lifeless space that the issue of the relationships between the crowd and the individual must be considered. It emerged during the nineteenth century with the development of industrial capitalism and technological progress. At the heart of this social, political and anthropological change, man tended to lose his individuality and melt into the crowd. From this point of view, the multitude had as its corollary 'the common man, the anonymous, undifferentiated man' (Fiori 1995: 95); in short, the man of the masses whose inevitable space is the city. The city thus becomes more and more disturbing totally different from the life of those who inhabit it, as Baudelaire shows in *Le cygne*:

> Le vieux Paris n'est plus (la forme d'une ville
> Change plus vite, hélas! que le cœur d'un mortel);
> Je ne vois qu'en esprit tout ce camp de baraques,
> Ces tas de chapiteaux ébauchés et de fûts,
> Les herbes, les gros blocs verdis par l'eau des flaques,
> Et, brillant aux carreaux, le bric-à-brac confus. (1976: vol. 1, 85–6)

> (Old Paris is no more (the form of a city
> Changes more quickly, alas! than the human heart);
> I see only in memory that camp of stalls,
> Those piles of shafts, of rough hewn cornices, the grass,
> The huge stone blocks stained green in puddles of water,
> And in the windows shine the jumbled bric-a-brac.)
> (Baudelaire 1931)

In these few lines, as with the Futurists, we can see the image of a changing city and, in both cases, it is interesting to note that the city has its own life. Consider Umberto Boccioni's famous painting with its dynamic

---

² See Heidegger ([1994] 2000: 64): 'Rather, by providing anew the essence of poetry, Hölderlin first determines a new time. It is the time of the gods who have fled and of the god who is coming. It is the time of need because it stands in a double lack and a double not: in the no-longer of the gods who have fled and in the not-yet of the god who is coming.'
³ See 'Le pain et le vin' in Hölderlin (1967: 813): 'et pourquoi, dans ce temps d'ombre misérable, des poètes?' ('and what, after all, is the use and purpose of poets in an age of darkness?').

title, *La città sale*, painted in the years 1910–11. Revealing the dynamism of the modern city, this painting shows, 'in a chaotic bric-à-brac', the frenzy of the industrial metropolises the Futurists favoured so much. Far from the concerns of naturalistic verisimilitude, Boccioni endeavoured to show and make us feel the energy, vitality and hustle and bustle of the city, in an endless spiral. Yet, paradoxically, the modern city, turbulent and overcrowded, is 'the great desert of men' of which Baudelaire speaks, he who, 'lost in this ugly world, jostled by the crowds' ('Fusées' in Baudelaire 1976: vol. 1, 667), feels rejected as the human being becomes a stranger to the city. And the swan is the allegory of this uninhabitability at the very moment in which, from a historical point of view, the city imposes itself as a place where man is obliged to live. Baudelaire fully grasped the essence of the modern city: a continuously changing, dynamic city, but a place of abandonment and solitude, reminiscent of the skinny, consumptive negress walking on the Parisian mud and joining, through the centuries, another exiled Andromache ('Le cygne' in Baudelaire 1976: vol. 1, 86–7). Hence the apparently paradoxical, yet fundamentally correct, definition of the city as 'a great desert of men' where the anonymous individual is returned to his solitude and irreducible otherness.

In this regard, two poets who started publishing in the 1910s have caught our attention: Camillo Sbarbaro and T. S. Eliot. If we associate these two *a priori* contrasting poets, although both were influenced by Baudelaire, it is because we have seen in their works the paradoxical dimension of sterility and solitude closely linked to multitude in a world where things, having lost any rational link, become fragments which no longer refer to a whole (Nietzsche 1993: 911).

As in Baudelaire, the one saying 'I', in *Pianissimo* by Sbarbaro, finds himself face to face with the crowd in the city. In his work, the multitude appears as a mechanical force into which the poet blends. The individual sheds his individuality and nullifies himself in the crowd to the detriment of any sense of responsibility and identification. According to Sbarbaro, immersion in the crowd means the death of the individual. The poet himself is a man of the masses and therefore of the desert, as the crowd is a caricature of the community as a whole, when the world can no longer be considered as a whole founded on harmony. In the age of modernity, the crowd is the result of the quantitative principle of aggregation. This is why, while wandering alone around the city, the poet meets grotesque figures, both familiar and unfamiliar, which he reveals in the expressionist manner of distraught deformation:[4]

---

[4] As regards the relationships between the mass and the individual, we have referred to and synthesized Umberto Fiori's (1995: 95–6) analysis.

> Fronti calve di vecchi, inconsapevoli
> occhi di bimbi, facce consuete
> di nati a faticare e a riprodursi,
> facce volpine stupide beate,
> facce ambigue di preti, pitturate
> facce di meretrici, entro il cervello
> mi s'imprimono dolorosamente. (Sbarbaro 1985: 32)

> (Balding heads of elders, unsuspecting
> eyes of children, the usual faces
> of those born to toil and reproduce,
> faces cunning stupid blithe,
> faces ambiguous of priests, painted
> faces of whores, are impressed
> on my brain painfully.) (Sbarbaro 2016)

Zoomorphic, dumb, happy, ambiguous or made-up, the faces can refer back to a typology which radically denies the individual. For this reason, at the end of the forementioned poem, the poet claims to be afraid 'of seeing that there are so many people' ('a vedere che gli uomini son tanti'; Sbarbaro 1985: 33). And this quantity, a concept we can also find in Eliot's work, corresponds to the standardization of destiny: birth, struggle, reproduction, without any other purpose, because life is a curse that ends with the obscurity of the void.[5] Sbarbaro, like Leopardi, pits pitiless lucidity against the illusions which enable Man to live. With no illusions regarding dead values and the crisis which has occurred, Sbarbaro knows there is no current or future community, and the city, in its stone stillness, is emblematic of a society of the masses and of petrified reality. The 'city of stone', 'incredibly vast and empty' ('immensamente vasta e vuota / una città di pietra'; p. 25) is an inhabited space where everyone is irreparably alone despite the chaos of the crowd: 'Talor, mentre cammino per le strade / della città tumultuosa solo' ('At times, as I walk along the tumultuous / streets of the city alone'; p. 32). Trams and taxis which – instead of uniting people – marginalize them, at the risk of crushing them (see the poem 'Trucioli' in Sbarbaro 1985: 84).

We can thus see in Sbarbaro's work the exact reversal of the Futurist ideal of vitalism, urbanization and victorious mechanization. Whereas the Futurists proclaimed their faith in the mechanical world and exalted the machine, speed and energy, Sbarbaro stressed immobility and desertification.

---

[5] Sbarbaro (1985: 32): 'E conosco l'inganno pel qual vivono, / il dolore che mise quella piega / sul loro labbro, le speranze sempre / deluse, / e l'inutilità della lor vita / amara e il lor destino ultimo, il buio' ('And I know the deceit for which they live, / the pain that set the crease / above their lips, the hope always / betrayed / and the uselessness of their bitter / lives and their ultimate fate, the darkness'; Sbarbaro 2016).

The Futurists' positive myth became a process of degradation, with the machine somehow Man's double, an automaton and sleepwalker, reduced to being nothing more than an object (Boarini and Bonfiglioli 1976: vol. 1, 125; Mengaldo 2003: 320). This explains why, in the soulless and memoryless city, only an existential feeling of abandonment and alienation, loneliness and nonsense can develop, reminding us of de Chirico's metaphysical paintings. It also explains why Sbarbaro created a body of work that was unconcerned with modernity and novelty, far from the principles and injunctions of the Futurists who, without being critical, showed their desire to take part in the process of the transformation of society.

If there is another poetic place from which elevation, transparency and blue are excluded, it is Eliot's city as it appears in the poem *The Waste Land*, the first part of which ends with Baudelaire's remark to the reader: 'You ! hypocrite lecteur ! – mon semblable, – mon frère!' (Eliot 1969: 60). With Eliot, similarly, it is the city and the 'waste' land, as they said in the Middle Ages, and it is very probable that, when choosing a title for his work, Eliot had in mind the 'paese guasto' of canto 14 of Dante's (1983: ch. 14, v. 94, 112) *Inferno*, with which he was very well acquainted.

In this poem by Eliot published, in 1922, just a few years after the catastrophe of the First World War, a real myth of degradation and aridity emerges. From this perspective, the city appears to be a phantom city, unreal 'under the brown fog', 'At the violet hour' (Eliot 1969: 72). Of the 'Fourmillante cité pleine de rêves, / Où le spectre en plein jour raccroche le passant' (Teeming, swarming city, city full of dreams, / Where specters in broad day accost the passer-by!), as Baudelaire (1976: vol. 1, 87) stated,[6] only sadness and desolation remain. In the general apathy of an inhospitable, vast, chaotic place, the city becomes, as for Sbarbaro, the place where multitude and solitude blend, as the big metropolis of the modern age is full of anonymous masses of living dead:

Unreal City,
Under the brown fog of a winter dawn,
A crowd flowed over London Bridge, so many,
I had not thought death had undone so many. (Eliot 1969: 60–1)

Evidently, in this vast, modern metropolis, the crowd replaces the individual, whose integrity is greatly threatened as he is exiled from himself, that is to say, a victim of alienation and depersonalization. As there is neither value to share nor transcendence, the result is the sterility of human relations and incommunicability:

---

[6] The lines quoted nevertheless remind us that Baudelaire cannot be reduced to the disenchantment of the world.

'My nerves are bad to-night. Yes, bad. Stay with me.
'Speak to me. Why do you never speak? Speak.
'What are you thinking of? What thinking? What?
'I never know what you are thinking. Think.'
I think we are in rats' alley
Where the dead men lost their bones. (p. 65)

Emotionless, unsociable, inurbane ... the city, as in Joyce's *Ulysses*, symbolizes alienation and abandonment. As for the phantoms who inhabit it, they are mostly nameless, related to a completely dehumanized social typology (the typewriter, the employee, etc.) in the barren, dull, everyday life of the desolate city. However, this negativity not only affects the city and those who remain there as automatons and living dead but also affects nature and the whole universe. As for the Expressionists, nature is not the positive counterpart of the city: 'the river sweats / oil and tar' (p. 76), it is stated. Nature is no longer a source of life and regeneration. 'The nymphs are departed' (p. 70) and the rain does not invigorate a land made sterile by drought:[7]

Here is no water but only rock
Rock and no water and the sandy road
[...]
There is not even silence in the mountains
But dry sterile thunder without rain
[...]
And voices singing out of empty cisterns and exhausted wells.
(pp. 82, 86)

Here 'the destructive power of modernity' (Luperini 1996: 202) is apparent. It makes not only the city but the whole world a place of human anonymity, loneliness, abandonment and alienation. And it is a human catastrophe we witness in this poem. Today, just a few decades later, Paul Virilio incontrovertibly states:

VILLES PANIQUES qui signalent, mieux que toutes les théories urbaines sur le chaos, le fait que *la plus grande catastrophe du XXe siècle a été la ville*, la métropole contemporaine des désastres du Progrès. (2004: 94)

(Cities of panics which signal, better than all urban theories on chaos, the fact that *the 20th century's greatest catastrophe was the city*, the contemporary metropolis of disasters of Progress.)

---

[7] As regards incommunicability and negativity, we have synthesized Boarini and Bonfiglioli's (1976: vol. 2, 228) analysis.

In this anonymous and inhospitable city, '*the 20th century's greatest catastrophe*', what is this representation of Man with which we are confronted? We have already mentioned individual–crowd relationships, which cause the wanderings, loneliness and lifelessness of the phantoms who have lost their individuality. Modern man is no longer sociable but a thing among things, totally alone and anonymous in the city of stone. It is a lifeless world which appears fleshless, even in the human body, and is very often perceived as a shadow or mechanism. With their inhuman bodies, the Futurists exalt mechanization and state that 'the pain of a man is as interesting as that of an electric lamp that sputters spasmodically and cries out with the most heart-rending expressions of pain' (*Manifeste des peintres futuristes*, 1910). And Giacomo Balla painted a *Lampada ad arco* (*Street Light*) which demonstrates the Futurists' love for electricity. Here, Balla used the Divisionist technique of painting sparks of light that give the effect of ocellated feathers. A crescent moon can be seen, high up in the sky, on the right, and imprisoned in the streetlamp, expressing the painter's irony. Everyone is familiar with the Futurists' loathing of pale, overly romantic moonlight, as well as their incomprehension of nature. And even if it is nothing more than an ideological attitude, this denial of nature and feelings is revelatory of the intense inhumanness that would lead during the Second World War to the rationally thought-out and organized extermination of entire populations who could be exterminated without any sense of guilt or hesitation because they had been denied their humanity.[8]

Resembling a 'plastic ensemble', Marinetti's *Selfportrait* also shows a denial of humanity, as the human figure is reduced to a geometrical mechanism, an articulated puppet. One can certainly see, with some irony, the desire to reject any sentimentalism, psychologism and, broadly speaking, humanity. We know, moreover, that Marinetti dreamed of a 'new Futurist sensitivity' for a new Futurist man whose prototype is Gazurmah, the 'sleepless hero', the mechanical man flying higher and higher in the sky, a mechanical son generated by Mafarka-the-Futurist (the eponymous hero of Marinetti's novel) without the aid of a woman.

Probably the most humanist of the Futurists, Boccioni in *Forme uniche della continuità nello spazio* (1913) also saw the human body as mechanical. His aim was to represent the aerodynamic effects of movement, that is to say energy, the force which identifies itself with form. This is why Umberto

---

[8] See Stephan Zweig (1943: ix): 'All the livid steeds of the Apocalypse have stormed through my life – revolution and famine, inflation and terror, epidemics and emigration. I have seen the great mass ideologies grow and spread before my eyes – Fascism in Italy, National Socialism in Germany, Bolshevism in Russia, and above all else that arch-plague nationalism which has poisoned the flower of our European culture. I was forced to be a defenseless, helpless witness of the most inconceivable decline of humanity into a barbarism which we had believed long since forgotten, with its deliberate and programmatic dogma of anti-humanitarianism.'

Boccioni studied the physical effects of the interpenetration of body and atmosphere, the pressure exerted depending on the speed. Hence the elastic deformation of certain parts of the body due to air resistance and the emphasis on joints.

Let us reconsider de Chirico. Regarding the human figure, or what was left of it, between 1910 and 1918, it underwent a continuous process of dehumanization and reification which was emphasized until it became the well-known mannequin. It was a tiny, disembodied black figure, a shadow of its own shadow, faceless and eyeless, just like the future puppet, a parodic, monstrous mannequin randomly split up and arranged with rulers, set squares, frames, wooden boards and other engineering tools, from which humanity is absent. Mechanical gears, 'orthopedic gods', according to Roberto Longhi's definition, *Ettore e Andromaca* (Hector and Andromache) both used props for an impossible embrace. This 1917 painting reminds us of the disabled, the shattered faces of the Great War, condemned to muteness and crutches, rejected because of the monstrosity of their wounds, no longer allowed to be human. Concerning the *Muse inquietanti* (*The Disquieting Muses*), they are abandoned on the stage of a theatre. Their ambiguous and composite nature made of columns, statues and mannequins reinforces the impression of reification and the human desert. Man is absent and the gods have fled. Incidentally, could god's breath still pervade the muse and inspire the artist? The world, using a Baroque metaphor, is a theatrical stage and, once more, Man is a puppet, unstably balanced on a plane that is excessively inclined forward, in a persistent and ironically solemn silence. And one of the muses has simply placed her head beside her, if ever she had it on her shoulders. In an age of a loss of totality and of impossibility aimed at infinity and eternity, the symbols of classicism, the myth has lost its power of life and truth, it is no longer the foundation. Only nostalgia remains. And the meaning itself has abandoned the world, a sterile, mineral and fossilized world which can be seen in dead cities, with their deserts and silent squares and their absurd buildings under a heavy sky which 'pèse comme un couvercle' ('weighs like a lid'; Baudelaire 1976: vol. 1, 74). The space is a lonely *no man's land*, enclosed and fragmented by buildings that resemble a fortress rather than an inhabitable place.

Despite his obsession with ancient Greece – he was born in Volos, the homeland of the Argonauts – de Chirico was very familiar with the notion that modern man had to deal with a cultural legacy whose intelligibility had been lost, since, from one assemblage to the other, the world resembled a large bric-à-brac, the meaning of which could no longer be perceived. And de Chirico spoke of 'a foolish and senseless world which accompanies us in this gloomy life'. In other works, he reconsidered the idea of nonsense: 'non-sense of the universe' and life as 'mere non-sense' (de Chirico 1994: 91, 119, 124).

Life as a mere nonsense, a city of stone, mechanical men ... After examining the modern age up to postmodernity, which genealogy do we belong to in relation to this representation of man and the world? Should we not make at least some comparisons with the Futurists? Speed, immediateness, simultaneity, ubiquity are all concepts that the new technologies – and in particular nanotechnology – implement through computers, GPS, satellites, mobile phones. Paul Virilio states that 'What's going up now [and it is interesting that he uses the title of Boccioni's painting], it is the advent of an "omnipolis": a city which is everywhere and nowhere' (2009b: 11), a city which consists more and more in 'a connection or a network of ports, airports, railway stations, telecom equipment, etc.' (p. 11). It is what he also defines as 'the OTHER-CITY'. Hence the idea, dear to him, that the elsewhere starts from here, as elsewhere and here are identical. The local is confronted with the global, and the individual is ultimately a body that is increasingly covered in the efficient technology that helps identify and locate it anytime and anywhere, without taking into account that the surveillance video cameras have developed considerably in a world where traceability replaces territorial and family identity. These technologies have given certain contemporary artists such as Stelarc the idea of modifying and enhancing their bodies through the use of these same technologies, carrying them not as mobile phones, telephones or credit cards but by attaching and connecting them to machines and robots.

The Australian artist Stelarc, considered to be one of the 'Post-Human artists', from the outset gained fame with performances where he hung his entire body from hooks piercing his skin, to prove the elasticity of skin. Pushing body art to the boundaries of auto-mutilation, Stelarc wanted to go further and become a bionic man for the post-industrial age. A few examples of his performances are enough to understand his position: Stelarc had a third ear constructed on his left forearm. It is a porous structure which encourages skin cell ingrowth so that the ear organically becomes part of his arm. At the time of the surgery, he had a Bluetooth-capable microphone implanted in his ear which should have made an internet connection possible but, due to an infection, the microphone was removed. Afterwards, he developed a third automated arm interacting with his body or with other factors, such as information from the internet. He has also presented his six-legged exoskeleton, a robot made with the help of a group of engineers from Hamburg which makes him look like a pneumatically powered machine-man. Stelarc explains that 'all his projects and performances study the prosthetic augmentation of his body, whether it is an augmentation by a machine, virtual augmentation or by a biological process, like the extra ear, they are expression of the same concept: the body as an evolving architecture and the exploration of an alternative anatomic structure'. And he adds: 'I don't see the body as the site of the psyche or of social inscription which presumes a sort of myself, but as a biological apparatus that can be redesigned.'

Going beyond Marinetti's craziest dreams, Man becomes a machine thanks to new technologies. And, from this perspective, it is evident that, according to Stelarc, Man must adapt to technology, not the other way round. He also states that a mobile phone should be implanted into all human bodies so that they can be in permanent contact with satellites.[9] The human being is reduced to an object, a modifiable and manipulable body, submitted to technological experimentations. Just like the Futurists, Stelarc is not concerned with the ethical aspect (Clair 1997) of his performances, nor with their economic and political implications, that is, that a man submitted to social and economic competition will have to be increasingly efficient and competitive. By means of body modifications, as Virilio (2009a) underlined, he will need to be more resistant to both ancient and modern plagues, more suited to infernal rhythms, pollution, radioactivity and so on.

We still need to investigate whether this process can be reversed, and if we can still escape this technological hell, the tyranny of performance, this crazy inhumanity, the fever of ubiquity and the frenzy of immediateness. Nothing is less certain, but nothing is as urgent.

References

Baudelaire, C. (1931), *Flowers of Evil*, trans. L. Piaget Shanks, New York: Ives Washburn, available online: https://fleursdumal.org/poem/220 (accessed 7 April 2021).
Baudelaire, C. (1976), *Œuvres complètes*, vols 1–2, Paris: Gallimard.
Bensoussan, G., (1998), *Auschwitz en héritage ? D'un bon usage de la mémoire*, Paris: Mille et une nuits.
Boarini, V. and Bonfiglioli, P. (1976), *Avanguardia e restaurazione*, 3 vols, Milan: Zanichelli.
Céline, L. F. ([1932] 1952), *Voyage au bout de la nuit*, Paris: Gallimard.
Céline, L. F. ([1932] 1983), *Journey to the End of the Night*, trans. R. Manheim, New York: New Directions.
Clair, J. (1997), *La responsabilité de l'artiste, les avant-gardes entre terreur et raison*, Paris: Gallimard.

---

[9] As regards all references to Stelarc in this and in the previous paragraphs, we have used the following websites: M. Lechner (2007), 'Le corps amplifié de Stelarc', *Libération*, 12 October, available online: https://next.liberation.fr/culture/2007/10/12/le-corps-amplifie-de-stelarc_103649 (accessed 4 July 2020); F. Lebas (2007), 'Stelarc performance', *Blog les Nodules Etranges*, April 2007, available online: http://lesnodulesetranges.blogspot.com/2007/04/texte-stelarc.html (accessed 4 July 2020).

Dagen, P. (1997), 'L'improbable rencontre avec Giorgio de Chirico', *Le Monde*, 31 December.
Dante (1983), *La Divina Commedia*, Milan: Hoepli.
De Chirico, G. (1994), *L'Art métaphysique*, ed. Giovanni Lista, Paris: L'échoppe.
Eliot, T. S. (1969), *Poésie*, édition bilingue, Paris: Seuil.
Fiori, U. (1995), *Poesia italiana del Novecento*, Milano, Mondadori,
Heidegger, M. ([1944] 2000), *Elucidation of Hölderlin's Poetry*, trans. K. Hoeller, Amherst, NY: Humanity Books.
Hölderlin (1967), *Œuvres*, ed. Philippe Jaccottet, Paris: Gallimard.
Luperini, R., Cataldi, P. and Marchiani, L. (1996), *La scrittura e l'interpretazione*, vol. 6, t. 1, Palermo: Palumbo.
Mengaldo, V. (2003), *Poeti italiani del Novecento*, Milan: Mondadori.
Nietzsche, F. (1993), 'Le cas Wagner', in *Œuvres*, vol. 2, Paris: Robert Laffont.
Sbarbaro, C. (1985), *L'opera in versi e in prosa*, Milan: Garzanti.
Sbarbaro, C. (2016), 'At times, as I walk along the streets', *Parallel texts: words reflected (blog)*, trans. M. Colarossi, 20 August, available online: https://paralleltexts.blog/2016/08/20/talor-mentre-cammino-at-times-as-i-walk-along-the-streets-by-camillo-sbarbaro/ (accessed 7 April 2021).
Virilio, P. (2004), *Ville panique. Ailleurs commence ici*, Paris: Galilée.
Virilio, P. (2009a), *Le Futurisme de l'instant*, Paris: Galilée.
Virilio, P. (2009b), 'Entretien', *La Croix: forum et débats*, 2 January.
Zweig, S. (1943), *The World of Yesterday: An Autobiography*, New York: Viking Press.

3

Literary Sardness: Between colonialism and postcolonialism, Creoleness and Creolization

Margherita Marras

Elaborating a key to understanding Sardness on the basis of the themes of colonial and postcolonial and, moreover, extending this interpretation to Creoleness and Creolization, may be a source of perplexity. In fact, while the term Sardness generally refers to a definition of identity located in a Western reality, that of postcolonialism refers to opposition to, and reparation for, the absolutism of Eurocentric thought, through which the West has imposed its supposed superiority on others. The same is true for Creoleness, in the sense meant by Jean Barnabé, Raphaël Confiant and Patrick Chamoiseau, the authors of the Manifesto *In Praise of Creoleness*,[1] and for Creolization, discussed by Glissant (1996) in his *Introduction à une poétique du divers*.

In both cases, it concerns literary theories stemming from postcolonial studies, which express the conflictuality of relations between Western centres of power and peripheral realities, and which build their thought on deep dynamics of diversity, of a historical, sociocultural, psychological and

---

[1] Jean Barnabé, Raphaël Confiant and Patrick Chamoiseau are the authors of the Manifesto *In Praise of Creoleness*, presented at a conference on 22 May 1988 during the Caribbean Festival of Seine-Saint-Denis (*In Praise of Creoleness* was published by Gallimard in 1989). The subject is the precious elaboration of the dissentive character that traces the path to follow for a cultural renaissance, made feasible by formulating and formalizing the basis for a new form of literature which takes into account the specific identity of the Creole islands and goes beyond the inherent flaws of their past.

linguistic nature. Nevertheless, far from being irrelevant, our comparative orientation allows us to highlight a new aspect of the composite and diversified reality of postcolonialism, whose critics steadily underline how opportune it is to avoid a one-track reading:

> colonization, decolonization and post-decolonization do not get told and do not get read the same way in every tradition. More essentially, we must admit that colonial and post-colonial history is not built the same way in every tradition. (Bessière and Moura 2001: 9)

In Italy, for instance, the word 'postcolonial' has a precise meaning referring to a series of historical factors, as well as to a new, geopolitical configuration of literature, which appeared with the powerful migratory flows that the country has faced since the mid-1980s and that Armando Gnisci considers as 'the Italian version of post-colonial literature's emergence in the European languages of the great colonization and the global parliament of migrant writers which characterizes this end of century' (Gnisci 2003: 83).

The relationship between postcolonial literature and the literature of migration is confirmed in the Italian case by the well-known fact that the writings of migrant authors are reminders of 'direct colonial responsibilities, neglected for decades' (Ponzanesi 2004: 29), highlighting an adventure forgotten by the collective consciousness, namely the presence of Italy in Africa and the violence committed (Gnisci 2003: 82). Gnisci considered this repression as typical in the culture and civic awareness of the Novecento,[2] and it has led Sonia Ponzanesi to talk about a *postcolonial unconscious*.[3]

Even though, ultimately, Ponzanesi affirms that the definition of postcolonial literature cannot be confused with the literature of migration, or more generally with transnational literature, she does not deny that there are many areas in which they are superposed:

> Strictly speaking, in the Italian context, the etiquette of 'post-colonial literature' applies to the emerging literature from former Italian colonies (Somalia, Eritrea, Ethiopia, Libya), or more broadly – as a literature of opposition that aims to destabilize the traditional canons and regimes of

---

[2] In 'Perdurabile ignoranza' (essay from 2001, published then in *Creolizzare l'Europa. Letteratura e migrazione*), Gnisci talks about two political phenomena, present in Italy in the post-unitaria era, and subject to a 'driving back' in the culture of the Italian Novecento: on the one side, emigration to the Americas where Italians were considered as the lowest ranking Europeans and, on the other, the colonial empire wanted by Italy for the country to be admitted as one of the European Imperial Nations (2003: 145).

[3] Sonia Ponzanesi considers that the Italian experience has been marginalized and forgotten by the Italian *Novecento* culture and indicates as one of the causes its short life, the limited geographical extension and the particularity of Italian imperialism: 'an imperialism in rags, more aggressive than strategic' (2004: 27).

representation of being Italian in front of the other – to all the different migrant writings in Italian (Albanian, Brazilian, Middle-Eastern, Slav and others). (Ponzanesi 2004: 29)

In light of the particularities of the peninsula's history, it is also possible to justify another, innovative, conception of Italian postcolonial studies – innovative in the strictest sense of the word, as well as in the broader sense evoked above – by spreading its meaning (political and cultural) to ancient peripheral Italian realities. This is an internal use of the term, referring to endogenous colonization, illustrated by a rich literature of varying quality and typology (sociological, anthropological, historical, political, etc.) and that, over the years, has noticed the inadequacies of the nation-state during the post-Risorgimento era, denouncing the results of a *piemontizzazione* that ignores regional differences.[4]

We are referring specifically to the South, which Tomasi di Lampedusa defined as a 'thousand-year-old colony [...] of the origins of the Mediterranean and Europe' (Gnisci 2003: 147), and as the Mezzogiorno assimilated by the post-Tridentine Jesuits with extra-European colonial territories, like an Italian India inhabited by ignorant woodsmen, as Ernesto de Martino (1961) stated.

The narrative works of several authors (from Giovanni Verga to Luigi Pirandello, from Tomasi di Lampedusa to Leonardo Sciascia, etc.) clearly show how this form of endogenous colonization has conditioned plots, topics and ideologies, as well as forged a subaltern society and culture. However, the impact of this history on Southern literature has largely been neglected, first by post-Risorgimento critique marked by the monolithic model of De Sanctis, then by a critique more inclined to catalogue works according to the fixed grid of canons and national currents, which has closed the way for proper appreciation of the variety in the Italian literary tradition. It is not the great names of widely known Italian literature who paid the price, but rather a multitude of writers from the Italian periphery, excluded because they are seen as 'atypical' in relation to the evaluation criteria elaborated by scholars.

To apply a model of postcolonial analysis to these contexts of Italian peripheral literature undeniably offers a new and richer possibility for taking into account the conditions of production (former or recent) of those realities, of assessing, elucidating and, if necessary, reconsidering different exclusions or even undertaking a new reading of the major authors' works, which have been widely commented on regarding the influence of

---

[4] During the second half of the nineteenth century, the imposition of the political and administrative system of the Piedmont to the rest of Italy following the unification of the country is known as the *piemontizzazione*, or Piedmontization in English.

colonialism, especially Southern colonialism, but more often according to a Western critical vision and/or by using the European tradition as a paradigm and the only evaluation criteria.

It is well known that the most famous representatives of postcolonial studies (Edward Said, Edouard Glissant, Fredric Jameson, Jean-Marc Moura, etc.) have chosen a critical examination of colonial relations in literature, leaving aside, if necessary, the real literary points of view and/or replacing them with a vigorous moral and political sense. This is in order to proceed towards critical decolonization by giving minorities their voice back and analysing the conditioning resulting from their cultural history, thus undermining the restrictive and normative definition of literature linked to the Western and Eurocentric literary canons (Moura 1997: 62).

In order to interpret literary creations, the importance given to the writer's values and conditions of existence, as well as to the environment in which the texts are produced and received, justifies the parallelism with the regionalist critique (with all the necessary precautions) which has taken place in Italy since the 1950s (see Eagleton 1983: 209). Through its demand to methodologically revise the motives of inclusion or exclusion of the works on strictly national criteria, this approach has undoubtedly given a first and salutary impulse to the knowledge and acknowledgement of geographical pluralism in Italian literary history. Thus, in the manner of postcolonial critique, Carlo Dionisotti's approach – as well as that recently of Alberto Asor Rosa in the chapter 'Le marche di frontiera' – refers to the similarities between deep 'historical-geographical-political articulations' and cultural ones, which make it possible to recognize a specific history and a defined space as a place of writing; and finally, history and space are the places where the text inscribes itself (Asor Rosa 1989: 57).

Obviously, as in the postcolonial view, the regionalist scope is not related to either the framework of the novel or the personal status of the author; on the other hand – as Asor Rosa wisely said – it is 'perceptible' and 'measurable' if the analysis of the text shows intellectual and environmental factors (historical, socio-anthropological, cultural) specific to the geographical area the author comes from and that influence and characterize its individuality or, if we prefer, factors transformed by this individuality (Asor Rosa 1989: 67).

Thus, the fact that a text is produced in a former area of endogenous colonization is no justification for immediately classifying either the author or their work as postcolonial. As Alessandro Carrera (2006: 255) clearly states, 'it is not the simple geographical localization that makes an author post-colonial, nor his [sic] proximity to or distance from the national language':

> In the Italian case, domestic post-colonial novels are born precisely when authors start to wonder what being a colony means, or what being a land of relegation means, despite being part of the nation state, and when they

try to explain themselves and their community in the court of a colonizer and hegemonic culture, which – therein lies the paradox – remains theirs. No matter if this hegemony is open or not to the problems of its colonies, and nor is it decisive that the ideology of the author opposes that of the central power. (p. 256)

Taking the definition by Francesco Orlando of Tomasi di Lampedusa's *Il Gattopardo* (*The Leopard*), Carrera develops his thoughts regarding the correct application of the word postcolonial, considering the ideological speech within the texts, which, in his opinion, should offer something vaster and more in common with all peripheral comparable realities which would transform the particularism of marginality into universality (p. 255).

Even if we agree with Carrera that there is plausibility in the conceptual path from marginality to universality, we consider it essential that the way authors organize their artistic material around the idea of enunciation (often inscribed in a native tradition, sometimes partially forgotten) and their own space (and its values), conceived as the heart of their political, literary and cultural research, be taken into account – a critical choice that is often made.[5]

In fact, upstream of the production of endogenous postcolonial (and colonial) authors, there is often critical reasoning: the number of literary texts can be considered the result of a true hermeneutical osmosis between theory and creation (seen as representation and narration) along with a reformulation of the question of identity. In this regard, Sardinia is an excellent field analysis, due to its long colonial history that conditioned the cultural policies and characterized the complex aspects of past and present literary production. Even though it is expressed in various forms, the clinical signs of the island's colonization are perceptible in the secular presence of a literature flatly imitating imported models; thus, from the fifteenth to the eighteenth century, most scholars representing the local literary culture were generally an expression of the official culture and Hispanic society.

This was a classic situation of cultural colonization and resulted in the weak presence of Sardinian in poetic creation (despite its ancient origins and its oral survival), with efforts to legitimate it as a language and/or to honour certain creative aspects of the local tradition perceived as vanity. The absence of any local literary field is emblematic of the secondary and subaltern position of a *Sardness* relegated to orality, which clearly becomes the expression of a popular culture 'defeated by history' (Muchembled 1978: 7) and of its positioning – according to Aimé Césaire's relevant definition – to the rank of *colonial subcultures*.

---

[5] According to Jean-Marc Moura, 'The post-colonial critique studies the way in which each author, each work handles his relation to the place and invests it with a specific method' (1999: 44).

This state of affairs did not change at all, or at least was not upset by the anticipated *piemontizzazione* that Sardinia suffered (the island passed to the House of Savoy in 1720) nor by the post-Risorgimento era. Even though the Sardinian *Ottocento* was traversed by a new social speech brought about by an intellectual class eager to regain and rebuild its cultural identity,[6] and despite the opening up of Sardinia (illustrated by the entry onto the island of literary and social trends from the peninsula, and by the diffusion of insular journals and newspapers at the national level),[7] there remain several abnormalities that underline the persistence of a consciousness strongly marked by its sense of belonging to a peripheral territory, negatively connotated and still subject to a colonial relationship. This is a common denominator in the various southern regions of the very young nation-state; however, here it was worsened by the particularity of the insular condition and by the painful historical and cultural contradictions inherited from prior dominations.

While there is no doubt that, from the *Ottocento*, Sardness marked the relationship between the Sardinian intellectual and their text, we are still confronted with behaviours that are the sign of a subaltern culture seeking legitimacy.[8] Some attitudes leave no doubt as to the sensitivity and acts of the intellectual suffering from redemption syndrome, perceivable in their defensive stiffness and in their need for acknowledgement in relation to the Other – and to the culture of the Other – as well as to their own identity, clearly perceived as fragmented and flawed (see, in particular, the *Falso delle carte d'Arborea*).[9]

In the same way, the weight of colonization is illustrated, on the one hand, by a servile attachment by novelists to national models (Pompeo Calvia, Enrico Costa,[10] among others), which moreover lags behind the

---

[6] According to Manlio Brigaglia, this intellectual class aims for 'quasi-codification of Sardness' (1982: 35). Sardness is considered as a category of the insular spirit and a way of being fully Sardinian.

[7] Among others, *Vita sarda* by Antonio Scano, *Stella di Sardegna* by Enrico Costa and *La Farfalla* by Angelo Sommaruga.

[8] As is evident from the number of works of different natures (historical, ethnological, anthropological, demoscopical, etc.) and, from the second half of the *Ottocento* (nineteenth century), poetic or narrative works conceived by the intellectual-writers as a tool for defending the specificity of Sardinian heritage and as an attempt to give a national dimension their insular culture.

[9] The *falso delle carte d'Arborea* refers to the smokescreen from 1845 by a monk in Cagliari who circulated and commercialized documents he pretended to have found in the archives of Giudici d'Arborea and which presented Sardinia as the cradle of the original Italian language. Such a 'discovery' would have imposed a 'Sardinian' rereading of all literary Italian history. For the historians Luciano Marrocu and Manlio Brigaglia, we can read within this manipulation the will of the insular intellectuals to promote the Sardinian cultural identity and their demand to see it perfectly integrated into the Italian system (see Marrocu and Brigaglia 1995: 47–8).

[10] Pompeo Calvia author of *Quiteria* (1902), Enrico Costa, author of *La bella di Cabras* (1887) and *Giovanni Tolu* (1897).

original literary context, and on the other, by a documentary-like narration that gives us the measure of their clear inability to master their own culture and make it aesthetically valid – despite drawing its material from the island and aiming for self-revalorization. On this subject, Manlio Brigaglia stated:

> The direct consequence in this vast movement of the island's discovery: whereas in Italy the historical novel arose – even if through imitation of Walter Scott – as part of a rediscovered sense of history, in Sardinia it was carried by the works of the 'greats' who gave material and encouraged the narrator's imagination [...] These novels, of low literary quality, became popular and had, in the formation of a new insular consciousness, the same importance of the Italian 'Risorgimento novel' in the diffusion of the ideal of Italian unification. Furthermore, as well as Guerazzi and D'Azeglio chose between all the possible events the ones that could show the survival of the ancient value at the heart of the Italians, likewise, Sardinian novelists chose among the events of the island, those – at the frontier between history and legend – which made it possible to highlight certain fundamental themes (the long servitude, the 'dignity' of the Sardinian people, the distinctive characteristics of regional civilization). (1982: 38)

In this literary past, placed under the theme of imitation of models derived from the centres, the dominators' places of provenance, we discover a first remarkable feature that is common to other colonized areas, such as the West Indies. Clearly, in spite of the diversity of their own histories, Creoles and Sardinians have in common the fact of having been excluded from their own destiny:

> Over-determined all along, in history, in thoughts, in daily life, in ideals [...] in a trick of cultural dependence, political dependence, economic dependence, we have been deported from ourselves in every piece of our scriptural history. (Barnabé, Confiant and Chamoiseau 1989: 14)

'Deported from ourselves', because of a colonial history which brought 'writing for the Other, borrowed writing [...] out of this land, and which, in spite of some positive aspects, did nothing but maintain in our minds the domination of an elsewhere' (p. 14). Applied to the Sardinian context, this critique explains not only the permanence of national models as tools for reproduction during the first part of the *Novecento* but also the use of the novel as a didactic instrument and of a political commitment where Sardness appears as a social and political referent, a contestation that is the basis of misleading stereotypes or, simply, a source of thematic narrative representations.

We find a significant example in the period following the First World War, when the novel summarized the junction between Sardness and a national-regionalist political creed, *Sardismo*, which can be considered the consequence of the rise of identity and communitarian awareness caused by the conflict.[11] This junction gave rise to a series of testimony novels to which the intellectual-writer entrusted the recreation of a regional community on the theme of Sardness, transformed into a repository providing certainties and values, based on a desire to exalt its belonging and conceived as a way of encouraging Sardinians to look forward (Pilia 1929: 164, 262).

The mission assigned to these writings gave them a precious documentary value. However, given their shaky form and the lack of refinement in their framework, our judgement of them is completely different if we analyse them from a literary and creative perspective. According to Egidio Pilia, in *Il romanzo e la novella*:

> Sardinian novelists, with no exception, were merely the reproducers and photographers of the customs and feelings of their time, without ever successfully rising to the dignity of intellectual creators capable of introducing into their regional reality a new way of thinking and considering life. Thus, more than the knowledge of their individual self, studying their work leads us to measure the psychological, intellectual, and moral state of Sardinia. (1929: 4)

If the evident inability to achieve aesthetic goals was a serious failing in Sardinian novels for a long time (except Grazia Deledda, who will be discussed later in the chapter), their role loses nothing of its significance if we consider them as a form of reaction that aims to achieve cultural decolonization (at least conceptually). This is a common attitude among many intellectuals within colonial contexts and which, in a way, made this narrative form capable of popularizing a privileged tool for rebuilding and reformulating identity. In this regard, we should not forget how in Haiti the *national novels* of Frédéric Marcelin, Justin Lhérisson or Antoine Innocent illustrated this same preference but also the inability to escape from a narrative rigidity, emerging through the linearity and simplicity of the plot. According to Ghislaine Gouraige:

> Haitian writers have cut away the seduction of the plot from the novel. After abolishing the imagination, they left the evidence, by conferring to

---

[11] The experience of the Sassari Brigade led to the creation of the Partito Sardo d'Azione in 1921, whose goals were the acquisition of political autonomy, judged to be essential for the socio-economic dynamism of the island.

the gift of seeing a more important role in the literary composition than the gift of creation. (1971: 149)

The political and didactic particularism that is characteristic of so many Sardinian novels from the first half of the *Novecento*, combining the exaltation of a newfound Sardness with activist *Sardismo*, erases itself through the darkest years of the Fascist dictatorship.

In the 1970s and 1980s, the junction between politics and identity, with its didactic intention, reappeared on the island's literary scene – along with unavoidable differences – as a deviant form: *Neosardismo*, fed by a claim for separatism and by *Sardidade* (Sardness, in the Sardinian language) becoming, for certain local intellectuals, the quirky equivalent of *négritude* (Pira 1978: 250); somehow, this is a simplistic view and a parallelism that a few objective motivations cannot justify.

The novels can certainly be part of an endogenous postcolonial perspective, if we consider them in the light of their narrative structures and their disturbing frameworks, the aim of which is to denounce the practices of old colonialism (see Zedda 1984) and the aberrations of new economic policies (see Masala 1986).[12]

However, it becomes impossible to do a comparative reading with categories such as Creoleness or Creolization because of the partiality of Manichean political denunciation of the opposition between colonized/colonizers, as well as of a rhetorical vision that is not objective enough with regard to the materials of self-representation and the roots of the crisis.

Sardness then became more radical following the weakness of the perception of its own identity as a category *per se* (in contradiction with the evolutionary principle of cultural identity proposed by Glissant [1981] 1997: 484), fossilizing into a conception of the Diverse incapable of going beyond a narrow-minded vision of difference, and above all, it did not interact with writing from the perspective of a dynamic project.

It was only in the 1970s, 1980s and mostly in the 1990s that Sardness found – with Giulio Angioni, Sergio Atzeni and Marcello Fois – a very modern connotation by changing the novelistic representation of identity. Like many Creole authors, these writers use language and the Sardinian heritage as work tools, reservoirs at their disposal, a cultural background on which to draw in order to renew the tradition, to reinforce, enrich and

---

[12] The argument focuses on the economic policies which, by the end of the 1940s, made people believe in an economic and social renaissance for the island, before turning out to be almost useless: the Piano di Rinascita – planned by the special Status integrated into the Constitution and approved on 1 January 1948 – and the developing industrial poles, which became a subject of the news by the end of the 1950s. Francesco Masala (1986) recounts in an apocalyptic way in *Il dio petrolio* the story of petrochemistry in Sardinia.

make more attractive the style and plots of their works. By giving their insular society a normative and cognitive value, they reserve the right to accept, transform or refuse certain aspects of their cultural history: using the Sardness reservoir goes hand in hand with a symbolic reappropriation of their own alterity but also with overcoming an emotional regionalism and rejecting any excessive dichotomy as endlessly repeated particularism.

However, before analysing the particularities of these writers, we must mention a heritage that no one can deny: Grazia Deledda. An authentic literary case in her time, not only in the narrow confines of her island but also in the much vaster Italian context as a whole, it is in fact impossible to position her work within the framework of Italian or even European literary currents. If we focus on the short stories set on the island that she wrote throughout her life – making it possible to follow how her career and thought evolved over time – we immediately see how much being part of both Sardinia and the insular and Italian cultural climate influenced and guided her narrative journey.

When Deledda wrote, the paradoxical situation of the island was characterized, as we have already mentioned, by an openness towards the continent which coexisted, in particular, with the persistence of evident manifestations of intellectual colonialism. Deledda was forced to denounce the sly, cultural resistance working on the island and to express her discouragement in the face of the failure of numerous literary attempts, given that when confronted with certain theses Sardinians were frozen in a scornful representation.

Thanks to her epistolary correspondence, we know how much Deledda, from her first literary attempts, felt the obligation to firmly fight this external condemnation, as automatic as it was unjustified, thus making the decision ('letter to Maggiorino Ferraris', 1891 in Deledda 1972: 249) to let go of 'the wild scenes, the bloody stories told to date by Sardinian authors, who make people see our dear Sardinia as a melting pot of hatred and killings'; and we know (from another letter to Ferraris) her desire to create 'by myself a totally and exclusively Sardinian literature' (p. 238).

Here, we have the announcement of a narrative project that, on the one hand, aimed to link the Sardinian universe (from which some of her formal, stylistic and conceptual tools were derived) with the Italian universe and that, on the other, led to the crucial choice to reposition the island culture from marginality in the past to a central place. The meaning of this subversion lay entirely in the author's decision to narrate Sardinian culture and history through its overlaps and to make it the heart of her creation. This can be seen in the last collections she wrote with the repeated use of autobiographical elements that clearly reveal that the project had somehow already been achieved, so much so that many interventions by the author – refined of any mannerisms and reviewed in the light of clear symbolism – led to a didactic meaning and tone, making the short stories a sort of spiritual testament.[13]

Deledda's clear references to Sardinian colonialism go hand in hand with evident clues of what today we might define as evolving postcolonial studies. These clues are easily accessible to analysis in all the short stories with Sardinia as the setting, an original core that, even diversely dosed over the years, is essentially composed of three inseparable elements: recuperation of the Sardinian linguistic heritage and oral tradition; elaboration of the concept of cultural diversity; and the conjunction between the narrator's role and the author's sense of belonging to the island.

When first reading these short stories, what is striking is definitely the use of a 'non-imposed' language which, for the writer born in Nuoro, was her mother tongue: Sardinian. Because of this choice, Deledda was unjustly relegated by certain critics to the role of 'stenographer' of social speech. These critics were unable to see how much her annulment of monolingualism and purism participated, on the contrary, in a much vaster writing and communication project on which her literature was based.

Moreover, the non-invasive presence of regional morphosyntactic and semantic calques such as *Che il diavolo ti scortichi, E non potevi squarciarti prima, Malata sono, Babbo grande* and so on, animates certain dialogues in the text, as well as the incidental proposition in Sardinian, mostly strictly in italics and translated into Italian, and wisely slipped into the linguistic texture of the short stories.

This literary technique is not only used to recount the insular world in its most precise details (social identification markers, traditions and customs) but also seems to answer a desire to defend Sardinian culture with regard to the official culture and plays a part in providing the narrative with sap and nerve.[14] Similarly, 'defending' himself from the French language, the Tunisian Abdelwahab Meddeb used, he said, the arabesque, the corruption, the deconstruction and an arbitrary language (Dejeux 1982: 87–8).

The same method was frequently used, in the second half of the *Novecento* in particular, by writers using another language (such as that of the French colonists in Africa) and other literary models (the Westerner novel), as Marina Guglielmi summarizes: '[those writers] appropriate the

---

[13] See 'A cavallo' in *Il sigillo d'amore* (1926), 'L'anellino d'argento' in *Il dono di Natale* (1930), 'Racconti a Grace' in *La vigna sul mare* (1932), in 'La grazia' in *Sole d'estate* (1933), 'Medicina popolare', 'Ballo in costume', 'Ferro e fuoco' in *Il cedro del Libano* (1939).
[14] Alongside the traditional social connotations (*bajana, maghiarje*), we also find the nicknames given to the characters by the community (*Tilipirche, Peppe Longu, Palasdeprata, Coeddu*). Moreover, we find food products (*casadinas, cascheddas, pirichittos, casizolos*), prayers and exorcism spells, the objects of popular medicine (*Sa medichina e s'istria, le collane di pedras de ogu, verbos*), curse words (*Mala jana ti jucat*).

existing model to revitalize it by decentralizing it, in order to combine the linguistic-literary ingredients and give birth to a new creativity' (2002: 174).

These theses and possibilities of analysis are confirmed by a narrative logic which includes, at the structural and formal level, many other non-academic practices that can also be found in retranscriptions of collective memory materials (legends, popular characters, beliefs, rituals, sayings, etc.), as well as in the storytelling techniques that respect orality.

It is crucial that the return to this heritage is condensed (more obviously and instinctively in the first collections than in the last) around a narrator who, by taking care of the literary mimesis found in the oral range, reveals to the reader the origin of the story told by showing, clearly, how it handles collective materials (see 'La dama bianca', *Racconti sardi* (1894) and 'Zia Jacobba', *Le tentazioni* (1899) in Deledda 1996: vol. 1).[15]

At the beginning of the short story 'Zia Jacobba', we read: 'What will seem to be a story told by the fireside (and this is what we call fables), on the contrary, is a true story, one that happened in a village of Baronia in Sardinia' ('Zia Jacobba' in Deledda 1996: vol. 1: 306). This approach goes hand in hand with the regular use of the 'us' form that Deledda uses to underline her role as interpreter and, at the same time, performer of the expressive but also behavioural codes of her community. She thus takes on the function of a modern-day *griot*, a type of storyteller with a strong presence in contemporary West Indian literature,[16] and one supposed to reorganize and readapt the tradition. In Deledda, this choice seems strictly linked to the concept of disagreement defined by Edouard Glissant, who insisted on the need to go beyond the servile imitation of the parameters adopted by the community the writer refers to, as 'literature cannot "work" by operating a simple return to "folklorized" oral sources' (Glissant [1981] 1997: 450).

In this regard, by following a diachronic path in Deleddian short stories, we realize that the reuse of legends, anecdotes and so forth is marked by readaptation and an increasingly complex inventive re-elaboration (see 'La leggenda di Aprile', *La casa del poeta* (1930) in Deledda 1996: vol. 5) that

---

[15] In 'La dama bianca', the novelist specifies that her short story goes over the story of zio Salvatore, an old Sardinian sharecropper: 'Here's the last story he told us, that many did not believe, but that really happened in this land of legends, bloody and supernatural stories, of impossible stories' (Deledda 1996: 154). And she specifies in a note: 'We tell it too, with some variations, in Gallura, and it seems that its founding principles aren't entirely legendary' (p. 163).

[16] Referring to the Creole novels, Daniel-Henri Pageaux affirmed: 'We have talked about the novel of the "us", insisting on the communitarian dimension of the narrative, on the presence of more collective characters than individual ones' (2001: 86). And as the Guadeloupean author Maryse Condé specifies: 'Writing is a collective act. Even when he says "I", the West Indian writer is supposed to think "us"' (1995: 309).

is both carefully done and sophisticated.[17] What does not change is her idea of culture: the confrontation between the Sardinian world's primitivism and continental civilization refers to the relationship between an archaic culture and a modern culture, yet still considered on equal basis. This principle anticipated another fundamental point in the Creole project: 'there is nothing in our world that is little, poor, useless, vulgar, unable to enrich a literary project' (Barnabé, Confiant and Chamoiseau 1989: 39).

In Deledda, the red thread of representation develops around an ethno-anthropological concept of culture, allowing her to get away from Manichean weaknesses of ethnocentrism – which negatively judges every value, conception and view of the world that distances itself from the perspective adopted by the group – as well as the imperfect and totalling will of cultural exclusivism.

This anthropological-literary vision cannot be separated from the central idea that goes along with the novelist's entire Sardinian production. Her vision of the island is a fundamental passage for understanding the essence of human beings: by looking at cultural differences and particularities, she said, she undertook a narrative journey which opened her up to a universal conception of humans and of the world.

'At heart, the human being is the same everywhere', she wrote in a letter to Piero Bessi. Thus, Deledda anticipated the narrative application of diversality (dichotomous annulment of *Diversity* and *Universality*), a term forged by the theoreticians of Creoleness who consider the literary exploration of their own tradition as an obligatory pathway for attaining 'the natural of the world' (Barnabé, Confiant and Chamoiseau 1989: 54) and affirming, in literature, the idea that it is with and within cultural differences that the world 'scatters' and recomposes. By refusing the despicable drifts of localism and navel-gazing that the mutilating categorizations brought from her country, Deledda integrated into her narration, almost a century earlier, the most complex aspects of postcolonial literatures, anticipating, without knowing it, the movement of *Creoleness*.

In her Sardinian short stories, the presence of ideas, narrative principles and topics defining her artistic-identity vision, gives these texts the value of a literary manifest. Despite the many imitations of the Deleddian model, none of the Sardinian writers who lived in the same period, or even immediately after, was able to appreciate and understand the deep reasons for her artistic conscience.

As we have already stated, to find the bases of such a narrative conscience, we had to wait until the end of the *Novecento*: Giulio Angioni, Sergio Atzeni and Marcello Fois did not hesitate to recognize the cultural debt they owed

---

[17] As shown in the several narrative retellings of Sardinian legends about hidden treasures (*iscussorgios*) in 'La dama bianca', in 'Il tesoro' (*Il flauto nel bosco* 1923 in Deledda 1996: vol. 4) and in 'Il pastorello' (*Il dono di Natale*, 1930 in Deledda 1996: vol. 5).

to their Sardinian compatriot, and, as Deledda did, they used Sardness as a writing engine, drawing from Sardinian culture – each with their own dosage and method – the objects of their representation, without expecting the complicity of the 'exotic researcher' and without pursuing the sterile goal of a simple affirmation of identity.

Those writers shared with Deledda, with Edouard Glissant and with the West Indians from the Creoleness movement the idea that no culture can live in isolation and that we must consider the complexity of its roots with a critical mind, without ever considering them as exclusive and unique; this conception is revealed in their methods for storytelling and their linguistic choices.

The first was Giulio Angioni, a writer and anthropologist with a gift for creative sensitivity that was clearly oriented by the abrupt change that occurred in Sardinia during the last decades (with the decline in the pastoral and peasant civilization) and whose consequences could be measured in the progressive dissolution of the components of the collective consciousness. During the long period of his narrative creation, Angioni (1992) elaborated a particular concept of cultural identity, based on the need for support. In *Una ignota compagnia*, a novel set in Milan in the 1980s, the object of the representation is the friendship between the African Warui and the Sardinian Tore Melis,[18] a pretext for asserting the idea, expressed by Glissant, of an identity where the Relative outweighs the Absolute, or a 'questioning identity, where the relation to the other determines the being without crushing it under an excessive weight' ([1981] 1997: 428). In Angioni's text, this guiding thread also manifests through a language enriched with Sardinian terms and phrases and by other languages coming from different cultures (Portuguese, Kikuyu, Arabic, Swahili, Milanese).

However, it is with Sergio Atzeni that the similarities between Sardness, Creoleness and Creolization become more suggestive and complex, probably thanks to the knowledge that the writer refined his style with a translation of *Texaco* by the Martinican writer Patrick Chamoiseau (published by Einaudi in 1994). It is in his posthumous novel, *Passavamo sulla terra leggeri*,[19] that he used ideological, literary and artistic processes, very similar to those of West Indian post-colonialism. Atzeni proposed a narrative re-reading of the

---

[18] Warui, a young African, and Tore Melis, a young Sardinian, work in Milan in the same company and live in the same house. In this city, presented as an artificial paradise, the two men become friends allowing them to get to know each other better ('with words I took him to my village, he took me in Africa'; Angioni 1992: 104), and discover similarities in both their cultures. The approach that shows itself to be fundamental for achieving acknowledgement of a more profound self-identity through others ('in his difference I found the things that were mine', p. 22).

[19] The title *Passavamo sulla terra leggeri* is a tribute to Patrick Chamoiseau; the sentence is taken from *Texaco* (Atzeni 1996).

island's history (from 2400 BCE to the fourteenth century), with the goal of representing a Sardinian community distinguished by and in the multitude of its different ontological landscapes (utopias, convictions, projects, beliefs). He proposed a perfect junction between the historical hypothesis, revisited with a powerful fantastical vein, and a mimetic illusion obtained thanks to the resumption of Sardinian cultural data.

He had a double goal: on the one hand, he tried to give meaning and to create a fictitious history with facts and traces of the island's civilization whose origins and development still remain controversial; on the other, his aim was to textualize a redesigned collective memory, affirming a modern concept of cultural complexity, where space and time, and mostly language, play an essential role.[20] On the one hand, time is recreated according to the settings of orality revised on a metaphorical register,[21] as well as adhesion to the real succession of historical facts;[22] on the other, the definition of space is made by following an imaginary transfiguration of the places. With regard to the language, Atzeni wanted to break free of the 'sterilizing neutrality'[23] of the 'official' language, as well as to rebuild the Sardinian language by adding in arbitrary and imaginative lexical choices, which can be seen, among other things, in the 'ancestors'' names.[24] Quite evidently, he voluntarily shifted his writing (forged on the transposition-transformation of the data specific to his original culture) towards an ethnographic, anthropological and, at the same time, identity project.

---

[20] The *bronzetti* are linked to a symbolic, historical recognition of the Sardinians as an ethnic group: '[the judge Mir] placed them in front of the cliffs and on the rocks along the paths. If someone had landed, eluding the surveillance, he would have understood that he was on the land of the horned men dancing on the cliffs' (Atzeni 1996: 21); the word *jana* referring to the pre-Nuragic testimonies of the *domus de janas*, is used to establish the existence of the tombs of Neolithic peoples installed in the centre of the island; the *nuraghi*, most representative monuments of the native civilization, are useful to Atzeni for pulling up hypotheses about the sacrality and mythical lifestyles of this warlike people: the writer talks about the building of the first '*n'u r a gh e*' (p. 25), made to defend against enemies coming from the sea, to then tell the different uses to which it was destined through the centuries.

[21] To tell the period of the origins, Atzeni uses numbers as well as a metaphorical speech ('Month of the wind that bends the oaks'; Atzeni 1996: 9; 'Month of the first flower on the snow'; p. 56; 'Month of the still sea'; p. 49), capable of creating a perfect mimetic illusion.

[22] Of which testify the passages from the prehistorical era to the Nuragic era, from the Phoenicians to the Etruscans, from the Ligurians to the Romans, from the Giudici to the Catalans.

[23] The concept of sterilizing neutrality was created by Edouard Glissant in *Le discours antillais* about the historical imposition of the French language on the Martinicans. For this reason, he invited the Creole writers to deconstruct the French language and raised awareness among them about the use of a shock-language, neither neutral nor provocative, through which to express the issues of the community.

[24] All the characters' names – from prehistory to the Nuragic era – are submitted to a syllabic crescendo (the prehistorical name S'U becomes Sul during the Ik invasion and then Sula in the Nuragic era). We notice in this crescendo the will of the writer to mark at the same time a time-related progression.

As Pageaux says, regarding Confiant and Chamoiseau's works, this approach leads to the 'appropriation and even re-appropriation of a culture: the writing becomes rewriting, reconquest' (2001: 88). This process is confirmed by the narrative structure of *Passavamo sulla terra leggeri*, where the main narrator (Antonio Setzu), guardian and caretaker of the collective memory, transmitted the facts concerning the Sardinian community to a young man, whose name (Azteni) and date of birth (1952) refer to the writer:[25]

> And now, here you are, the guardian of time, says Antonio Setzu. [...] You will be able to add new explanations to the ancient facts told in the story that was entrusted to you, but also to tell the memorable events of your thirty-year-watch, provided that you are clear and concise. (Atzeni 1996: 211)

This passage clearly shows the role that Atzeni gave to the writer, who was called upon to unify orality and writing, and to give meaning to his story on the basis of creative and interpretative freedom but also on a conception of identity that refuses any drift that might lead to its closure. For these reasons, we can consider *Passavamo sulla terra leggeri* as a 'Sardized' model of Creolization, founded on the free resumption of collective memory materials and on Glissant's idea of disobedience.

This principle is shared by Marcello Fois, a novelist and great admirer of Deledda and Atzeni, who also shows great sensitivity towards speeches about minorities and historical submissions.[26] First, with *Gente del libro* (Fois 1996), set in a North African context at the end of the nineteenth century, he publicly accused Western imperialism and Eurocentrism; then, with *Sempre caro* (1998), *Sangue dal cielo* (1999) and *L'altro mondo* (2002), he transferred his polemics to the Italo-Sardinian area, by telling the painful confrontation that began during the post-Risorgimento era, with a *nation-centred* ideology, historically considered as responsible for the worsening gap between Italy and Sardinia.

These three detective and historical novels are part of the author's ambitious project, planning six tetralogies set in Nuoro, whose historical reconstitution started at the beginning of the nineteenth century and should

---

[25] 'I was listening to the story on the 12th of August 1960 in the kitchen at Setzu's, in Morgongiori, between 3 p.m. and the 13th stroke of midnight, when Antonio Setzu pronounced the last word [...] I was eight' (Atzeni 1996: 7).

[26] Marcello Fois recognizes the merit of Grazia Deledda to have used the traditional heritage, going beyond the folkloric limits of the pastoral and exoticism, see Marcello Fois, in his 'Prefazione all'Edera' (in Deledda, 2005: 7). Furthermore, he considers Sergio Atzeni to be the first Sardinian author to introduce, in the island's literature, a key to Creole reading (see Marras 2009: 182).

end in our times. Currently, it includes the three abovementioned novels and also *Ferro recente* (1992), *Meglio morti* (1994) and *Dura madre* (2001), in which Fois tells the story of the city of Nuoro at the end of the twentieth century. The common denominator is a relatively flexible detective story that Fois adapts to his needs as a Sardinian author and to the realization of his narrative project. Both cycles present an original double perspective; a parallel reading shows the direct relationship between the political and sociocultural contradictions, dealt with in the historical novels, and the devastating effects of globalization on Nuoro's community in the contemporary period.

In the historical cycle, Fois organizes his novels around two inseparable lines: the first cleverly combines detective and historical structures, which makes it possible to formulate critical discourse on Sardinia's colonial past; the second, more pragmatic and constructive, is conceived as the cultural, linguistic and aesthetic promotion of Sardinian alterity. The same structure can be found in *Dura madre*. In this novel, the author proposes, on the one hand (and as in *Ferro recente* and *Meglio morti*), a representation of the city of Nuoro fully declining at the social and cultural level, ravaged by the endemic ills revived by abject new crimes, and, on the other, he uses a 'Creolized' writing (still in an embryonic state in the first two novels), developed during a long narrative journey.

In *Sempre caro*, *Sangue dal cielo* and *L'altro mondo*, the plot and the detective structure are supported by considerations and events presented from an anti-colonial perspective: Fois establishes a direct relationship between the socio-genesis of the crimes perpetrated in Sardinia and the precarity of the economic, social and political conditions of the island. To link this double formulation (both historical and police-related), the writer uses a special detective, Bustianu, a character built around Sebastiano Satta (a real lawyer and intellectual from Nuoro), to whom he gives the task of resolving the criminal mysteries as well as the task of expressing judgements on the disastrous effects of the *piemontizzazione* in Sardinia.

We thus find all the hotspots and weaknesses of the island's history, dealt with by a great number of specialists of the *Questione sarda* (among others, Giovanni Maria Lei-Spano, Emilio Lussu and Leopoldo Ortu). Opportunely arranged in the texts, the historical events give structure to the narration and allow the composition of a local sociocultural cartography, where we find, as the main guilty party, a State that is indifferent to Sardinian issues. Thereby, Bustianu denounces how badly the island is integrated at the national level,[27] how minority cultures are reduced to subcultures (because

---

[27] Bustianu affirmed: 'Italy is too young a nation, it will need time before we can speak the same language. And I am not talking about a language *per se*, I am referring to this culture which, in good and in evil, is our common heritage. We weren't led around by the nose when we built this Italy! Here's what I say: leave us some time to choose how we want to be in this nation. I think we would be better Italians if we could enter it as Sardinians' (Fois 1999: 32).

they do not meet the 'official' vision of the world),[28] the corruption of the legal system and the inability to fight the *omertà* and so on.

However, it is definitely in *L'altro mondo* that this denunciation becomes more tragic, also thanks to the almost symbolic combination of detective and historical plots at the cost of the exasperation and alteration of historical data. The plot of the novel deals with the presumed murder of Elena Seddone, a murder that is closely linked to the realization of a secret protocol for chemical experiments on Sardinian land.[29] It is about a project developed, after the defeat of Adwa, by the Italian secret services and supported by complicit deputies, in anticipation of a resumption of the colonial policy on the African continent. Thus, while the arrogance of the central authorities becomes the backdrop for murders, the disastrous national-colonial policy becomes the subject of dissection to find the solution to the mysterious crime. Fois does not hesitate to give audacious comparisons which clearly show his purpose of deeply evaluating Italian colonialism, by decomposing it and then summarizing it, in the tragedy of the two dimensions (endogenous and exogenous) where the colonies' destinies of Africa and Sardinia cross paths. This is clearly illustrated in the presentation of the soldier Mari, a survivor of Adwa and one of the executors of the criminal protocol in Sardinia:

> He has things to tell, Mari: he can talk about Africa-Africa and Africa Sardinia which, anyway, are inhabited by the same kind of animals. He can talk about the brilliant, imperial future, the invincible weapon which kills when we breathe it, the elite corps, the divine males, the superb warriors, the chosen races. And he can also talk about some sacrifices, sacrifices of people who are, after all, useless, such as the Africans, the Sardinians, as is true for all the Africans and all the Sardinians on earth. (Fois 2002: 183–4)

---

[28] We find, in *Sangue dal cielo*, a revealing comparison between Sardinia, the Indies and other colonized lands: 'I was thinking about Christopher Columbus [...] about a sentence that has always made me laugh. Even if, at heart, it is sad. He wrote it to the King of Spain, from the Indies or America, whatever. [...] The power of language. And it says a lot about the behavior of conquering cultures. Do you want to hear it? [...] He had found some indigenous people [...] and decided that it was worth it to put them on a caravel to Spain to show them to the King. Then came the doubt, maybe the indigenous people did not know a word of Spanish, and that could be seen as an offense not only with regard to the sovereign but also to the culture, the only culture that he incarnated [he thus wrote:] "If it pleases Our Lord, as comes the time to leave I shall bring six of these men to Your Highness, so that they can learn how to speak" [...] do you understand? I insisted. "He didn't say: 'so that they can learn how to speak Spanish'; he said: 'so that they can learn how to speak'"' (Fois 1999: 98–9).

[29] At the end of the novel, we discover that the woman was poisoned with the chlorine used for the protocol experiments, but the investigation was manipulated by high representatives of national politics, who organized (with the help of the military and some Sardinians) a false reconstruction of the death. The mystery was solved thanks to Bustianu, but Fois does not give the reader the certitude that this truth will ever become public.

However, as we said earlier, this denunciation is supported by pragmatic and constructive writing in which the similarity with the Creoles is expressed in a more capillary way. We observe the presence of a linguistic mix in which the mother tongue underlines the cultural specificity of the narrated world and, at the same time, actively participates in the construction of literary models.

In Fois, as well as in Creole literature, the focus is on submitting the linguistic instinctiveness to conscious formalization and moving on to a transformation of the mother tongue into a stylistic mark.[30] The most meaningful example can be found in *Sangue dal cielo*, the writing of which is scattered with morphosyntactic and lexical regionalisms, pleonasms and sentences in *nuorese*, alternating with Italian by switching role, sense and function (Fois 1999: 6–7).

Fois's choice to not formalize this passage by means of a diversification of the typographic typefaces, expresses his will to refuse the hierarchical opposition between spoken language and written language, a disagreement which undermines the principle of diglossia imposed by history.

As in the historical tetralogy, the narrative dimension of *Dura madre* is marked by very refined linguistic and stylistic research. The Sardinian-Italian mix, inaugurated with *Sempre caro* and absent from both *Ferro recente* and *Meglio morti*, finds its place once again. However, this time, all the occurrences of the Sardinian language are marked by italics or accompanied by explanatory comments. This new formalization finds a logical explanation in *Dura madre*: the Sardinian sentences and phrases, presented in this way, reinforce the plot and bolster the representation of the city of Nuoro (where the tradition is 'now watered down and reduced to folklore'; Fois 2001a: 48).

Fois gives his 'literary-curative' answer to this state of things: he reproduces the configuration of the oral tale and of the typical mechanisms in Nuoro's mentality. For instance, the narrative wanderings inspired by metaphors and parables (such as the story of Gaspare the dwarf, to explain the servile spirit of Sardinians),[31] or the 'literary constructions of a pre-literary heritage'

---

[30] Marcello Fois took a reflexion by Milan Kundera about the linguistic choices of the West Indian Chamoiseau, which he defined as 'the expression of liberty of a bilingual who denies the absolute authority of one of the two languages and has the courage to disobey both of them' (back cover of *Sempre caro*, 1998); Marcello Fois explained: 'me, I don't speak Italian or a dialect, I speak two true languages. [...] I think that "one more language" is not a capital loss, nor a clue of provincialism: quite the opposite, since Italy is also multiplicity of expressions and expressiveness, it can only be an element that enlarges the culture' (2001b). The point of view is very similar to that of Edouard Glissant: 'the Creole language that is natural to me intrigues at all times my practice of French, and my language comes from this symbiosis, without a doubt stranger to the craftiness of mixing, but wanted and directed by me' (([1981]1997: 554); see also Marras (2009: 46,131).

[31] Fois said he had the idea of the story of Gaspare the dwarf after he saw a photograph of a little man on a cart.

(quoted in Marras 2009: 183), which he uses, he says, 'to revive the Sardinian oral tradition' (p. 47). By giving visibility and an active function to the 'cultural and socio-linguistic particularities of this world of which he tells the end' (p. 183), Fois performs a practical demonstration (poetic, but also sociological and anthropological) of resistance 'to the dangers of cultural assimilation and alienation: the reconstruction after the deconstruction' (p. 183). It is clear that, as for the West Indians in the *Creoleness* movement, Fois does not see his role of narrator as that of an identity relator, but, on the contrary, he considers himself a re-constructor and conceiver of his cultural space.

Conclusion

A cross-referenced reading of Sardness and Creoleness cannot be limited to the similitude of critical discourse in the conflicts between centres of power and peripheral realities. The more organic reasons for this comparison can be found in a shared deep reflection on cultural diversity, combining artistic creation with a major political and cultural project. The commitment of Sardinian and Creole authors is marked by their attitude regarding the constitutive intolerance of nationalisms and, simultaneously, by their refusal of all alienation of settled identity. The literary Sardness of Deledda, Angioni, Atzeni and Fois, as well as the Creolization and Creoleness of Glissant, Chamoiseau, Confiant and Barnabé, open a path towards tolerance and self-conscience, proposing a way of living the identity under the sign of openness, disowning the concept of cultural purity and affirming the need for a multicultural and mixed-blooded conscience:

> If we talk about mixed-blooded cultures (like those of West Indians), it is not to define a category per se, which would be in opposition with other categories (of 'pure' cultures), but to affirm that today opens for the human mentality an infinite approach to the Relationship, as conscience and as a project; as theory and as reality. (Glissant [1981] 1997: 428)

Marcello Fois, for his part, confirms the fundamental significance that he gives to cultural difference: 'I am terrorized by purity which, biologically, is death. Whereas a mix is growth and life' (quoted in Marras 2009: 188).

These authors conceive their own island as an open space from which they draw the elements to enrich their imaginary and to create an aesthetic which absorbs philosophical, anthropological and ideological principles, promoting a diversal vision of the world (Pageaux 2001: 84). Their common artistic, political and cultural goal is well explained by the motto adopted by the theoreticians of Creoleness: *subsist in diversity* (Barnabé, Confiant and

Chamoiseau 1989: 53), which means to maintain the consciousness of the world in the exploration-construction of their original cultural complexity. Marcello Fois affirms:

> This concept has defined something that we Sardinians, and especially the most sensitive intellectual Sardinians, can feel perfectly but are unable to express in words, to set, to baptize: 'subsist in diversity' is a concept as simple as it is gigantic, a concept that answers the need to give body to a thought which had stayed too abstract until then. [...] It is a selective concept that shows the need to make our critical sociocultural sense work and to differentiate what should be kept in the tradition and what should be modified; the tradition is not a dogma but it can become one in the hands and spirits of involute cultures. Tradition and memory are phenomena that are not at all passive, but active. (quoted in Marras 2009: 182)

'Subsist in diversity' organizes itself around a double movement which promotes creative vitality, while opposing the most dangerous principles in colonial cultural history:

> we know that no culture is ever an achievement, but rather a constant dynamic searching for unseen questions, new possibilities, one which does not dominate but which becomes a relation, which does not plunder but promotes exchanges. A dynamic that respects. It is Western folly that broke this natural way. Clinical sign: colonizations. (Barnabé, Confiant and Chamoiseau 1989: 53)

Colonialism and imperialism are expressions of a weak culture. Empires collapsed when emperors believed that stability came from suppressing differences. The intellectuals and the enrolled economies did the rest. But this type of model does not last. Even when it seemed that the only possibility was a dying model, it is in difference that survival can exist (Marras 2009: 187).

In the first pages of this chapter, we talked about the relationship, in Italy, between postcolonial and migrant literature. Given what has been said, it is obvious that such a relationship gets an 'other' sense thanks to these authors, partisans and promoters of a Creole and Creolized Sardness. It is no coincidence if, in the areas of the Mediterranean subjected by the past to internal colonialism, this 'West Indian regionalism' was affirmed, with a transnational impact. Angioni's, Atzeni's and Fois's novels are undoubtedly precious indicators of our times: as for other writers in the Italian periphery, they contributed to giving a new impetus to literary perception of national identity, by pushing critics and readers to consider the national borders of literature as 'lungs and not barriers' (Gnisci 2003: 111). This lets us make an interesting link with migrant writing, which Gnisci recognizes as 'that that is produced by authors writing in a (national) language different from their own origin' (p. 8). Given the extent of this phenomenon, subdivided into several phases and typologies, we will refer here to writers from former Italian colonies and, in a more precise manner, to the generation for whom Italian was the language of instruction. Despite the diversity in the choice of genres (a form of autobiographic narrative still predominates in migrant writing), the areas of contamination and the similarity with narrative logics linked to Sardness remain bountiful. One example is given to us by Maria Abbedù Viarengo (born in 1949, in Ethiopia, to an Oromo mother and a Piemontese father), who emigrated to Turin in 1968 and wrote an autobiography (partially published in the magazine *Linea d'ombra*) in which she tries narrative experimentation, using elements from her culture of origin and calling on an original mix (Oromo, Italian and Piemontese) to build a narrative speech capable of affirming a concept of open and heteroclite identity (Ponzanesi 2004: 31).

In the Italian context, literary Sardness thus should be conceived as the expression of an endogenous postcolonial, Creole and Creolized culture, which played a part in preparing the ground and the foundations for a more just comprehension of this migrant literature and *non solo* (not only that). It is indeed unquestionable that the writers of Sardness, as is the case for those of Creoleness, by affirming their acknowledgement of cultural complexity through a hybrid and syncretic vision of the modern world, have transformed the literary space into a place of confrontation and of welcoming differences.

References

Angioni, G. (1992), *Una ignota compagnia*, Milan: Feltrinelli.
Asor Rosa, A. (1989), *Letteratura italiana. Storia e geografia III: L'età contemporanea*, Turin: Einaudi.
Atzeni, S. (1996), *Passavamo sulla terra leggeri*, Milan: Mondadori.
Barnabé J., Confiant, R. and Chamoiseau, P. (1989), *In Praise of Creoleness*, Paris: Gallimard.
Bessière, J. and Moura, J.M. (eds) (2001), *Littératures postcoloniales et francophonie*. Conférences du séminaire de Littérature comparée de l'Université de la Sorbonne Nouvelle, Paris: H. Champion.
Brigaglia, M. (1982), *La Sardegna*, vol. 1, Cagliari: Edizioni della Torre.
Carrera, A. (2006), 'Il "grande stile" di Salvatore Satta', *Nuova prosa*, 44: 238–56.
Condé, M. (1995), *Penser la créolité*, Paris: Karthala.
De Martino, E. (1961), *La terra del rimorso*, Milan: Il Saggiatore.
Dejeux, J. (1982), *Situation de la littérature maghrébine de langue française*, Alger: Office des Publications Universitaires.

Deledda, G. (1972), *Versi et prose giovanili*, A. Scano (ed.), Milan: Edizioni Virgilio.
Deledda, G. (1996), *Novelle*, vols 1–6, G. Cerina (ed.), Nuoro: Ilisso.
Deledda, G. (2005), *L'Edera*, Nuoro: Ilisso.
Eagleton, T. (1983), *Literary Theory: An Introduction*, Hoboken, NJ: Wiley Blackwell.
Fois, M. (1992), *Ferro recente*, Bologna: Granata-Press.
Fois, M. (1994), *Meglio morti*, Bologna: Granata-Press.
Fois, M. (1996), *Gente del libro*, Milan: Marcos y Marcos.
Fois, M. (1998), *Sempre caro*, Nuoro: Il Maestrale.
Fois, M. (1999), *Sangue dal cielo*, Milan: Il Maestrale-Frassinelli.
Fois, M. (2001a), *Dura madre*, Turin: Einaudi.
Fois, M. (2001b), 'Interview', available online: http://www.ilportoritrovato.net/HTML/biblio824b.html (accessed 6 July 2020).
Fois, M. (2002), *L'altro mondo*, Milan: Il Maestrale-Frassinelli.
Glissant, E. ([1981] 1997), *Le discours antillais*, Paris: Gallimard.
Glissant, E. (1996), *Introduction à une poétique du divers*, Paris: Gallimard.
Gnisci, A. (2003), *Creolizzare l'Europa. Letteratura e migrazione*, Roma: Meltemi.
Gouraige, G. (1971), 'Le roman haïtien', in *Le Roman contemporain d'expression française*, Sherbrooke: Presses de l'Université de Sherbrooke.
Guglielmi, M. (2002), 'La traduzione letteraria', in A. Gnisci (ed.), *Letteratura comparata*, 155–84, Milan: Bruno Mondadori.
Marras, M. (2009), *Marcello Fois*, Fiesole, Florence: Cadmo.
Marrocu, L. and Brigaglia, M. (1995), 'La perdita del regno' in *Intellettuali e costruzione dell'identità sarda tra Ottocento e Novecento*, Roma: Editori Riuniti.
Masala, F. (1986), *Il dio petrolio*, Cagliari: Castello.
Moura, J.-M. (1997), 'Francophonie et critique postcoloniale', *Revue de Littérature comparée*, 1.
Moura, J.-M. (1999), *Littératures francophones et théorie postcoloniale*, Paris: PUF.
Muchembled, R. (1978), *Culture populaire et culture des élites dans la France moderne (XV–XVIII siècle)*, Paris: Flammarion.
Pageaux, D.-H. (2001), 'Créolité antillaise entre postcolonialisme et néobaroque', in J. Bessière and J.-M. Moura (eds.), *Francophonie et postcolonialisme*, 83–115, Paris: H. Champion.
Pilia, E. (1929), *Il romanzo e la novella*, Cagliari: Il nuraghe.
Pira, M. (1978), *La rivolta dell'oggetto*, Milan: Giuffré.
Ponzanesi, S. (2004), 'Il postcolonialismo italiano. Figlie dell'impero e letteratura meticcia. La letteratura postcoloniale italiana. Dalla letteratura dell'immigrazione all'incontro con l'altro', *Quaderni del '900*, 4.
Zedda, F. (1984), *Rapsodia sarda*, Cagliari: Troisi.

4

From house to archipelago: Ways of inhabiting Mediterranean worlds

Clément Barniaudy

> *A house is created by cutting doors and windows in walls, but it is only the empty space within which creates life.*
> LAO TSEU, *TAO TE KING*, CH. 11

Between dazzling sunlight and breaking waves, the perched villages of the Aegean Sea and their white houses encrusted in the rock faces shine out to the horizon from the open sea. Elsewhere, there are Alberobello *trulli* (Apulia, Italy),[1] M'zab Valley mud houses or Provence farmhouses ... or even the modern pyramids of La Grande Motte or indeed city skyscrapers ... On the shores of the Mediterranean, mankind has felt the need to create internal spaces, living spaces. While this habitat is a reflection of the sedentary lifestyle of human beings and their time on Earth, it is also a place for a cosmic link, a place for recollection and the point of departure to the elsewhere.

This is because, beyond the material aspect of housing, no matter where a human being may find themselves in the world or at what time of their life, there is a need to 'inhabit'. To inhabit the world, to inhabit the Earth, is to 'be at the heart of', 'to be exposed to', 'to be there' which can be achieved in

---

[1] A *trullo* (plural, *trulli*) is a traditional Apulian dry stone hut with a conical roof.

so many ways. Through different forms of dwellings in the Mediterranean basin, it is possible to identify ways of being there, of thinking of ourselves within the world and of having a relationship with the Earth. The meaning of inhabiting goes beyond forms of spatial organization, architectonic and urbanist principles. We can say that invisible principles that have led to designing and building in different ways have also appeared. What is the thinking behind the architectures of Mediterranean worlds? What ways of inhabiting are there?

Flux and holds: The birth of a dwelling

In order to comprehend the birth of a dwelling, a first simple diagram can be drawn up. A diagram made up of four lines which interweave more than they follow each other. In the beginning, there are fluxes and human beings in the face of fluxes. Directed fluxes and modulated line speeds: material, ideological, natural and cultural fluxes ... This is how information, winds, water courses, merchandise, migrants, values and arms circulate in our world ... Flux is by nature deterritorialized, even if it crosses territories. Flux, however, does not float above our heads without ever being taken hold of. This is the second line in composing a house: human beings reach out and take hold of fluxes. Here, perception and sensation play an important role and it is they that produce holds. However, appropriation is not fully determined and depends more on intuition. I adopt such or such an idea, such a habit by listening to my feelings, I choose such a place out of affinity. Flux is the object of precognitive selection.

Very soon this intuition is relieved by reason. Reason makes it possible to liberate the third line: consolidation of a world. Medial holds (Berque 2004) lead to the construction of a shelter. The shelter acquires a certain autonomy through its consistence and stands out from the ensemble of the exterior elements. An inner world comes into being, a dwelling is born. This abode, this individualized world, can, however, only really take shape by being closed and opened simultaneously. Thus, if walls are built, it is the windows and doors that make possible a certain relation with what lies outside, creating an opening. The dwelling is once again open to fluxes and the individualized world is transformed by exchanges between the inside and outside worlds.

This oversimplified diagram obviously needs elaboration. A journey to the Mediterranean will help us question this setting up of an abode, its functions, its processes of fabrication. It will therefore be necessary to study ways of inhabiting, ways of setting up a space in the heart of the world and of creating a relation between this space and the world. What relationships exist between the inside and the outside? How can we conceive our sense of place and how can we think of ourselves in the world? How to give meaning to one's time on Earth, to one's geographical experience, to one's manner of inhabiting the Earth?

To have in order to be: The importance of the dwelling

First stop on our Mediterranean voyage is in front of an ancient Greek house. Whether an original hut or a shelter of fortune, this house appears at first sight to fulfil a certain number of basic functions: protection from the cold, from the rain, from wild beasts, a place to store victuals, hoard assets and, lastly, a place of rest. Let us stay with this last idea. Rest implies calm and well-being, and thus a place and time away from the hustle and bustle of the world. The home's primary function is therefore to gather, to conserve … it is a place of retreat and separation which makes possible a different use of time. Levinas explains this to us better than anyone:

> Recollection, a work of separation is concretized as existence in a dwelling [...] Because the *I* exists recollected, it takes refuge empirically in the home. Only from this recollection does the building take on the signification of being a dwelling. (Levinas [1971] 1988: 164)

The dwelling is necessary. It provides not only this all-important shelter in the sense of material accommodation but also the possibility given to the *I* to exist as an entity that requires recollection, which in turn requires a dwelling, thus creating an anchorage. Recollection, however, in no way leads to withdrawal. In return it allows expression. This is the real meaning of the French word *ménager* (to set up home, to conserve): in order to create, in order to perform a task, in order to withstand amid the chaos. It provides the impetus to accomplish a task, it opens up possibilities of expression. *Ménager* is in this sense a source of 'poietic', creating a link between the world and *I*.

> The privileged role of the house does not consist in being the end of human activity but in being its condition, and in this sense, its commencement [...] Recollection is hospitality. (p. 162)

It is by building a world, through one's dwelling, that the individual opens themselves up to others. From here stems the richness of the term 'hospitality'. Connected to the home, hospitality is what allows recollection and the desire to interact with others (the *désir d'autrui*) to converge. In short, to create a space where one can welcome others. Let us return to our Greek house now, what else hides behind its form, beyond its functions?

On closer examination, two elements can be identified. The house both sets the world in order and makes communication between Human, Earth and Sky possible. Setting the world in order helps pass from *chaos* to *cosmos*. It is the role (already well investigated) of the great cosmogonies to transform the world of chaotic currents into a habitable place for humans. In ancient Greece, a divine couple intervened with the purpose of organizing the space: Hestia and Hermes. Hestia was the goddess of the home, she mobilized the space, the centre. She was the incarnation of femininity (in the broad sense, in both sexes) which encouraged hospitality, dear to Levinas. *Hestia* gives a place, an *oikos* to the human community. Members of the same family are thus under the protection of a goddess and are united by the home's fire, *omphalos*, which makes it possible to keep the chaos outside, beyond the house's walls. But Hermes came to break the domestic retreat by opening up the *oikos* to the outside space. Hermes was a messenger. God of the shepherds and travellers, he represented movement within space, a passing through, a contact among foreign elements. That is why he occupied pastoral spaces, crossroads and border regions (*eskateia*). In the home, his place was on the doorstep, and in general he was always to be found on the fringes of towns and communities. His presence above the *oikos* joined the inside and outside together, in the space of Myth.

The two divinities were on the same level; they really existed for the people of that time. To Hestia belonged the inside, the enclosed, the fixed, the inward looking of the group. To Hermes, the outside, the open, movement and contact with people not of one's own. Tension between stable, oriented space and, on the other hand, moving space generated a complex notion of inhabiting, where the perpetual balance of the forces (the principles of permanence/principles of movement) facilitated man's becoming open up to the world.

But communication between the worlds does not stop there. From birth, human beings are dislocated and begin to build territories where the framework of the home plays a regulatory role. This is why the house is first of all square (symbol above all of stability) and allows the forces of Gaia to resist those of Chaos. The home also offers the route for exchanges between the gods from below with those of above: the axis which passes through the fire and the top of the roof brings communication between the different parts: the sky and the earth, human beings and their environment. The image conjured up is one of a mast deeply rooted on the deck of a boat shooting up to the heavens (Vernant [1965] 1996).

The basic square house of the ancient Greeks with very few openings therefore reflects a way of living where human beings take their place alongside earthly and cosmic forces (see Figure 4.1). The dwelling makes possible recollection and departure in relation to the outside environment. But what happens when the Gods leave the household? How does the specified space for living rebuild itself to provide rest and harmony?

FIGURE 4.1 *Sketch of a primitive house under Mount Ida (Crete).* © *Michel Rouvière, 2010.*

Connecting with the world through transcendent principles: Transcendental arithmetic and perfect proportion in the modern home

Second stop on our Mediterranean trip: Le Corbusier's Cabanon in Cap Martin (1951), an apparently simple building, devoid of any artifice but which satisfies basic human requirements: to be housed, to work, to wash. However, the simplicity of its form hides a special conception of the log cabin's architectonic principles. The cabin is in effect the product of harmonic organization. But the harmony between the hut and the world is no longer the act of a polytheist transcendence. It is not that the transcendence – which makes the harmony possible – has evaporated but rather that it has in fact been replaced by transcendental arithmetic. The log cabin, like Le Corbusier's other buildings or designs, is in effect built on precise measurements (see Figure 4.2). Each door, wall and window has been regulated by a 'range of harmonious measurements to suit the human scale, universally applicable to architecture and mechanical things' (Le Corbusier [1953] 2006: 178).

This range, called 'The Modulor', transforms the log cabin into the archetype of a minimalist dwelling where human beings can live according to their size (dimension). Appropriate size (dimensioning) provides a relationship of adequate proportions between human beings and their habitat, and more broadly between human beings and the cosmos. This

FIGURE 4.2 *External and internal views of the Cabanon in Cap Martin (France).*
© *FLC/ADAGP. Photo: O. Martin-Gambier, 2006.*

range provides a principle of construction which allows harmonization of the human body and, by extension, its shell (the architectural body) with the world.

Le Corbusier was inspired by several sources before conceptualizing the 'Modulor'. Between each segment of the scale one notes, on the one hand, the presence of the golden ratio (by multiplication or division; phi = 1.68 ...) and, on the other, that of the Fibonacci sequence ($n3 = n2 + n1$, $n4 = n2 + n3$ ...). Based on the height of a 6 ft tall man (which is that of Anglo-Saxon characters in novels), he calculated measurements which allow use of the space for normal human activity. Each segment of these scales follows a logical sequence combining that of the golden ratio with that of the Fibonacci sequence.

The precise details of this scale are not really important here. What is important is the access to perfect proportions. Le Corbusier was part of an ancient philosophical and mystical tradition, borrowing from Pythagoras, Plato, Vitruvius and even Leonardo da Vinci. The harmony highlighted by these great authors makes human beings resonate together with their environment in cosmic concert. The architect thereby gives us 'the measure of an order which we feel is in accordance with that of our world'. A feeling of well-being is imparted by this divine order, these perfect, unchangeable proportions, hidden in nature, based on numbers; harmony arises from transcendental arithmetic.

Is the amazing feat realized by Le Corbusier effective? Le Corbusier claimed to house human beings in the cosmos, laying claim to a new form of humanism (adapting that of the Renaissance to his context) but was his ruse not simply an adulteration?

The next stop in our grand tour is in front of the Cité Radieuse in Marseilles (1947–52). A large housing block, this building is characterized by a repetition of its elements, 'pure' shapes, a total absence of adornment and its huge scale (see Figure 4.3). Its harmony is once again founded on the Modulor scale, but a primitive, mathematical language also regulates the plans. On visiting the building, the pervading right angles and lack of curves (a reflection of the 'language of asses', according to the author) are striking; the block is ordered geometrically and in an austere way. Benoit Goetz (2002) points out that, in fact, Le Corbusier was looking for ethics which allow human beings to inhabit space in a better way. *His ethics meant placing man in safe housing where he can stand up to outside aggressions, providing him with 'savoir habiter' (knowing how to inhabit).*

The driving forces of this stability were geometry and transcendental arithmetic. By using these criteria as the basis for harmony, Le Corbusier seemed to detach the dwelling from the outside world and make it autonomous. This can be seen both by the presence of concrete stilts, which support the building, and by his own words expressed from 1923 onwards about the need to build 'a house that is this human limit, surrounding us, separating us from the natural antagonist phenomenon, giving us our human milieu, to us human beings' (Le Corbusier [1923] 1995: i).

FIGURE 4.3 *Marseilles' Cité Radieuse (France)*. © FLC/ADAGP. Photo: P. Kozlowski, 1997.

We can see here the idea of separation from nature, being considered as the outside environment. However, this statement must not make us focus our attention on Le Corbusier, the man. Functionality of space, the use of standardization and the discordance between the building and its site teach us more about a conceptual context specific to an era rather than an original and subjective intention. Each individual, each habitat becomes just like the others and the building loses its connection with its environment, its sense of landscape. This movement reflects modern thinking: belief in progress, domination over nature which merely serves as a resource or support, taming the uncontrollable, the fluctuating, rationalizing each little piece of land, denial of emptiness and chaos. This is because if a building frees itself from its immovable context, from its territorial prominence, it is so that it may reterritorialize as standard form, a work which asserts itself down through time.

Modern projects and the rational treatment of space: When the dwelling becomes autonomous

It is possible to recognize in the architecture of the Cité Radieuse the premise of existential anguish that occurs when confronting technological breakthroughs. From here stems the need to fill, control and organize to the point of obsession, so as to leave nothing to chance. From here, too, the reduction of possibilities, especially regarding change of use, poetic effraction. The models used are scientific but come from normative science which does not create something new but tends more to reproduce ('royal science' according to Deleuze and Guattari: 1980). Harmony comes from numbers, and inside space is separated from the wild outside not suitable for human beings. It is not by chance that hygienism and Nazi or fascist concepts of identity developed at this time. Human beings inhabit spaces in opposition to their surroundings. The limit is no longer where things begin but where they end; they disappear in the uninhabitable.

This type of housing and thinking lasted the whole century. But people quite quickly began to protest against this collective programme for humanity with its imperfections ironed out. Le Corbusier's vision holds a wealth of contradictions, a richness which should be brought up to date, because modern beliefs quickly become obsolete.

Architects fairly rapidly understood the risks engendered by this way of conceiving housing. As in Bentham's Panoptic, the architectural use of space can lead to a levelling and moulding of human behaviour (Foucault 1975). It is in this sense that we should take heed of Heidegger's concerns regarding the 'prefabricability' of human beings (Heidegger 1958: 9–48). The modern Western vision aims to unify space through total control and grid lines. Space thus becomes without limits, unified but leaning towards an extensive and intensive process of banalization: 'The world holds no more unknowns, no imperfections. The same building can be planned in Oslo as in Rio. It is a paradise of norms and "*objets types*"' (Portzamparc and Sollers 2003: 77).

Archetypes, norms and technological models clash with and fight against the spaces around them. It is through this struggle that human beings exist and inhabit the Earth, and the use of machines (planes, ferries) goes hand in hand with an architectural will to overcome the environmental resistance human beings face in their space, and themselves affirm in space by making grids, oversizing and creating solid volumes, symbols of the technological *logos*. The world in which they are immersed claims to be humanized, too much so, in the sense that every inch of space is designed and rationalized.

It becomes obvious that space loses its richness, because human beings' senses can wither with the disappearance of discovery and surprise. One loses the desire to be elsewhere, inside space becomes banal, shaped by the same influences, the same conception. The inhabitant loses their connections with non-human forces, with the powers of the Earth. All possibility of poetic effraction is wiped out, reduced or banished. Some have, more or less consciously, taken note of all these consequences of the modern architectural model. Not the Postmodernists, where the paradigm of 'Everywhere the same thing' is replaced by 'no matter where, no matter what', but those who differ and sometimes find it difficult to make themselves heard.

Settling into the folds of the Earth: Immanent freedom and presence in the world

Le Corbusier himself conceived works which contradicted his earlier affirmations; for example, near the end of his life, the Rob and Roq project (1955) in Cap Martin, on the Mediterranean coast. Something had changed in his architecture. The building is no longer independent of its surroundings but slots halfway into the slope of the landscape. The choice of materials, curved shapes, a roof terrace; the dwelling – destined for tourists – no longer asserts itself as mastering the land but fits into the space as a singularity. The site, which is halfway up the slope, makes an opening possible through inflexion, a suspended territory which juts out. For Bernard Cache (1997), it is the main contribution of the modern vision.

But what is also surprising here, beyond the rapport between the building and its surroundings, is its size. And one can recognize, beyond this formal approach, the influence of Mediterranean vernacular architecture. Le Corbusier was struck both by the architecture of rural villages in the Alpes Maritimes *département* (Roquebrune, Vence, etc.) and their alleyways but above all by the architecture of the Aegean Sea islands. Shapes are reduced and are closer to nature. Everything seems to relate to the landscape, not restrain it, but to interact with it, from the inside out. To receive in order to transmit. This architecture gives the measure, the rhythm of a simple, harmonious lifestyle, suited to song and dance. One moves towards a totally different concept of inhabiting, whereby human beings and the cosmos are no longer in harmony thanks to a resonance formulated by numbers but because of an immediate and corporal relationship. The new measure becomes that of experience, and it makes immanent freedom possible.

Let us move swiftly on in our Mediterranean voyage: 'masures' (farmsteads) made from Santorini volcanic stone (see Figure 4.4), Epirus stone villages, Puglia *trulli*, Moroccan clay architecture, Haute Provence dry stone huts and farms ... There are numerous examples of vernacular architecture in the Mediterranean, displaying a sensuous relationship between mankind and the world in which he lives. More than anywhere else perhaps, human beings have been able to interact with their surroundings in order to produce housing which is in harmony with the landscape, as André Ravéreau (2003) points out regarding the M'zab. What is hidden behind this architecture?

In response, our hypothesis is once again based on philosophy and in particular on the concept of immanence. Its origins can be found with Anaximander, a pre-Socratic Greek philosopher from sixth century BCE from Ionia (Anatolia's Aegean shore). He proposed a most interesting theory about the relationship between man and the cosmos. Anaximander broke with transcendental thinking which had prevailed until then (Vernant [1965] 1996).

FIGURE 4.4 *Architecture and landscape on the island of Santorini (Greece). Photo: C. Barniaudy, 2009.*

Kratos (power, domination) belonged traditionally to the gods (Hesiod) or to one of the Elements (Thales, Anaximenes) and later to a Demiurge (Plato). But Anaximander bestowed *kratos* to what he called *apeiron*.

Apeiron is a principle which can be translated as *limitless* or *infinite*, one which makes it possible to toy with relative realities. As a Milieu of absolute immanence, *apeiron* does not in any way constitute *kratos* but the core common to all realities without identifying itself with them. By placing *kratos* within *apeiron*, Anaximander reproduced what was happening in the city space, where the power was transferred to the Agora, in such a way that no one could be totally dominant and that there was one justice for all. Anaximander's revolution made possible a universe without transcendence, founded on a balance of forces, on the reciprocity of positions and common measurement (*apeiron*, limitless). By disengaging earthly space from any particular domination, Anaximander committed to the fields of immanence and uncertainty. Human beings, Earth (relative immanence) and infinity (absolute immanence), these are the players which interweave in inhabiting.

A place, thought or work will be considered harmonious as soon as it allows an interpenetration between the finite and the infinite. Everything becomes possible, depending on situations, perception and understanding of what is close by and far away. The rules about habitable space are no longer dictated by another world but respond to spatial proximity that is sensitive to human experience of the world. But, if no superior being comes to consecrate the space, does the world become a flat universe without qualities? And how is it possible for infinity to penetrate the finite?

A way to live through immanence: Heterotopia and the Japanese archipelago

To further consider these reflections on an immanent relationship between human beings and the cosmos, we need to look at heterotopia and move towards the Far East and Japan. According to Augustin Berque, the Japanese archipelago has a long tradition of immanence:

> To say that the identity of 'place-moment' is more important than that of the person, in Japan (Pre Modern in particular) does in no way signify that people have less of a personality; but that this personality is affirmed by the immanence of its relationship with the world, whereas in the European tradition, other criteria have prevailed (noticeably the relationship with a transcendental God, who is at the origin of the Cartesian 'I think, therefore I am'. (Berque, Ferrier and Sauzet 1998: 26)

The art of a place is a complete cultural expression which is concentrated in the traditional Japanese house. This dwelling gives us our feeling of being present in the world, of 'being there', united with a whole that we call Earth. It hinges on an unbroken movement between full and empty where darkness follows light. Traces of this can be found in the West, but it differs in that Emptiness is at the foundation, as in Taoist teachings. The world in front of human beings becomes part of their flesh, and architecture avoids conflict with nature, so that, on the contrary, the building becomes part of the landscape.

This interweaving of inside with outside comes from an ensemble of elements: sliding partitions, gardens, counter-space ... One must go with the flow, let the process take place without obstruction. The separations vanish, the inhabitant learns to coexist with the outside world (see Figure 4.5). The architecture borrows from the landscape and the highest cultural ideas join together with those of nature. 'Leave barbarians and beasts far behind and follow nature, return to nature' (Bashô quoted in Sauzet 1996: n.p.).

No emptiness to be filled, no space to be furnished but, on the contrary, it is emptiness which allows man to inhabit it. Space is created, sacralized

FIGURE 4.5 *Human beings between inside and outside, at one with their environment source.* © M. Sauzet, 1999.

by harmonious breaths of air and the architecture reflects the sense of forms moulded into their surroundings.

Modernism, Postmodernism: Desert, falsification and dislocation

In the Mediterranean, as in the East, traditions therefore exist which allow man to live in the world to suit himself, reconciling the space within with that without. The Earth insinuates itself into the territories, and the territory throws itself at the Earth in ever-changing relationships. It would appear that, at present, there is a distinct lack of relationship with the cosmos. Returning to Heidegger's (1958) conclusions, the housing crisis facing society today can be seen as just another facet of a far deeper crisis: that of inhabiting and the lack of a real vision regarding inhabiting, which is a fundamental part of being. The philosopher Gilles Deleuze's lucidity confirms this: 'The world awaits its inhabitants who have lost themselves in neurosis' (1985: 268). Why has it become so difficult to inhabit this Earth? Which strategies should be adopted for re-enchantment of the territory and a harmonious way of inhabiting?

The reduction of space-time and the contraction of geographic distances (note the 'end of geography': Virilio 2009) have radically changed the problem of inhabiting. Fluxes speed up, mobility intensifies, whether desired or not. Deterritorialization exceeds settling, to the point of annihilating its function of 'creative destruction' (Biancofiore, Chapter 1, this volume) and generates fluxes that traverse bodies without organs, vectors of multiplicity devoid of all cohesion. These lines of deterritorialization fill the bodies with a magma of mediatized clichés. The dislocated body struggles to consolidate itself, to be in tune with its milieu whilst space offloads its qualities.

At the same time, another contradictory movement is developing: irredentism, a fanatical attachment to a piece of land, glorification of national, regional or local identity ... As if something were disappearing and generating instead a far harsher fixation. The loss of one's points of references, the loss of the meaning of our presence in this world ... The only solution often proposed to return a sense of place to individuals and society is to hark back to the past. Hence a total 'myth-ideology' that is continually gaining in strength and which distinguishes between the clean and the unclean, the others and us. The rhetoric of indigenous population and of murder identities has made a comeback with its potentially bloody consequences (Detienne 2005). Between these two extremes, excessive deterritorialization and the irredentist reterritorialization, does there not exist a means for territorial production that can control chaotic fluxes but which can also remain open to outside forces?

Ritornello and territory: Artistic composition and consistency

If we have taken a quick look at the first simple plan of a dwelling, we now need to go deeper into the mechanics at the beginning of the formation of a territory. Gilles Deleuze and Félix Guattari explain that 'milieu and rhythms are born out of chaos, the concern of ancient cosmogonists' (1980: 384). Four types of milieu are released into the living: the outside milieu (material), the inside milieu (composing elements and composed substances), the intermediary milieu (membrane and boundary) and appendage milieu (energy source). Each milieu is vibratory and open to the chaos by which it is threatened. But the milieu's riposte is the rhythm which joins the chaos in the in-between, forming a *chaosmos*. The rhythm is not a measure or cadence but instead a live changing of milieu. But the territory is not yet established if one remains with milieu and rhythms alone.

> Territory is an act which affects milieu and rhythms ... Territory takes shape when the components of milieu cease being directional (indication, function) and become dimensional (expression, motifs). (p. 386)

The emergence of means of expression or intrinsic qualities defines the territory of a living being. Colour, song, posture and smell all undersign the territory. Deleuze and Guattari adopt ethology's analysis of the markers of an animal's territory. For these authors, the birth of art is coextensive with that of territory. Ritornello, body lines and colours define means of expression which undersign a proper noun, a piece of land. A flag is planted in the ground and this ground becomes the bedrock of forces from within and from inspiration and cosmic forces. However, one needs to go beyond the signature.

A new assemblage made of counterpoints and motifs is soon added to the signs already on display. The signature is transformed into a style and the markers become rhythmic characters or melodic landscapes. This new assemblage is brought about through the interaction between the inside milieu of impressions and the outside milieu of circumstances. Territory is precisely this place which makes possible the meeting of interior and exterior forces (chaos, terrestrial and cosmic forces) in a hand-to-hand clash of energies. From chaos to earthly forces, from reverberating blocks to rhythmical expression, one goes from milieu to territory. The passage from one to the other is performed by a 'ritornello', a child's nursery rhyme in the dark or a bird's song in the forest. Ritornello allows both the creation of a territory (inside space) and its openness to other territories (outside space). The problem of territory is therefore a question of distance (if someone ventures onto my corner of the pavement, apportioned to me by the forces, I complain) and particularly of consistency.

Territory is never enclosed if you consider this process of formation. Deterritorializing forces are effectively going to create new assemblages: 'There is no territory without at least partial vectors for exiting the territory and, in turn, reterritorialization operates on deterritorialized assemblages' (Deleuze in *L'abécédaire de Gilles Deleuze* [film] 2004).

The consistency of a territory is based on ways of holding together the components of territorial assemblage. The authors proposed a 'Rhizome' model rather than an arborescent one (the tree still being hierarchical). Strengthening occurs from the outside towards the inner core (Dupréel 1961). A body organizes itself as the inside of the outside (Foucault [1966] 1986); this strengthening occurs in the in-between, by growth in the middle, by developing gaps and superimposing disparate rhythms without imposing cadence or measure.

This dwelling where human beings inhabit the world – in the sense that they are at the core of it – can in this way become their home. But considering this process, the territorial monad always remains open at the margins but also through the gaps and the in-between which allows permanent contact and enrichment with other territories. As clouds of spots with blurred edges, territory is the product of consistent multiplicity. A territorial unit is the result of the assemblage of expressive matter into milieu. In conclusion, territory takes its form from an artistic composition peculiar to each individual.

This composition can become harmonious from the moment at which the territory is enlightened, when it becomes a clearing region (*lichtung*) with an expressiveness that becomes open to cosmic, chaotic and terrestrial forces.

Considering territory in this manner means opting for an immanent way of inhabiting, which is formed through impregnation, with an ambience full of flavours and colours. Architectural designs convey this concern regarding openness and consistency.

Numerous architects, apart from those of the traditional vernacular, have chosen to espouse architectural principles which respect the milieu. The objective being to design a dwelling which expresses a sense of landscape, which slots into the folds of the Earth, thus becoming part of the landscape. Such is the present trend for bioclimatic architecture which is rediscovering harmony by merging the inside with the outside. We shall not go into this trend in detail, but it is practised by many well-known and lesser-known actors. Numerous examples of this architecture can be found in the Mediterranean: vegetal, green, stone, wood, earth and even brick.

An example of this architecture which deals with its climate, its environment, receiving lines from outside and transmitting its own signals into the environment, can be found on the south coast of the Mediterranean. Many houses in Tunisia have wind towers. Wind, by definition, constitutes an outside force, creative or destructive. However, thanks to the ingenuity of the master builders, wind has been brought into the home for the benefit of its inhabitants. A complex system of low and high pressure has been created. It evacuates hot air, replacing it with cool air, thus creating a ventilation system which cools the house. In winter, the cold currents stay outside or are used in the opposite way. Whilst air conditioning is

FIGURE 4.6 *The wind towers of Yazd (Iran)*. © A. Taveneaux, 2015.

being developed all around the Mediterranean basin, certain architects are attempting to put these methods to use to satisfy the heating and ventilation requirements of its inhabitants and tourists (Culot and Pirlot 2006). Such is the case of the Yazd (Iran) wind towers which transpose this technique for living in hot climates (Figure 4.6). Design that uses alternative methods to those used by Modernists is thus helping the house to breathe and open it up to desert breezes.

Rhythm and inhabiting: The house which breathes

A particular artistic and philosophical thought, as a metonymy of this kind of architecture, addresses the logic of a dwelling which breathes. Through Cézanne's works or the Hagia Sophia in Istanbul, Henri Maldiney ([1973] 1994, [1985] 2003) shows that it is rhythm that gives human beings their home on Earth. As soon as the matter is animated by a rhythmic presence, space is inhabited by a climate, by an atmosphere which varies according to its dimensions. Rhythm is immanent in emerging existence. It is an articulate presence which makes possible the cohesion of heterogeneous elements and the creation of active voids which thus bring about an opening. Rhythm is the way to open up a place to be, where emptiness becomes a reserve, latent energy. Architecture thus comes into being from the moment the home takes in the infinite landscape which envelops it. Two opposing movements fall within the same cycle: diastole opens systole. A dynamic vitality emerges which gives us this perceptual faith, this sense of place.

Let us stop once more on the banks of the Mediterranean at the Hagia Sophia, the masterpiece of Byzantine art. When Maldiney narrates his experience at the Hagia Sophia, he explains how he was at first hit by a dizzy spell. Very quickly, however, this dizziness changed, and his body adjusted to the ever-present space. The secret of metamorphosis is emptiness, a non-place (Augé 1992) par excellence, a reserve out of which the existing appears and articulates itself. The dome and the pendentives create a rhythm:

> Only Emptiness, only Nothingness make possible this absolute departure which, in spite of Aristotle, is at the very beginning of any self-movement of space-time and which is rhythm. (Maldiney [1985] 2003: 210)

In painting, it is Cézanne who offers us the example of an interesting use of space and landscape. The painter from Aix excluded intimacy, enclosed areas and things with well-defined contours. He painted in dabs. Cézanne ceaselessly endeavoured to bring together several milieux (air, water, earth ...) to fight ferociously against geometric, configured, enclosed and enclosing drawing. Each colour enables one to attain *apeiron*. The brushstrokes form a blended ensemble where each part opens up infinite dimensions, where the inside meets the outside, in a discordant harmony. Cézanne makes us feel the 'there is' of the world through the rhythmic handling of space and colour, where the heart of nature resonates from beneath its forms. This process transforms the configuration of a soil situated between earth and sky into an open space, a place of tension between inside and outside. There is, however, no rational calculation to arrive at this resonance but instead just a liberation of the powers of the senses:

> All great landscapes have a visionary character. Vision is the invisible becoming visible ... Landscape is invisible because the more we conquer it, the more we lose ourselves within it. To achieve landscape, we must sacrifice, as far as possible, all time, space, and objective elements; but this abandonment does not only achieve its objective, it affects us equally. In landscape, we cease being historic beings, in other words beings that are themselves objectifiable. We have no memory for the landscape, neither do we have for ourselves in the landscape. We dream in full daylight, eyes wide open. We are stripped away from the objective world but also from ourselves. That is feeling. (Cézanne quoted in Gasquet 1926: 113)

It is therefore through this feeling that the work can emerge. But this process is not only limited to artistic spheres. The painter's reflections invite us to experiment with this rhythmic freedom in our everyday life. Perhaps only a 'rhythm analysis' would enable us to become aware of inhabited spaces (Lefebvre and Lourau 1992). It is the powers of feeling rather than those of imagination which will allow a defined space (my territory) to reverberate with undulating fields from outside, composing our new territories. A house in itself is no doubt no longer sufficient to transcribe this way of inhabiting. It would seem that the archipelago represents a better model of this polyrhythmic habitat.

Inhabited diversity: The enchanted archipelago

The Mediterranean is a fragmented sea sprinkled with islands which form archipelagos: the Cyclades, the Ionian, the Dodecanese, the Aeolian and the Balearic islands ... Life on an archipelago is that of a moving form, connecting with the outside. It is criss-crossed with lines of escape and return, fresh water supplies and momentum. In the harbours, bubbles of space-time related to the cosmos (sea, mountains) evolve. Boats, crinkled by the water, carry the inhabitants far out on sea routes. The journey is as inhabitable as the point of arrival. The journey matters more than the destination, and the detours and the impromptu stop-offs are a source of delight. Thanks to the creative abilities of the carrier, the territory becomes filled with meaning. A veritable archipelago can be formed within a town. Yannick Haenel, in *Cercle* (2005), takes his narrator on a stroll in the heart of Paris. Very quickly, space accumulates qualities. Characterless places become harbours for the narrator and encounters bring a new territoriality. The urban sea links up these islands, these distinctive places, giving them a consistency. It is here, too, that the sense of feeling (dear to Elytis) permits man to inhabit as a poet. Hölderlin says nothing less than this, when he writes, 'Full of merits, yet poetically, man dwells on this earth' (quoted in Heidegger 1958: 47).

For poetry is perhaps the starting point which makes interpenetration possible between me and the elsewhere. It feeds a body with cosmic forces. An artistic body traversed by another's voices, by all the others' voices. The logic of feeling is not an intentional aim but a communication with the world. It allows the creation of world moments, in other words, spaces where we remain, where we inhabit. The boat is no doubt a reflection of this way of inhabiting. Sailing from one island to the next, Odysseus was always mindful of his surroundings. The desire to return, 'nostos', turns into song and allows him to stay in the same place whilst travelling. Bubbles and lines, clearings and paths, form the narrative's thread, like man's experience in the world. Human experience thus takes the form of a labyrinth. Nietzsche reminds us that: 'If we wanted – and could dare – an architecture appropriate to "our" kind of souls (we are too cowardly for it!) – the labyrinth would have to be our prototype' ([1881] 1993: 1071 [§169]).

A path which doubles back, which forks off in another direction, the labyrinth belongs to the order of the unknown, of surprise. It is for this reason that it continually satisfies man, as for him, 'everything is detour, return, discourse, everything is a string of destinations, everything is a chorus of endless verses' (Bachelard [1957] 2005: 193). With the labyrinth, one enters a tectonic of paths belonging to the becoming and opening-up of possibilities. Space is fragmented between gaps, pieces where discovery and the fulfilment of life take place. To find one's bearings in a labyrinth, one's hearing must become more acute. Man follows the music of his soul and step by step captures the meanderings of existence. Walking is no longer enough; one must dance and occupy the space in a dynamic fashion. Another time opens up at the same time as space is discovered. Interposed time, infinite time, like that of the garden of forking paths:

> Unlike Newton and Schopenhauer, your ancestor did not believe in a uniform and absolute time. He believed in an infinite series of times, a growing, dizzying web of divergent, convergent, and parallel times. That fabric of times that approach one another, fork, are snipped off or are simply unknown for centuries, contains all possibilities. (Borgès [1941] 1993: 507)

What remains important for the inhabitant is to invent his territory while creating it. Calvino showed that imaginary geography was in fact poorer than real geography: 'a methodical greyness spreads out over the Utopian cities from Francis Bacon's Bensalem to Cabet's Icaria' (2003: 485). Poetry makes possible this inhabited journey, this geographicity where Earth speaks to Man and Man addresses the Earth and speaks for the Earth (instead of and at it). Language is perhaps this refuge, this treasure to dispense where every sentence awakens a corner of space. Inhabiting is embodied in speaking, singing, playing and creating in a language interspersed with human and natural forces. Maybe a rug or a coat would suffice as a point of departure for expression which creates a territory:

> It is in the weaving of rugs that nomads lay out their know how: light, brightly colored objects which are spread out on the bare ground wherever they stop to spend the night and which in the morning are rolled up to be carried away with them. (p. 557)

To inhabit, thus, as a poet, a dancer or a nomad, is never to affirm one's territorial identity or to claim one's property but rather to affirm one's belonging to Earth ... Belonging to the spaces between myself and Earth ... Every time man creates a territory based on fixed criteria (soil, blood, etc.), the same battles resurge and, with them, conflicts about purity. To claim a free, smooth space conducive to departure, to journeys and to arrivals is to sail the world into open singularities. Inhabiting the world, inhabiting the Earth, is akin to creating a work of art, giving birth to harmonic rhythm and to penetration of the finite by the infinite.

References

Augé, M. (1992), *Non-lieux, introduction à une anthropologie de la surmodernité*, Paris: Seuil.
Bachelard, G. ([1957] 2005), *Poétique de l'espace*, Paris: P.U.F.
Berque, A., Ferrier, J.P. and Sauzet, M. (1998), *Entre Japon et Méditerranée, architecture et présence au monde*, Paris: Massin.
Berque, A. (2004), *L'espace au Japon: vivre, penser, bâtir*, Paris: Arguments.
Borgès, J. L. ([1941] 1993), 'Le jardin aux sentiers qui bifurquent', in *Œuvres complètes*, vol. 1, ed. J.-P. Bernès, trans. Paul Bénichou, Jean Pierre Bernès, Roger Caillois et al., 499–508, Paris: Gallimard.
Boutang, Pierre-André (Dir.), *L'abécédaire de Gilles Deleuze* (2004), [Film], France: Montparnasse.
Cache, B. (1997), *Terre meuble*, Orléans: HYX.
Calvino, I. (2003), *Défis aux labyrinthes*, t. 1 (1955–78), trans. J.-P. Manganaro and M. Orcel, Paris: Seuil.

Culot, M. and Pirlot, A. M. (2006), *Architectures autrement*, Brussels: AAM Éditions.
Deleuze, G. and Guattari, F. (1980), *Mille Plateaux*, Paris: Minuit.
Deleuze, G. (1985), *Cinéma 2, L'image-temps*, Paris: Minuit.
Detienne, M. (2005), *Les Grecs et nous*, Paris: Perrin.
Dupréel, E. (1961), *La consistance et la probabilité constructive*, Brussels, Palais des académies.
Foucault, M. (1975), *Surveiller et punir*, Paris: Gallimard.
Foucault, M. ([1966] 1986), *La pensée du Dehors*, Montpellier: Fata Morgana.
Gasquet, J. (1926), *Cézanne*, Paris: Berhheim-Jeune.
Goetz, B. (2002), *La Dislocation, architecture et philosophie*, Paris: Les éditions de la Passion.
Haenel, Y. (2005), *Cercle*, Paris: Gallimard.
Heidegger, M. (1958), *Essais et conférences*, trans. J. Beaufret, Paris: Gallimard.
Lao Tseu (2002), *Tao Te King*, trans. L. Kia-Hway, Paris: Gallimard.
Le Corbusier ([1923] 1995), *Vers une architecture*, Paris: Flammarion.
Le Corbusier ([1953] 2006), *Oeuvre complète 1946–1952*, t. 5, ed. W. Boesiger, Basel: Birkhaüser – Editions d'architectures.
Lefebvre, H. and Lourau, R. (1992), *Eléments de rythmanalyse*, Paris: Syllepse.
Levinas, E. ([1971] 1988), *Totalité et infini*, Paris: Le livre de poche.
Maldiney, H. ([1973] 1994), *Regard, parole, espace*, Lausanne: L'âge d'homme.
Maldiney, H. ([1985] 2003), *Art et existence*, Paris, Klincksieck.
Nietzsche, F. ([1881] 1993), 'Aurore', in *Œuvres*, t. 1, ed. J. Lacoste and J. Le Rider, Paris: Robert Laffont.
Portzamparc, C. (de) and Sollers, P. (2003), *Voir, Ecrire*, Paris: Gallimard.
Ravéreau, A. (2003), *Le M'Zab, une leçon d'architecture*, Arles: Actes Sud.
Sauzet, M. (1996), *Entre dedans et dehors, l'architecture naturelle*, Paris: Massin.
Vernant, J.-P. ([1965] 1996), *Mythe et pensée chez les grecs*, Paris: La Découverte.
Virilio, P. (2009), *Le futurisme de l'instant*, Paris: Galilée.

5

Pasolini and the Mediterranean: Lost cultural worlds and the reappearance of archaic worlds

Matthias Quemener

> *I hear people say: Italy, the Mediterranean, ancient landscapes where everything is on a human scale. But where is this? Show me the way. Let me open my eyes and seek out my measure and my satisfaction! What I see is Fiesole, Djemila, and ports in the sunlight. The human scale? Silence and dead stones. The rest belongs to history.*
> ALBERT CAMUS, 'LE DÉSERT', *NOCES* (1996: 65)

In order to understand and define the relationship between Pasolini and the Mediterranean, it is useful to look closely at his works because the importance that the *mare nostrum* increasingly takes throughout them greatly outstrips simple curiosity and the simple desire to be immersed in the azure waters of a cultural area brimming with history. There is indeed the possibility of two Mediterraneans: there is the concrete/actual place, the Mediterranean which lives, breathes and hears, and there is an abstract Mediterranean where the limited space is pushed out into a 'poetic space of creation', unlimited, where myths and ideas take shape, where representations are forged and historical legacy sets imagination on fire. The Mediterranean is present in most of his films. It is implicitly present like a link, an *origin*, a specific space-time. Pasolini used it as a vehicle for communicating with his audience, to rediscover, through words and images, characters freed from the neurosis inherent to modernity: 'Complete men, un-mutilated' (Bataille 1954: 36).

This type of research and thinking imbibes Pasolini's polymorphous work, as if he were in search of the *essence of man*, which modernity had destroyed during its cultural development. This desire to represent cultural worlds constantly shaken by doubt can first be seen in his interest in the Roman subproletariat and his *Ragazzi di vita* whom he frequented in the early 1950s and who featured in his works from that period.[1] This proletarian world, full of people marginalized and excluded by society, was a way for him to get to the heart of a *violent but honest reality* which, in its specifically cultural aspect, reminded him of the farming world of his childhood in Frioul, although the confrontation with the reality of the suburbs was far harsher than the peaceful nature of that of the country. But just like peasant farmers' culture, *borgate* culture does not lie, it is *true*, in its limitations as much as in its *shape*: the *knowledge* acquired by the simple fact of living life carnally and viscerally. A life which henceforth becomes violent. This new confrontation led him in a direction where the question of a cultural future was at the heart of his thinking, because he realized that it was in the process of cultural change that real political fracture – the cardinal point of *distorted reality* – was to be found.

Confronted by a previously unknown world, but recognizing in this universe slices of the life encountered in his youth in Frioul, with the same difficulties for survival, Pasolini made this once totally foreign to him place his *own*. This *concrete experience of otherness* was to inspire and suffuse the body of his cinematographic and literary works: the culture of the Roman underclass was to take pride of place, thus bursting the abscess of scandal in the middle classes who had only a vague and ill-informed idea of this class.

Pasolini united with them, exposing, describing and illustrating the everyday life of a world affected by the rejection and *shame* of not being born in the middle classes, in a 'petit-bourgeois universe' (Pasolini [1976] 2000: 199). The choice of language, the Roman dialect, which he used as much in his films as in his novels from that period, affirmed this preoccupation with reproducing the reality of this existence, and not transforming that reality into a representation that the bourgeoisie might have had of these people, instead re-presenting them just as they were and just as they lived, with the culture they expressed and which was an integral part of Italian culture: 'Thus, whilst I originally chose the dialect for subjective reasons, as a purely poetical language, when I arrived in Rome, on the contrary I made

---

[1] Novels: *Ragazzi di vita* (1955), *Una vita violenta* (1959); Films: *Accattone* (1961), *Mamma Roma* (1962), *La ricotta* (1963).

an objective use of it as the dialect of the local sub-proletariat, in order to arrive at the most precise description possible of the world which I faced' (Pasolini 1992: 42). This linguistic issue is fundamental. Pasolini lent it great importance because he knew that it is also through language that cultural change takes place (just as it is through *erotic experience* that it imposes its codes and rules); indeed, he was aware that the Roman dialect he used in his films would disappear in its classist and sociological form: 'No kid from around Rome will be able to understand my novels' slang in 10–15 years. Oh the irony of it! They will have to consult the glossary like a good, old bourgeois Northerner!' ('Etroitesse de l'histoire et immensité du monde paysan', 8 July 1974, in Pasolini [1975] 1987: 87).

The anthropological change that he witnessed thus reinforced this visceral attachment to cultural diversity, a diversity that can only help each man understand himself and give himself a *space to exist*. Because it is in the very flesh that he feels this heartache which links him to a cultural world slowly disappearing, just as it is through the body that bourgeois cultural rules impose their principles and values: 'the cultural model offered to Italians (and indeed to all the world's inhabitants) is unique. It is above all in the lived experience, the existential, that conformation to this model is to be found, so also in the body and behavior' (Pasolini [1975] 1987: 86). This first concrete experience of *otherness* was to have consequences on Pasolini's inspiration and aspirations. His search for a *view of reality* inevitably confronted him with the *most violent and most crude but also the most sublime reality*, like the two sides of a weigh-beam.

The cultural issue is fundamental for understanding the transformations that reality underwent during these years of change in Italian society. It was this consciousness of '*anthropological mutation*' *in action* (see 'Etude sur la révolution anthropologique en Italie', Pasolini [1975] 1987: 72, emphasis in original) that the author's new artistic creations defined, in his books as well as in his cinema, and which prompted him to film in countries and regions that had not yet been profoundly affected by cultural change. Pasolini therefore enlarged his field of knowledge by integrating into his general theory elements of a linguistic, behavioural, social, ethical, sexual and cultural nature, all of which he believed brought transformation to Italian society; he perceived the globalization of this process well before many intellectuals who only became aware of it when the *mutation* had been truly embedded as a universal cultural form. It was through the signs, which formed the cultural base, that this '*new culture*' ('Letter to Calvino' in Pasolini ([1976] 2000: 218) gradually became the sole cultural horizon and thus a common space of expression and exchange to confront. Baudrillard succinctly summarized this culture. The sociologist, who was a contemporary of Pasolini, here used eroticism to reveal the concrete functioning of this semiotic system which did not place reality at the centre of the world but rather an indefinite profusion of signs:

the ethics of beauty which is that of fashion can be defined as the reduction of all concrete values, values of usage, of the body (energetic, gestural, sexual) into one single functional value of exchange which alone summarizes, in its abstraction, the idea of the glorious, accomplished body, the idea of desire and delight – and which also naturally denies them and forgets them in their reality to become drained in an exchange of signs. (Baudrillard 1970: 207)

From then on, it was to Mediterranean countries that Pasolini turned as it was there that he was able to find a quintessence at once ancient, archaic and sincere, the same simplicity and authenticity that he could feel in the peasant farmer world of his native Frioul or indeed in the Roman *borgate*. He already had a presentiment that the representation he made of the *borgate* was destined to disappear; apart from the progressive rehabilitation of the *borgate* in the urban fabric of the capital from the 1970s, which made accessible these areas which had previously been left to their own devices, it was a way of life and a view of life that was gradually disappearing. The perception he had of the underclass, the characteristic that he found in the simplicity of the people, in the kind of love of life despite poverty, was something he discovered on his journey to India with Alberto Moravia and Elsa Morante for example (see Pasolini [1962] 2007). Pasolini talked of it in his collection of poems *La religione del mio tempo*, edited in 1961. This collection gathered together texts written by the poet between 1957 and 1959, poems about people from the *borgate romane* as well as the rural world of Frioul:

> to the refined and the under-class come
> the same hierarchical order
> of feeling: both outside history
> in a world with no way out
> except through sex and the heart
> with no profundity except in the senses
> In which joy is joy and pain pain ('La ricchezza' in Pasolini 1961)

'*Joy is joy and pain pain*': reality is the reality of the senses, the reality of a feeling which cannot be betrayed as it comes from the most profound layers of one's being. Pasolini's consciousness of this fundamental transformation indicated in his mind a rupture in his own vision of Italy and its historical future. This is why he turned to countries where cultural traditions were still alive and in use, to find *a still quite strong cultural base*, which he could no longer find in modern Italy, unless in very specific but minority geographical areas, especially in southern regions, such as Sicily.

His vision of this poor, exploited social class filling the *borgate* can sometimes be seen as poetic, linked to a mythical vision of the class war. More than mythical, these poor, uneducated people – who did not have access to compulsory schooling and had thus not been exposed to *bourgeois cultural integration* – were, for Pasolini, the poetic but very real symbol of a way of life and of seeing the world that was totally opposed to that of the deeply profane middle classes: a more vibrant temporality, more in tune with the earth, a *sacred reality*. Pasolini believed that this *reality* was disappearing as fast as *capitalist entropy* was destroying all that man could possess and that linked him to *history, to a past which made him conscious of who he was, and affirmed his singular place in the world*: these fundamental pillars upon which man leant, Pasolini detected them in values which still existed when industrial civilization had not yet made itself the only way of evolving.

Life revolved around the seasons, morality, common values, shared and sanctified rituals which brought together the community, giving it its meaning and its reality. Even values from the creation of nations and the different nationalisms developed in the first part of the twentieth century, fatherland, family, order – already bourgeois values – were no longer values that were viable in hypermodern societies (see Marcuse 1963; Lipovetsky 2004). It was not just a break from our origins, with the *archaic principle of life*, which Pasolini confronted, but a still more radical break which effaced history itself along with more recent cultures:

> the nationalized and therefore falsified 'values' of the old agricultural and paleo-capitalist universe suddenly no longer count. Church, country, family, obedience, order, saving, morality no longer count. They no longer survive even as false values. They survive in a marginal clerico-fascist culture (even the M.S.I. – 'Movimento sociale italiano' – repudiates them for the most). They have been replaced by the 'values' of a new type of civilization, completely 'other' compared to the old peasant and paleo-industrial societies. (Pasolini [1975] 1987)

Pasolini's theory about this historical change, this *cultural mutation* through new instances of socialization and the production of signs peculiar to *new culture*, came about gradually. But it first came into being through the Pasolinian experience, through the realization that this change came from the heart of the *borgate* and that the life he had been trying to portray as close to reality as possible, was itself transforming gradually. Pasolini denounced collective integration into bourgeois culture and planning ahead, presented henceforth as an 'inter-class' model but still maintaining the idea of distance and differentiation through some elementary signs, thus perpetuating the ghettoization of this popular class. This intuition, this realization, took on more and more significance in Pasolinian thinking. Thus, from the late 1950s, Pasolini turned to anthropological and philosophical works which helped him to acquire the theoretical tools necessary for understanding and explaining this vast cultural phenomenon, the slow cultural decline behind the hedonistic and conformist finery of the new culture. Of the authors he read, particularly noteworthy are Bataille, Eliade, Durkheim, Frazer, Lévy-Bruhl and De Martino whose works played a significant role in the formation of his theory on *cultural apocalypses* and his vision of the contemporary world. We therefore find a continual progression in his theory of culture, a theme which had always fascinated the artist from his very first poems on the vibrant and ritualized world of the Frioul countryside.

It was the changes Pasolini experienced in Italy, this *cultural mutation*, which erased all trace of the country he had known and loved, in which he had felt alive and now felt a foreigner, which made him search for places and people who had not yet suffered *capitalist entropy* and were therefore quite capable of representing fragments of reality still capable of incarnating the archaic model that had vanished and *recomposing* it. In this way the Mediterranean became for Pasolini the place to regenerate, even symbolically, a vision of the world from a long time ago but which had survived up till now. The sense and essence of a bygone civilization had suddenly been buried with only ruins remaining, onto which could be built new values imposed by the *production of signs on a large scale* which I would even qualify as on an *industrial* scale. To take the idea of *neo-reality* which Jean Baudrillard analysed just like Pasolini, even if he did so in a more artistic medium, 'it is out of the question that truly symbolic or didactic processes come into play (in mass communication), because that would compromise collective participation which is the point of this ceremony – participation which can only happen through a liturgy, a formal code of signs (produced by instances of use/consumption) carefully emptied of all meaning' (Baudrillard 1970: 155–6). In short, 'it is the historic and structural definition of consumption to extol the signs on the basis of a denial of things and of what is real' (p. 16).

Facing this forced *acculturation*, the Mediterranean assumes a heavily cultural valence through the historic unit it represents. In each of his films, the Mediterranean can be sensed, defined by the spectator through the earthy atmosphere of the horizon, through the people and their way of life which is discovered, through the persistence of the sun forging faces and bodies. It is this vast space which Pasolini depicted, sometimes in an almost documentary-like fashion, like a camera filming landscapes not for what they are really but for what they speak to us about, what they represent: 'My cinematographic taste is not of cinematographic origin but figurative [...] And I can only conceive images, landscapes, compositions of silhouettes from my initial passion for painting, that of the Renaissance, which has man at the heart of every perspective' ('Diario al registratore' in Pasolini 1998: vol. 2, 1846).

Like painters, he seized the archaic continuity of the places in which he found himself, a feeling he could only capture in places where industrial civilization had not yet supplanted in its entropy ancient social and cultural structures. Places and landscapes whose dusty and desert-like character Pasolini used to indicate, behind vast open spaces, a horizon which he could no longer find in his native land. Basically, the author was animated by constant opposition, an opposition which he felt 'in his body', between his desire to recapture a lost, *sacred* unity with the world around him and the disillusionment or worse still the disgust at seeing the world, his world, his own universe crumbling in a semantic ensemble which created false social relationships: 'each group or individual, before even ensuring his survival, is in desperate need of giving himself a meaning in a system of exchanges and relationships' (Baudrillard 1972: 76). It was at this level of inter-individual relationships that the signs of the *new culture* came into play, a *hoax* culture, as it was totally out of sync with different local realities and was attached to a *globalized semiotic matrix*. A production of signs, detached from all historical context but fixed in a hedonist present, leading to a new form of unifying dictatorship, that of conformity, eliminating all forms of class culture to create a new one, a sort of bourgeois culture which now belonged to everyone and therefore to nobody.

Pasolini's world, *his world* – the world he linked to the peasant-farmer class of his childhood, that of Frioul, but also that of Calabria, Sicily and their particularistic ways of life – could only be recreated by means of a geographical and cultural space charged with history. The Mediterranean was this age-old space, from which the greatest discoveries came marked by movement and continual exchanges. The Mediterranean maritime opening is essential for commerce and colonization and thus for cultural contacts and confrontation with *otherness*. The Mediterranean and the ancient rigidity of its traditions and its way of life. The Mediterranean is a condensed version of life, this sea matrix of cultures, joining three continents, which discovers in its waves a type of unity. The Mediterranean is this *summary of natural poetry*, whose aesthetic resonances awakened in Pasolini a kind of wonder which was at the basis of the opening to *otherness*.

This was why Pasolini gave so much importance to location scouting from an artistic and personal perspective, because it was a way for him to come face to face with as yet unknown countries and cultures, guessed at by the poet but not truly experienced at that point, interiorized by *experience*. Such was Pasolini's desire, and in a sense his hope when faced with the irreality of an Italian society in total transformation, when he undertook his journeys: to reimmerse himself in a *popular and true reality*, to come face to face with countries that had not yet been fully afflicted by *progressive cultural destruction* and to feel alive in this space in order to be able to observe it from within, like an anthropologist who immerses themselves in a society for their studies. For Pasolini, it was the *concrete experience of otherness*. He was searching for this permanent confrontation with otherness which he knew or had known, preferably alone, as he says in The Scent of India, 'it is only alone, lost, dumb and on foot that I can manage to recognize things' ([1962] 2007: 60).

Recognize: this is the key word for Pasolini's hunger for life and experimentation, a way for him *to be and to act in the world*. *Re-cognize* is to rediscover in the *elsewhere* something which the poet already knows, which he has already experienced, seen, felt, but which he can no longer get hold of in today's Italian society. It is not simply the cultural differences of which he writes at length in *The Scent of India* which are striking in Pasolinian experiences of travel and meetings, but paradoxically, the meeting points in the way of occupying nature, of *being present in the world*, between populations from different countries and popular and rural Italian cultures. He rediscovered a human essence, a universal culture of necessary existence, made roughly with simplicity: 'it is this enlightened peasants' world, pre-national and pre-industrial, which survived until recently which I regret (it is not for nothing that I live as far away as possible, in a Third World country where it still survives, although the Third World itself is undergoing so called development)' (Pasolini [1975] 1987: 86).

When Pasolini spoke of the Third World, a theme to which he returned more and more, notably in his references to the *capitalist revolution*, in short when writing about his position regarding changing reality, it was not just countries previously known as 'underdeveloped' and known today as 'developing' which were at the centre of his thinking. It was the issue of the North/South split that interested him, whilst noting that obvious economic differences between the two poles went hand in hand with a type of cultural colonialism no longer based on violence and direct submission but on a techno-media network, supported by economic directives founded on neoliberal theories imposed by international economic organizations (notably the IMF). The whole of the Mediterranean basin was thus incorporated into the term 'Third World': Central/Southern Italy, Greece, the Middle East and Northern Africa. It was in the heart of this area that the author did most of his travelling. It was not just a geographical area, but more of an abstract concept. It was a *poetic space for wandering* which knew no frontiers and which stretched as far as Uganda and Tanzania, where Pasolini made his documentary *Notes for an African Orestes* (*Appunti per un'Orestiade africana*, 1969), location scouting of sorts, for a film with Aeschylus's *Orestes* as the starting point.

Pasolini revisiting an ancient classic and wanting to relocate it into a contemporary time period and place, Africa, is revelatory of a new link that the filmmaker and poet was weaving between the contemporary reality of the Third World and ancient Greece, the foundation of Mediterranean culture and civilization. Pasolini had translated *Orestes* (1988) between 1959 and 1960, at Vittorio Gassman's request and already in his translation Pasolini had modernized the original text, in order to make the story more relevant and be better heard, not by modernizing the essence but its form: thus, for example, Zeus becomes God and the Temple, the Church. Naturally, Pasolini's translation concentrates not on the literary but the setting, which is an important part of Pasolini's theory; in his *Manifesto per un nuovo teatro*, he stated his affiliation with or his return to the origins of ancient theatre of 'Athenian democracy', the theatre in ritual form, totally ritualized, religiously, politically and socially (Pasolini 1968a). He saw in the archetypical and complex characters of the Greek tragedies 'a means to express ideas and concepts theatrically: in a word, to express what we now call an ideology' (Pasolini 2003: 1008–9), in other words, a principally political perception. Pasolini's objective was the articulation between ideology and myth, ideology allowing a profound transformation of society through revolutionary action, so subversive compared to the norm, underlining the universality of the myth and its centrality in the cultural edifice of collectivity.

Pasolini's updated translation of *Orestes* thus aimed to return the meaning – *its historical and sacred meaning* – to Aeschylus's work, because there could not be any real understanding of the founding principles of the original text without reference to contemporary reality. In this way, Pasolini brought the ancient world back to life, not by representing it as such and by cutting it off, so to speak, from the transhistorical nature of myth and Greek tragedy, but by echoing the idea of Kandinsky who thought that 'to attempt to revive the principles of ancient art, can only lead to the creation of still-born works' (Kandinsky 1989: 51). It is by updating Greek tragedy, whilst obviously retaining the evocative power of Aeschylus's work, that Pasolini was truly able to 'bring back to life' the issues, notably political (in the comparison established between the birth of Greek democracy and contemporary Italian democracy), contained in the trilogy, without which this text would remain, in the spectator's mind, an ancient work, an out-of-date classic, which could no longer speak to us. The writer thus believed in the topicality of myth and Greek tragedies (which are a kind of representation of myth) (see Vernant and Vidal-Naquet 2002).

The central idea of *Notes for an African Orestes* is more or less identical and was initially based on Pasolini's translation for Gassman. The author's intention was, however, more wide-ranging: this work was to be used in a cinematographic project entirely dedicated to the Third World, *Poema sul Terzo Mondo*, that was to include five episodes on five countries, with five different but similar situations (India, Central Africa, the Middle East, South America, the US and black American ghettos). *Notes for an African Orestes* finally became a documentary, commissioned by the RAI (Radio Televisione Italiana; but who later rejected it), which took part in a broader cultural deliberation on the historical future of central Africa and more generally Third World countries. Transposing Aeschylus' tragedies into contemporary Africa was once again a way for Pasolini to bring Greek myth back into contemporary reality, and notably into the political and cultural reality of underdeveloped societies in full-blown structural and cultural transition.

Pasolini's interest in Aeschylus's trilogy, and in Greek tragedy in general, whose themes he brought up to date, was political, like his theatre, 'Teatro di Parola' (Theater of Word) (Pasolini 1968a), where it is through the body that our most buried, most primitive and most archaic feelings resurge. In all his theatrical works, particularly in *Orgia* (1968), *Bestia da stile* (1965–74) and *Affabulazione* (1966–9), it is body language which prevails whilst 'words are totally de-sanctified, better still, destroyed in favor of pure physical presence' (Pasolini 1968a), and this is also why Eros, essential in Pasolinian thinking and central to his theory of *cultural mutation*, incessantly interferes with his characters' lives, in his plays just as in his films, especially the later ones. For the poet, sexuality as it was considered at the time of cultural mutation, 'is in reality a convention, an obligation, a social duty, a social anxiety, an inevitable characteristic of the consumer's quality of life' ([1975] 1987), it is a fundamental vehicle for behavioural change. The author knew that the themes developed by the myths are not simply a reflection of ancient Greek times, of a fallen antiquity, but concern archetypical situations that can be transposed into modern times because Pasolini believed in the 'timelessness of myths' (Fusillo 2007). By transposing Aeschylus' tragedy into the African area, by running two historical times and two opposed geographical areas in parallel and by operating a kind of mimetic overlapping, the poet achieved a transformation of the work whilst preserving the context of opposition represented by Aeschylus. He put into question *the future of modernity and its values* by presenting archaic worlds beset by trouble and change.

In this way, the filmmaker rediscovered in modern Africa, through an almost anthropological view, a social and political situation similar to that described in Aeschylus' tragedy, bringing to life the truth of the myth and its topicality for a society confronted by a *new future*, with the presence of Europeans and their culture, totally opposed to that of traditional Africa. At the same time, we witness in *Orestes* the birth of the first democratic institutions in the first tribunal in history, presided over by Athena, judging Orestes for his matricide. Aeschylus puts new Athenian democracy centre stage as a replacement for tribal justice. It is the emergence of the 'world of polis' (see Biancofiore 2003, 2007), the 'civilized and democratic' world which sets the foundations for a new society and announces the gradual disappearance of archaic Greece. In the same way, Africa sees its traditional way of life suddenly being swept aside by civil and apparently democratic institutions, through the intervention of colonial powers.

By means of this fundamental opposition – the historic birth of democracy versus the ancient cultural world – the author raised the question of the *permanency of the sacred*, his permanency in a world which erases all traces of naturally scandalous elements linked to the sacred (erotism, death, abjection and stain ...). We could analyse Pasolini's works through the prism of the sacred: the myth expresses, in a non-exclusive manner, the permanency of a *sacred reality* which the writer referred to as desacralization of the modern world. Thus, his denunciation of bourgeois entropy was linked to the loss of expression of the sacred which he noted and whose principles he tried to bring back into being through his works. He denounced the inability of the bourgeoisie to accept the reality of the world, its *inevitable tragic side*, because of its marked tendency towards repression.

It is the subject of the book *Teorema* (Pasolini 1968b), which later became a film, where the arrival of a stranger in a Milanese family radically transforms the meaning of their existence. *Teorema* describes the irruption of the sacred into a bourgeois Italian family typical of the 1960s through the almost Christ-like character of the stranger, played by Terence Stamp, who reveals, by his presence alone, the fears, wishes and desires of each person. He makes their true essence burst out, the smothered aspirations of each member of the family beyond their bourgeois conformist attitudes which hinder the expression of being. Eroticism, which is a specific form by which the sacred can express itself, plays a big part in this film, as a vehicle for transcendence which until then is suppressed by bourgeois social duties, and which an element marked by *the stranger's seal* (the stranger) suddenly awakens, bringing about a total reversal of the initial situation.

With Pasolini, the upsurge of the sacred often occurs through eroticism and it plays a big part in Greek mythology. The author even believed that it was through eroticism and changing erotic behaviour that the 'new culture' brought about the mutation:

> in the first phase of the cultural and anthropological crisis, which began around the end of the 60s, when the unreality of the sub-culture of mass media began to triumph and therefore mass communication, the last rampart of reality seemed to be made of 'innocent' bodies, with the ancient violence of their sexual organs. Indeed, the representation of Eros, seen in a human context just recently overtaken by history, but still physically present (in Naples, the Middle East), was always something which fascinated me personally, individually as an author and as a man. (Pasolini [1976] 2000: 82)

This perception of the 'popular' body, freed, a body which *lives*, a body which accepts itself in its nudity when the bourgeoisie finds it vulgar, Pasolini discovered this again in the Mediterranean: it was a solar body, open and not closed, which did not fear nudity, or *endangerment* to use Bataille's (2001) terminology.

It was in the Mediterranean space and culture that Pasolini set off in search of the sacred. He did it with Greek mythology in mind, and notably, we have seen at the crucial historic moment when civilization replaced archaic or 'barbarous' Greece, when the first tribunal, to return to the Aeschylus' tragedies, replaced the law of 'an eye for an eye' which was practised at that time. The Italian writer exploited Mediterranean stories, culture and mythology in most of his films and literary works. He signed up to the long tradition of the great Greek thinkers feeding on their texts and ideas in order to reinvent them: the fixed point of his stories was the permanent opposition, either directly (*Teorema*) or implicitly (*Medea*) present, between the world of bourgeois reason and the sacred, mythical universe of the modern underclass.

The latter universe was represented as the *people*, enamoured of their rituals and the places which surround them: naked places, desert-like, symbolic for the poet-filmmaker of virgin, natural spaces, a world close to the earth, a vital source, a chthonic world, where presence becomes concrete, where the sacred can express itself. Unlike in the anonymity of cities, where it loses itself. Thus the ancient world becomes a *universe of reference* for the author, myths offering archetypes that can act as a general representation of existence, often through allegory or metaphor, but always with the view to offering a vision of the world promoting constructions, origins or even cultural fractures.

The chthonic, desert-like landscapes represent the *archaic sacred universe* in Pasolini's cinema. They are especially present in *Medea* and *Oedipus Rex* (1967). *Medea* was filmed, amongst others, in Syria and Turkey, namely in the region of Cappadocia, with its troglodytic dwellings and its ashen earth, whilst *Oedipus Rex* was filmed in Morocco and Italy. The author followed the original storyline of the tragedy but each time his own interpretation of the myth superimposed the original work, renewing the meaning of the original story. The topic addressed in *Orestes* was taken up again in *Medea*: the distinction between the two worlds represented is even more marked, two paradoxical worlds which conflict with one another, when in fact it is only by unification that the contradictory forces which rock the world and collectivity can be balanced, and *coexist*.

The foundations of the rupture are expressed here, the impossibility of allowing our own ambiguity facing *Eros* and *Thanatos* to exist in the world with our cultural principles: because 'life and death are to be found to the same degree in a being, like thesis and antithesis. So something superior rises above them, values and tensions of our existence which are above life and death and which can no longer be reached by opposition, but only through them life comes into its own, with its supreme meaning' (Simmel 1988: 174). It is only through sacred space that this ambiguity can be represented and surpassed because it is there that our 'accursed share' (see Bataille 1967) is exteriorized, accursed because it threatens the profane universe. In *Medea*, we find Jason's world, a metaphor for the modern world, 'dominated by speech, de-sacralized [...] pragmatic, moving forward in a straight line towards progress, in other terms, towards rational ripening which should allow the young hero to retake power' (Fusillo 2007: 161). Medea's world, subject to the seasonal cycles and suffused with rituals, magic, dreams – *signs* – is an *archaic religious world* from which Jason's world has detached itself. An 'archaic, hieratic, clerical universe' (Pasolini quoted in Naldini 1991: 335), a chthonic world which expresses itself through fertility rituals of the earth, the first scene in the film, and the sacrifice, the culmination of *sacred logic*. The representation of two temporalities and two spaces colliding is, once again, the sacred world which is that of Medea, the great priestess, and the profane world of Jason, marked by *politics* and *power struggles*.

Pasolini's film and his vision of Euripides is supported by all the anthropological theory to which we have already alluded, notably Mircea Eliade, as Fusillo (2007: 161) points out. The filmmaker attempted to capture the effects provoked in Medea by the priestess's uprooting from her chthonic universe, with her own culture, so different from Jason's, indeed almost opposites, a wrench which she feels as soon as she descends to Argos on the land of Iolcus, Jason's country. Driven by the power of her love for Jason, she sacrifices the environment which gave *a meaning and a logic to her existence* ... The humiliation which she later endures when Jason offers his hand in marriage to Glauce, daughter of Creon, King of Corinth, along with his ambition to seize power, increases her frustration and anger. It is therefore a profane pragmatism which drives Jason to *betray* Medea whose vengeance will be all the greater because of the sacrifice she made to follow Jason. It is the ancient world of Medea which gradually disappears before resurging when the thread of their love is broken. Thus, 'infanticide is the inevitable consequence of Medea's uprooting from her sacred universe, from her sexual "perdition" for Jason [...] Jason's error is to have not grasped Medea's cultural differences' (Fusillo 2007: 161).

Medea's unleashed anger is just as much the fruit of Jason's betrayal as her uprooting, the loss of her cultural references, removing from her actions the sacred meaning they had in the *archaic and vital environment, linked to natural movement*, and which give her anger an apocalyptic dimension leading her even to commit infanticide. Her now boundless fury becomes almost unhealthy and she can no longer be *integrated into the world*. She is an 'empty, unnatural repetition' (Fusillo 2007: 170). It is *reversed energy*. Her anger thus loses the framework it needs to express itself and overflows with rage. It is the confrontation between two worlds, symbolically representing modern anthropological change for Pasolini, two notions of life which have separated so far as to become opposites. *Manifestation and expression of the sacred* become the central core of cultural mutation for it is here that fundamental anthropological modification is to be found.

Beyond national borders, beyond the natural frontier formed by the Mediterranean sea, Pasolini extended countries and cultures to create a network of places and landscapes which, although far apart, were linked by a common thread which history had perpetuated and which was represented by the cultural unity of each region. According to the author, the Mediterranean, its culture and its spaces were the reflection of a perception of the world and of a way of living, from times gone by, a popular culture, proletarian to use class terminology, of the whole of the Third World. It was a proletarian culture from before cultural mutation, before the norm of bourgeois life became what should be the aim for the poorer classes, who assumed their condition with a kind of pride, a conscience. The bourgeois norm exploded this pride into shame, shame of the proletarian condition, an existential obligation to adopt bourgeois ways, thus destroying popular cultures which had existed for centuries. They had been a part of this state of 'true and shining joy' (Pasolini [1975] 1987: 96) because they did not go against the dominant culture: through their variety they formed the dominant culture, they were active, they created the presence of the poorest classes. And as Pasolini said, 'when the classical world is exhausted, when all the peasants and craftsmen die, when our post-industrial world has made the production cycle irreversible, it is then that our history will end' (quoted in Naldini 1991: 260). The classical world, according to Pasolini, reverberates in *'the peasants' and craftsmen's'* universe but also in the world of the proletariat, the proletariat that is conscious of his condition and proud of it, despite the difficulties it brings.

It is this world, which had become *'ancient'* out of necessity, which Pasolini continually sought out and represented in order to confront his spectators with reality's violent change, a change so rapid that it has met with no reflection at any point in humanity's history, notably because the tools that make cultural diffusion possible have strengthened so much as to create a uniformity of a totalitarian nature (see Chomsky 2001). But during his Mediterranean travels, the writer rediscovered these existences linked to the movements of the earth, these sacred as opposed to reasoned spaces, where ritual, myths, gestures, the body and music are in tune with the sometimes violent, sometimes *mystical* reality of the world. Greek myth once again proposes life's inherent contradictions, as much in their social form as on an individual, *ontological* basis. Pasolini was not nostalgic for a bygone era: he highlighted the gradual loss of space for expression, for a large part of mankind, and it was here that *anthropological mutation* strictly speaking existed, one not opposed to a logic of reason, of *Logos*, but which was the main element that helped to give meaning to the logic of reason (Pasolini ([1981] 2006). *Logos* and *Eros asserted themselves as two combined perceptions to discover the reality of the world, a non-fragmented reality*. A society cannot survive without the sacred universe (Caillois 1950), it cannot eliminate mankind's and the world's ambivalence, but culture must help to denote this ambivalence, in order to integrate it and bring it to light. Death, sex and violence are unavoidable elements in this world; it is impossible to try to deny or eradicate all trace of them: a *sacred space* is *needed* for them to be represented as *existing*. Numerous Mediterranean civilizations have existed based on this principle, this unavoidable contradiction that is at the heart of the world made visible and palpable. It is this contradiction that

Pasolini ceaselessly represented, in his writings and his films, taking a caustic view of the modern world with its uniformity but particularly its loss of space for expression of the sacred, emptied of any *significance*.

References

Bataille, G. (1954), *L'expérience intérieure*, Paris: Gallimard.
Bataille, G. (1967), *La part maudite*, Paris: Minuit.
Bataille, G. (2001), 'L'anus solaire' in *Œuvres complètes*, vol. I, *premiers écrits, 1922–1940*, Paris: Gallimard.
Baudrillard, J. (1970), *La société de consommation*, Paris: Denoël.
Baudrillard, J. (1972), *Pour une critique de l'économie politique du signe*, Paris: Gallimard.
Biancofiore, A. (2003), *Pasolini*, Rome and Palermo: Palumbo.
Biancofiore, A., di (ed.) (2007), *Pasolini: pour une anthropologie poétique*, Montpellier: Presses universitaires de la Méditerranée.
Caillois, R. (1950), *L'homme et le sacré*, Paris: Gallimard.
Camus, A. (1996), *Noces*, suivi de *L'été*, Paris: Gallimard.
Chomsky, N. (2001), *Propaganda and the Public Mind*, Cambridge, MA: South End Press.
Fusillo, M. (2007), *La Grecia secondo Pasolini: mito e cinema*, Rome: Carocci.
Kandinsky, W. (1989), *Du spirituel dans l'art, et dans la peinture en particulier*, Paris: Denoël.
Lipovetsky, G. (2004), *Les temps hypermodernes*, Paris: Grasset.
Marcuse, H. (1963), *Eros et civilisation*, Paris: Editions de Minuit.
Naldini, N. (1991), *Pier Paolo Pasolini*, Paris: Gallimard.
Pasolini, P. P. (1961), *La religione del mio tempo*, Milan: Garzanti.
Pasolini, P. P. ([1962] 2007), *L'odeur de l'Inde*, Paris: Denoël.
Pasolini, P. P. (1968a), 'Manifesto per un nuovo teatro', *Nuovi Argomenti*, 9: 6–22.
Pasolini, P. P. (1968b), *Teorema*, Milan: Garzanti.
Pasolini, P. P. ([1975] 1987), *Ecrits corsaires*, Paris: Flammarion.
Pasolini, P. P. ([1976] 2000), *Lettres luthériennes: Petit traité pédagogique*, Paris: Seuil.
Pasolini, P. P. ([1981] 2006), *Les dernières paroles d'un impie : entretiens avec Jean Duflot*, Paris: Gutenberg.
Pasolini, P. P. (1988), *Orestiade*, Turin: Einaudi.
Pasolini, P. P. (1992), *Pasolini su Pasolini: Conversazioni con Jon Halliday*, Parma: Guanda.
Pasolini, P. P. (1998), *Romanzi e racconti*, vols 1–2, Milan: Mondadori.
Pasolini, P. P. (2003), *Tutte le poesie I*, Milan: Mondadori.
Simmel, G. (1988), *Tragédie de la culture*, Paris: Rivages Poche.
Vernant, J.-P. and Vidal-Naquet, P. (2002), *Mythe et tragédie en Grèce ancienne*, Paris: La Découverte.

6

The Mediterranean panorama through migrant writers

Vittorio Valentino

> 'o sciore cchiù felice è 'o sciore senza radice
> corre comme 'o cane senza fune, 'o sciore senza padrune.
> o sciore cchiù felice è l'ommo senza radice
> corre comme 'o cane senza fune chist'ommo senza padrune
> nuje simmo senza padrune
>
> (The happiest flower is the rootless one,
> it runs like an unleashed dog, flower without a master
> The happiest flower is the man without roots
> it runs like an unleashed dog, this man without a master.
> We do not have a master)
> Almamegretta, 'O sciore cchiù felice', Sanacore, 1995

There is, in our simple way of observing a geographical map, a process for attributing 'differences' between different parts of the planisphere before our eyes, which might exist, through automatisms in our mind. Automatisms that certainly come from our subjective knowledge, and from the impressions that we experience. Objectively, we can always take into account elements of diversity, first physical (territory size, population) and then cultural (language, traditions, morals, religion).

However, in our era of wide-ranging communications and the transit of capital and goods, one specific area is making itself heard more than any other, the economic dimension. This dimension, more than climate, conflicts or colonizations, shows us, through the directions taken by migrations, a world more than ever divided into two parts, as ideal as they are geographical: the North and the South.

Although a dichotomy has always existed, today it relies not only on poverty and colonization but also on the consequences of it: mediocre decisional opportunities, a very low level of instruction and infrastructures, and a very difficult postcolonial situation. Here we are talking about the South(s) of the world, whose borders are evidently nuanced but can be located around and below the Equator, a line-creation that is as imaginary as it is effective.

Of the numerous areas in which those considerations are applicable, the Mediterranean basin is a perfect example, thanks to its own, unique specificity and reality, for understanding North–South dynamics in recent years, in a very complex panorama caused by very different cultures, sensibilities and religious beliefs. In just a few fundamental words, Paul Valéry summarized those places which belonged to him. As a thinker, poet and philosopher, he talked of this range of intellectual energies, of forces and potential in his text 'Inspirations méditerranéennes':

> These people kept up relations of all sorts: war, commerce, trade (whether voluntary or not), of things, knowledge, and methods; they mingled their blood, their speech, their legends and traditions. The number of ethnic elements thrown together or in contrast throughout the ages, their customs, languages, beliefs, laws, and constitutions have engendered an incomparable vitality in the Mediterranean world. (Valéry [1933] 1975: 33)

The concomitance of intellectual elements and exceptional materials make this closed basin an example of exchanges and interactions; indeed, whether desired or not, migratory flows have always characterized the 'human and political morphology' of these coasts since antiquity, through slavery or the search for vital resources. Forced changes for these populations can be attributed to deep fractures from even further afar – from religious wars or the exploitation exerted on colonies by European powers – and linger still in our time, hanging over all future perspectives.

To this day, the never-solved conflicts highlight the differences, even more than the common features; thus, international events such as the collapse of the Soviet Union, the Balkan War, the Israeli-Palestinian conflict, or the September 11 attacks, are reflected in this sea and amplify the contrasts. Those contrasts are followed by the backwardness of the countries located to the South of the basin in relation to the countries of the North, which are also at odds with Northern Europe. The writer Predrag Matvejević enlightens us about this topic in the Mediterranean:

The image that the Mediterranean is offering us is far from being comforting. Indeed, its Northern coast presents some backwardness in comparison to Northern Europe, its Southern coast in relation to the North. The whole basin is struggling to tie up to the continent, both in the North and the South. Can we consider this sea as a real ensemble without considering the ruptures that are breaking it down: Palestine, Lebanon, Cyprus, Maghreb, Balkans, former Yugoslavia? ([1996] 1999: 83)

This vision simultaneously asks the question of the whole and of a sea-border, given the numerous fractures between States. Matvejević thus wants to denounce a European closure towards the Mediterranean.

There is a sort of nationalism that creates a distance, one that can form a permanent gap, due to the lack of any real North–South dialogue. A dialogue bridge could be the meeting point between traditions and the future: on this topic, Matvejević explains that 'an identity of the being, by amplifying itself, overshadows or repels an identity of the making, badly defined' because 'the retrospective continues to prevail over the prospective' (p. 84).

Thus today, at the turn of the twenty-first century, the situation has basically evolved very little. The great masses of population therefore travel mainly from the Southern to the Northern coasts, but also from East to West, with similar motivations: the search for another life, a job more suitable for survival, the preservation of life itself, jeopardized by wars or political or religious persecutions.

To understand the amplitude of this phenomenon we above all need men and women whose real experience of this situation can be seen on their skin. Who, today, could shed light for us on the present situation? What measure can we use to estimate the depth of the impact of this mass migration on the habits and territory of those who leave and of those who receive these immigrants?

I strongly believe that books, authors, critics and essayists, written stories or just told stories, are the fundamental measure for perceiving this type of change, in a world, a given universe, such as the Mediterranean. Contemporary academic researchers have implemented initiatives for discussing and promoting the point of juncture of this area-basin composed of a wide range of cultures. The idea of the presence or not of a whole, as formulated by Predrag Matvejević, for instance, or the Southern thought of Franco Cassano, are a proof of this. The latter, who teaches the sociology of knowledge, proposes a 'thought from the South, a South that thinks the South, a South that wants to achieve maximum autonomy from this gigantic mutation, [...] A thought from the South must no longer think of the South or the Souths as lost and anonymous peripheries of the empire'

(Cassano 2012: 2). Feeling like one belongs to the South means looking at oneself with the potential, strength and knowledge that one already has. Being part of an ancient strength is a sign of progress and openness:

> Southern thought is the thought one feels welling up inside, there where the sea begins, where the shore interrupts all land-based fundamentalisms (especially those related to commerce and development), at the time when one discovers that the borderland is not a place where the world ends, but where those who are different come into contact, and the relationship game with the other becomes difficult and real. [...] Southern thought was truly born in the Mediterranean, on the coasts of Greece, with the opening of Greek culture toward conflicting discourses, toward the *dissòi lògoi*. In the beginning, there is never just the one, but two or more. We can never reunite the two in one: [...] we must just ensure that the two do not go their separate ways to the point of wanting each other's destruction; we must ensure that they keep talking to each other. (p. 3)

In his essay, Franco Cassano highlights the need for movement and dialogue, as well as the rise of awareness. Each word, whether on paper or not, carries a voice; each voice reflects the change realized within ourselves to live better with the 'other'.

Taking the voice of author-migrants requires appropriation, using the gifted experience of these men and women, travellers, workers, activists or refugees, who decided to bring their lives with them, to write their stories, in the form of novels, poems or something else. This comes out of necessity, as a testament, a permanent guide, after their journey.

In the last few years, it has become extremely difficult in the Mediterranean basin to collect all these voices. Some of them have unfortunately disappeared into the abyss of this sea that unites peoples, this sea that also drowns some of them during their journey, a journey that is very often made with makeshift means: in the last twenty years or so, there are an estimated 30,000 victims (dead or missing) of the journeys in the Mediterranean from South to North. These are the voices that will stay eternally silent. But it is also difficult because of the 'encounters' between migrants from so many countries, creating incredibly important crossroads.

If the elements that bring us to this migratory phenomenon are due to actual fractures in this densely inhabited space, it is precisely here that a new voice, a literature, a philosophy, issued from immigration, can intervene and affirm itself as an answer to the great fractures that divide the States. In fact, this voice comes from far away, starting with the thinkers from the beginning of the last century, such as Valéry, who travelled and explored the coasts and an idea emerged, a concrete *thought*. Valéry, in the text we quoted earlier, found a certain perspective of unity, in a common cultural dynamism from ancient times, like a foundation of everything that forms our contemporary way of life:

> Whether in the realm of natural or civil laws, the type itself was defined by Mediterranean minds. Nowhere else was the power of language, conscientiously disciplined and directed, so fully and usefully employed; language ordered by logic, [...] It was here that science broke away from empiricism and practical use, here that art cast off its symbolic origins, that literature was clearly differentiated and divided into distinct genres. ([1933] 1975: 34)

Through the importance of this common word, which goes beyond languages and countries, we can reach a common thought relating to a real sense of belonging, as well as to the development of this area. This thought transforms and adapts itself to our time through new writers, thinkers and researchers, who can act to create a reconciliation between 'us' and the 'other'. A new word of unity, one that acts from the inside, by using immigration as an experience, and the power of words as a weapon to denounce intolerance but also to observe all the phenomena that occur in relation to cultural diversity, in our times. Speaking in this context, as we observed in Franco Cassano's thought, means expressing a vision of the components of our time. The writer expresses himself severely, and his word also acts as a weapon; this is to awaken the conscience, to highlight secularization and the immobile individualism of Mediterranean society:

> Freedom and happiness have come to be equated more and more with the exclusive care of our private well-being, with the warmth of our domestic spaces: even as public, open spaces deteriorate, we can always decorate our balconies, and perfume and purify the air inside our homes and cars while making it unbreathable outside; we can listen to sermons against consumerism between TV commercials, and go far into the night for serious programming, bewildered refugees in a world where thought is seen as the intermediate state between depression and repression. (Cassano 2012: 13)

With these words, Cassano denounces the presence of a mentality and a way of living specific to the South, which has led a great number of individuals to leave it as a result. But it also marks the realization of the contemporary intellectuals who stride along many paths: the ideological and the philosophical, but also the social and historical. We are in fact talking about the serious consequences of migration, but also the sea, and the poetry linked to its inherent danger. In the same work, for instance, we found the strength of a thought that blends poetry and social data:

The sea makes possible a breakthrough that opens the mind to the idea of leaving, to the experience of betrayal that makes faithfulness more uncertain but also more valuable and complex; that invents nostalgia, the inward pain and longing for one's homeland that is the companion of every traveler. It makes every human being a foreigner and every foreigner a human being, turns separation into companionship, allows more than one soul to inhabit us. (p. 11).

We have here the presence of intellectual literature, which knows how to combine the humanist with the scientific point of view in order to explore the migratory phenomenon. I do not think that this sensitivity from an Italian intellectual is solely the fruit of a simple coincidence, because the Italian case is surely one of the most significant in this human and cultural panorama. The geographical position of the Italian peninsula, standing in the middle of the sea like a bridge, its arm outstretched to all the Mediterranean coasts, makes it a privileged observation base. The past twenty years, we have witnessed a radical change in Italy: the country has gone from being a 'country of emigration' to a 'host country', confronted with a phenomenon of massive immigration, mainly from Eastern Europe and Africa. No intellectual could remain silent, as Angela Biancofiore showed, when she summarized the situation with lucidity, in 2006 in the review *Narrativa:*

Le nostre coste, soprattutto la Puglia, la Calabria e la Sicilia, stanno vivendo da alcuni anni e con un ritmo serrato l'arrivo di popolazioni straniere. La situazione è carica di tensione, sia con le forze dell'ordine, sia con le popolazioni locali che non sono pronte ad accogliere un tale flusso migratorio in regioni spesso caratterizzate dalla povertà e dalla disoccupazione. (2006: 100–1)

(Our coasts, especially those of Apulia, Calabria and Sicily, have been subject to the rapidly growing arrivals of foreign populations for several years. The situation is very tense, whether in terms of law enforcement or the local populations who are not ready to welcome this migratory flow in regions often characterized by poverty and unemployment.)

The great wave of the 1980s, and especially of the 1990s, left a very strong sign, because it changed the identity of the country as a whole, giving it simultaneously the extent of its limitations: a lack of resources and feelings of insecurity, which in certain local contexts could be even harsher, such as Southern Italy. That is why Italy remains a fundamental example, because it knows (and has known) many specific cases: first, the phenomenon of emigration concerning the whole country, then the transformation into a host country, and this in a situation of major North–South disparity. But what about the authors we have quoted? What have they dealt with? What is their message?

In order to answer these questions, we must deal first with the situation in Italy, from the emergence of this new reality, taking into account two distinct interdependent aspects. The first aspect to be explored is certainly that of the Italian writers who looked at the migration question after having lived through the experience themselves, and we cannot exclude Erri De Luca, a Neapolitan writer, worker and activist who emigrated from his native South and who traces an exemplary and fundamental social panorama.

He actually completed a series of journeys all around the Mediterranean to work or to provide humanitarian aid. De Luca tells us about his emigrant situation, but also his condition as a common man who came into contact with the 'other', so close but sometimes so far. After Africa, Eastern Europe or the Middle East, he decided to write down his words and show his impressions, his observations, to recount without prophetism, the beauty and difficulties of the populations he met. His view acquires increasing importance over the pages because it reveals the story of a man, who left a harsh, transforming South, to join another, more complex, tougher South. The years of his left-wing militancy bring a lucid, critical look to the present, but also to the possible future of the whole Mediterranean basin. In 1995, in *Pianoterra*, De Luca detected the change that was happening:

> Un tempo, anche noi nati sotto il Volturno ci dicevamo del sud. [...]. Fornivamo braccia a buon mercato alle Americhe, alle miniere, alle acciaierie. Vendevamo sale, lavoravamo da bambini e sul lungomare tiravamo reti lontane con corde grosse come braccia. [...]. Non dovevamo più partire verso l'inferno straniero, ora ce l'avevamo in casa. Eravamo ancora del sud e ci piaceva dirlo, scrivercelo addosso quando con quel nome di fabbrica passavamo nelle piazze d'Italia intorno a un palco. Eravamo la Questione Meridionale. (1995: 25)

> (In the past, we too, born at the foot of the Volturno River, used to call ourselves Southerners. [...]. We provided cheap workforce to the Americas, to the mines, and to the steel mills. We sold salt, we worked at an early age, and standing on the seashore, we pulled nets from afar with ropes as thick as arms. [...]. We did not have to go to the foreign hell anymore. Now we had it at home. We were still Southerners, and we liked to say it and to brand ourselves as such when we walked around the squares and stages of Italy. We were the Southern Question.)

In the mid-1990s, De Luca gave us a parallel with his militant 1970s and traces of a significant parable: the South as he knew it at the time had changed; it had moved and thus created new disparities. The Italian case is an example because it marks this frontier of change. Despite the still difficult situation in Southern Europe and in Italy, the real poverty, expressed by the shift of masses of population, moved house and marked its difference through a wall of water, that of the Mediterranean, a wall to jump over, completely, to start to live and hope. De Luca further states:

> Intanto le nostre città si popolano di un sud mobile. Le stazioni, le prigioni, i ponti, i sottopassaggi e i semafori ci mostrano a domicilio il sud. Noi non lo siamo più. (p. 25)

> (Meanwhile, our cities are getting populated by a mobile south. The stations, prisons, bridges, underpasses and traffic lights show us the south at home. We are not it (the South) anymore.)

This mobile South thus represents a significant part of our population, which today lives off expedients and clandestineness. De Luca's poetry denounces a situation which, ten years later, still has not changed: in 2005, the writer published *Solo andata: righe che vanno troppo spesso a capo*, in two parts: a novel in verses ('Solo andata') and a series of poems ('Visite'). He stages part of the Mediterranean social landscape, with its suffering and indignation at the injustices. De Luca imagined the tragic trip by a group of illegal immigrants heading towards the Northern coasts:

> Non fu il mare ad raccoglierci,
> noi raccogliemmo il mare a braccia aperte.
> Calati da altopiani incendiati da guerre e non dal sole,
> traversammo i deserti del Tropico del Cancro. [...]
> Dicono: siete sud. No, veniamo dal parallelo grande,
> dall'equatore centro della terra.
> La pelle annerita dalla più dritta luce,
> ci stacchiamo dalla metà del mondo, non dal sud. (2005: 11–13)

> (It was not the sea which received us,
> but we received the sea with open arms.
> Down from the high plains burned down by wars and not by the sun,
> We have crossed the deserts of the Tropic of Cancer. [...]
> We were told: you are the south. No, we come from the same great parallel,
> from the equator, center of the earth.
> The skin darkened by the straightest of lights,
> we detach ourselves from half the world, not from the south.)

Those same individuals who accomplish these exhausting journeys sometimes decide to undertake a work that may be 'cathartic': that of recounting. Here we are talking about another aspect of the literature of migration, of these men and women who have decided to write in the language of their host country to talk about their leaving experience, their arrival and their integration into this new life and, in this new state or sometimes world-continent, that of hope.

The phenomenon started in the early 1990s, in countries where immigration was new: this was the case for Italy, Spain and Greece for instance. Looking at the Italian peninsula is a way of once again having the example of a mixed culture under construction, absolutely 'in the making', worthy of all our attention, as a perfect exploration area (see Pasolini 1964; Abate 2006).

However, we must quote those, like Armando Gnisci, who collected the first migrant writings when they first appeared. Gnisci understood the importance of the first wave of migrants, their possibility for expression and their narrative potential, as a means of exploring the migratory phenomenon at its best. This university teacher of comparative literature at the University of Rome La Sapienza was the first, in Italy, to use the term Creolization to describe the advent of the literature of migration, in his work *Creolizzare l'Europa*, published in 2003. In the introduction to the book, with a very explicit title 'Prima ondata' (First wave), we find the importance and weight given to these changes:

> In Italia viviamo in diretta e all'urto l'esperienza della prima ondata dei migranti e dei loro scrittori e artisti. Essi vivono tra due mondi e, a voler essere precisi, non appartengono a una "prima generazione", che sarebbe (e che sarà) piuttosto quella generata sul nuovo suolo, "prima indigena e creola". Parlo, invece, propriamente di scrittori della migrazione in Italia di prima ondata, perché essi portano con sé e comunicano l'esperienza di chi ha vissuto, e continua a vivere nella memoria la prima parte della propria esistenza altrove, un altrove che era, e rimane, comunque patria, e la seconda la vive da qualche anno in una nuova lingua. (2003: 7)

> (In Italy, we are living directly and as a sort of shock the experience of the first wave of migrants and of their authors and artists. They live between two worlds and, to be precise, do not belong to a "first generation", which is (and will be) those born in the new land, "first indigenous and Creole". I'm talking, on the contrary, truly of authors of migration in Italy coming from a first wave, because they carry in them and communicate the experience of the one who lived, and continues to live in the memory of the first part of his existence elsewhere, an elsewhere that was, and that remains, anyhow the homeland, and the second homeland, for some years, in a new language.)

First, Gnisci realized the situation and talked a few lines later of the possibility of 'gathering in a contemporary way and participating in the phenomenon of the birth of a form of Creole literature'. We find ourselves faced with a dynamic effort of active participation and not waiting and observing. This realization implies an absolute help in the birth and flowering of this new form of writing. Once again, Gnisci stresses the possibilities of the 'Italian case' we talked about earlier:

> Da un certo punto di vista, insomma, siamo indietro rispetto all'Inghilterra, alla Francia e alla Germania, che conoscono una letteratura della migrazione di seconda e terza generazione, ma, per altro verso, siamo all'avanguardia, perché in quelle nazioni il fenomeno non fu colto fin dal primissimo apparire. [...] come italiano e come letterato, ho risposto mettendomi in corsa al suo primo manifestarsi all'inizio degli anni Novanta del secolo scorso. (pp. 7–8)

> (From a certain point of view, all in all, we are behind the times compared to Great Britain, France and Germany, which have second and third generation literature of migration of, but on the other hand, we are avant-gardiste, because in those nations the phenomenon was not perceived as soon as it appeared. [...] as an Italian and a scholar, I responded by putting myself in the race at the first demonstrations in the early 1990s.)

In his essays, the author expresses his willingness to understand the new phenomena of his time. He is thus the impetus behind a new trend of studies recognizing the importance of migrant literature in the Mediterranean as a whole.

There is a continuity, through a series of less studied passages and mutations from the first generation towards the new, which gives this concept of Creolization life. In his work, *Nuovo Planetario Italiano*, Gnisci talks about integration without any barriers, the result of a history which is henceforth shared:

> Sostengo che i migranti, e i migranti scrittori così come gli scrittori-migranti, sono definiti nel loro importante ed eccezionale destino da loro stessi [...]. Chi, invece, scrive, suona o fa cinema ed è figlio/a di migranti, partecipa direttamente alla incipiente creolizzazione dell'Europa. Fa parte di una nuova e importante storia comune, che comincia appena ad essere narrata. (2006: 31)

> (I believe that migrants, and author-migrants as well as migrant writers, are defined in their important and remarkable destiny by themselves. [...] The one who, on the contrary, writes, plays music, or makes films, and is the son or daughter of migrants, directly participates in the incipient Creolization of Europe. He is part of a new, significant shared story, which is just barely starting to be told.)

Creolization does not only concern the Euro-Mediterranean region, but for those who perceived its importance, and as the common use of the word indicates, it does go beyond this area. On this topic, we can quote the Caribbean writer and philosopher Edouard Glissant, who, throughout his career, participated in the crossing of cultures. In an interview for *Le Monde 2*, he mentioned a phenomenon concerning the whole world, beyond our Mediterranean area:

> We live in a perpetual disruption where civilizations interweave, large parts of culture turn and mix, where those who are afraid of interbreeding become extremists. That is what I call a chaos-world. [...]
>
> Creolization is an interbreeding of arts, or of languages, which produces something unexpected. It is a way of transforming ourselves in a continuous manner, without losing track. Creolization applies not only to organisms, but also to cultures. And cultures are more complex bodies than an organism. [...] When I say that our world is Creolizing, all cultural creation does not necessarily become Creole, but it is becoming surprising, complicated, and inextricably mixed with other cultures. The Creolization of the world is the creation of an open and inextricable culture, it occurs in all domains, music, visual arts, literature, cinema, cuisine, at a vertiginous speed. (2004: 26–9)

Even so, the real step forward is the one that transforms a 'desire' into an 'editorial desire'. The fact of giving space and visibility to new migrant writers does not always represent a source of important income in the editorial field, especially in comparison with the writers native to the host country. In that case, the work of Gnisci for Italian Creolization has been fundamental:

> Si tratta della poetica che da anni vado sperimentando, della mutua decolonizzazione tra europei e stranieri migranti, anche attraverso la produzione di opere comuni. Questa via va in direzione opposta o antagonista rispetto a quella della critica, soprattutto giornalistica, che parla, dall'alto delle tribune del potere mediatico, di 'ghettizzazione' degli scrittori migranti dentro alcuni miseri contenitori editoriali o promozionali a loro specialmente dedicati, osannando i 'prodotti', sia pur rari dei grandi gruppi editoriali. (2006: 34–5)
>
> (It is a question of the poetics that I have experienced for years, of mutual decolonization between Europeans and foreign migrants, also through the production of common works. This path goes in the opposite or antagonistic direction to that of critics, in particular journalistic critics who, from the rostrum of media power, talk about the ghettoization of

migrant writers within miserable editorial or promotional containers specially dedicated to them, praising the 'products', although rare, of large publishing groups.)

The decolonization Gnisci is talking about is the way, as intellectual as it is personal, of freeing oneself from the direct or indirect influence exercised on the colonies, since the great colonial powers officially left them. The liberating power of speech, the expressive possibility of the new language frees the writers from their past and 'traditional' official languages such as French. Still in the anthology *Nuovo Planetario Italiano* and with this mind, one of the North African migrant writers who affirmed herself in Italy, Amara Lakhous, tells us:

> Le opere letterarie prodotte dalla migrazione maghrebina [...] presentano alcune caratteristiche comuni. Prima di tutto il fatto di non essere scritte in francese, la lingua dei colonizzatori, ma in italiano [...] L'altro che in questo caso è soprattutto la lingua della nuova terra [...] alla quale nelle pagine di questi autori è riservato un posto speciale proprio perché rappresenta la chiave d'ingresso all'inaccessibile mondo degli altri, l'Italia. (2006: 157)

(Literary works produced by Maghreb migrants [...] have some common features. First of all, the fact that they are not written in French, the language of colonizers, but in Italian [...] Secondly, in this case, it is mainly the language of the new land [...] to which these authors reserve a special place because it represents the key giving them access to the inaccessible world of others, Italy.)

Maghreb constitutes a great base of departures for Mediterranean migration but also an important testimony of elements linked to migration and integration. As a matter of fact, many writers are intensely active in terms of literature, and this transcends borders: Tahar Ben Jelloun, for instance, has written in French and Italian and has been translated into dozens of languages. Other authors with less visibility still forge links between their origins, present and future, in their mother tongue and most of all, as we have already said, in the new host language.

The situation of Arab migrants, far from their country for various reasons – economic, ideological or political – takes on its full meaning through contact with the other migratory realities around Italy and Europe. We have to consider other major upheavals, which have caused the mobility of the populations from the Balkans, following the fall of the Soviet Union, the end of Hoxha's regime in Albania or the war that inflamed the former Yugoslavia. These political disintegrations, which led to massive migratory movements, spread over more or less short periods, made Western Europe the prime destination. As the main themes are the same, all those new realities have many common points: the new life of these men and women facing 'others', differences, the memory of their former life, the suffering and sensations felt on both the personal and moral levels. Their own notions of daily life have been transformed by the distance from all that represents their known world. The autobiographic narrative thus remains the most commonly used for recounting their practical, everyday life, but also the spiritual one for making their voices heard and reaffirming the presence, existence and the integration journey followed by each one in their new culture, in the new country, in a transversal way, no matter what the origin of the individual.

All the desire to tell first goes through a journey in which many migrants have lost much, even sometimes their loved ones, their hope and their dignity. But regardless, this impetus comes from a strength and from a need to write, maybe, in order to build and rebuild oneself completely. The weight of the journey or the imprisonment in the past, in nostalgia, do not inhibit travellers, who become, over words, more than individuals who are carrying a heavy baggage behind them. They are, in the end, militants for a better South, in which there would not be room for a sea-wall or devastating and uncertain crossings.

Migrant writers are the link between the philosophical idea of a common Mediterranean and the modern idea of opening and integration, which has emerged in the last twenty years in Europe, through awareness of the consequences, and causes, of migration. This is a possible link facing the impossibility of understanding the 'other', and the unadapted policies implemented to this day, which feed only on hatred and repression, without any real harmony between departure and host countries.

Although in our research our unit of measure is found in migrants' words, it is today fundamental that these words be considered not only as literature but also as a real call for another South, because this South of the world is not – and must not be – the only South possible.

References

Abate, C. (2006), *Il mosaico del tempo grande*, Milan: Mondadori.
Biancofiore, A. (2006), 'Stranieri al Sud: per una ridefinizione delle frontiere', *Narrativa*, 28: 99–118.
Cassano, F. (2012), *Southern Thought and Other Essays on the Mediterranean*, trans. N. Bouchard and V. Ferme, New York: Fordham University Press.
De Luca, E. (1995), *Pianoterra*, Rome: Quolibet.
De Luca, E. (2005), *Solo andata*, Milan: Feltrinelli.
Glissant, E. (2004), 'La créolisation du monde est irréversible' (interview), *Le Monde 2*, 31 December: 26–9.
Gnisci, A. (ed.) (2006), *Nuovo Planetario Italiano*, Troina: Città Aperta Edizioni.

Gnisci, A. (2003), *Creolizzare l'Europa*, Rome: Meltemi editore.
Lakhous, A. (2006), 'Maghreb', in A. Gnisci (ed.), *Nuovo Planetario Italiano*, 155–87, Troina: Città Aperta Edizioni.
Matvejević, P. ([1996] 1999), *Mediterranean: A Cultural Landscape*, Berkeley: University of California Press.
Pasolini, P. P. (1964), 'Profezia', in *Poesia in forma di rosa*, Milan: Garzanti.
Valéry P. ([1933] 1975), *Collected works*, vol. 15, trans. by M. Mathews and J. Mathews, Princeton, NJ: Princeton University Press.

7

The other Mediterranean: Italian migration poetry

Flaviano Pisanelli

> *esser vasto e diverso*
> *e insieme fisso:*
> *e svuotarmi così d'ogni lordura*
> *come tu fai che sbatti sulle sponde*
> *tra sugheri alghe asterie*
> *le inutili macerie del tuo abisso*
>
> (to be vast, to be diverse,
> yet to be fixed:
> and so to empty myself of all uncleanliness
> just as you do when you toss upon the beach
> among cork and seaweed and starfish
> the useless rubble of your abyss)
> Eugenio Montale, Mediterraneo

The Mediterranean space as the 'centre' of the world

For centuries, Western critique and historiography played a part in elaborating a rather static and homogeneous image of the Mediterranean around which the Europeans have, on the one hand, established a set of limits and boundaries and, on the other, learned to interpret the rest of the world from their own point of view. Becoming an 'immutable centre' beyond which 'other' civilizations and 'other' unknown (or very little known) lands developed, the Mediterranean space imposed itself as a measure, a 'filter', a 'uni-verse', a perspective from which Western people have told and orientated their own history, as well as that of the 'Others'.

Since ancient times, Europeans have considered the Mediterranean basin as a closed space within which Western culture, identity and imagination have been able to elaborate a true Eurocentric view of the world. This world view has been questioned by postcolonial critique and literature in recent decades. Introducing new concepts, such as cultural blending and interculturality, has profoundly altered the nature and dynamics of the everchanging relations between the worlds which form – according to Edouard Glissant's renowned definition – the current 'chaos-world'.[1]

The expression *mare nostrum*, used by the Romans with the aim of building a huge and homogeneous empire around a sea which should have represented its centre, its vital point, the source of endless richness, explains the geopolitical meaning the Europeans have attributed to the Mediterranean since ancient times and long before the development of a real European identity. Thus, down through the centuries, the Mediterranean was considered the centre and identity pivot of a developed civilization capable of simultaneously confronting the underdeveloped, tyrannical culture of Asian peoples, organized around a very hierarchical society and little accustomed to exchanges, and the spatial void the Greeks had established in the Strait of Gibraltar, where they had located the well-known 'Pillars of Hercules'.

Until the fall of the Western Roman Empire, the Mediterranean sea was the 'centre' of the civilized world and, at the same time, the *limen* between the known and the unknown worlds. In other words, it represented a symbolic, geopolitical space of justice where order, sense of proportion and happiness prevailed. This image of the Mediterranean as the 'centre-frontier' of the world endured due to the spread of Christianity. Reinterpreting Roman and Greek polytheism from an allegorical point of view, and with the end to the dream of a continuing Roman Empire through the strength of a religious

---

[1] Edouard Glissant develops the concept of 'one-world' which he opposes to the contemporary phenomenon of globalization which risks erasing a certain number of populations and civilizations not included in the economic and political logic imposed by dominant cultures. The concept of 'one-world' is based on the notion of globalization which favours the elaboration of a centrifugal identity based on the power of mutual 'relations' between the different cultures and identities in the world. This essentially poetic approach to the notion of identity denies the Eurocentric model of root-identity, in the name of which mankind has often undergone various conflicts and sufferings. By the expression 'one-world' or 'chaos world', Glissant means a cultural blending which cannot be limited to the *melting pot* concept. Indeed, it summarizes and achieves the cultural complexity of a contemporary world able to transform itself in accordance with the relations and exchanges the different cultures establish (see Glissant 1996: 60 et passim).

doctrine, Christianity aimed at imposing itself not only on Europe but also on the Southern and Eastern coasts of the Mediterranean.

The challenge of creating a 'Christian space' which could unite a certain number of peoples around the *mare nostrum* was first achieved by Charlemagne, who founded the Holy Roman Empire after being made emperor by Pope Leo III. This episode caused a breach between the northern and southern Mediterranean coasts, with the former Christian and the latter Arabic and Islamic. As a result of this breach, a true European identity – later confirmed by the birth of the various nation-states – started to assert itself and spread.

After witnessing the development of ancient Greek civilization based on polytheism, a sense of the tragic and a philosophy that sought infinity and the multiple sense of existence, as well as witnessing the birth, around its coasts, of the world's three major monotheistic religions (Christianity, Judaism and Islam), the Mediterranean basin gradually transformed itself into a 'space-frontier' of exclusion and separation, ignoring its original vocation of exchange and cultural permeability.[2] The increasing political power of the Catholic Church, along with its desire to impose itself as a universal religion (hence the etymology of the word 'Catholic'), was one of the first stages in Eurocentrism, based on a belief in cultural superiority which justified any abuse of other civilizations, as Armando Gnisci states:

> In che senso il cristianesimo imperiale romano rappresenta un vero e proprio capitolo della storia dell'eurocentrismo ? Direi che esso inaugura propriamente e veramente la mentalità eurocentrica, unendo il segno

---

[2] Franco Cassano claims that the ancient Greek cultural system is based on the dialectical relationship between a land profoundly connected to the sea which, in turn, allows communication between the different civilizations living in these lands: 'Il rapporto tra le differenze (con le loro dinamiche complesse, conflittuali e spesso tragiche) è qui sin dall'inizio il problema. Questo mare ad un tempo esterno e interno, abitato e guadato, questo mare-confine produce un'interruzione del dominio dell'identità, costringe ad ospitare la scissione. Qui la terra con la sua ossessione per la fissità, la sicurezza e l'appropriazione urta sempre contro un limite, qui è stata da subito più difficile la confusione tra il governo di una città e il potere del proprietario. E questo grazie all'insinuarsi e all'interporsi del mare, alla sua capacità di custodire e collegare le differenze con la loro talvolta irresistibile resistenza a federarsi, che solo il grande nemico comune (l'impero persiano) riesce a smorzare.' ('The relationship between the differences (with their complex, conflicting and often tragic dynamics) is here the problem since the very beginning. This sea, at the same time external and internal, inhabited and forded, this sea-boundary, produces an interruption in the dominance of identity, forces to host the division. Here the land with its obsession with fixity, security and appropriation always bumps up against a limit, here the confusion between the administration of a city and the power of the owner was immediately more difficult. And this is due to the insinuation and interjection of the sea, its ability to keep and connect differences with their sometimes irresistible resistance to federation, which only the great common enemy (the Persian empire) manages to soften.') ([1996] 2005 : 23–4).

dell'impero dei Romani [...] con una religione che pretende di essere 'universale' e di discendere dall'unico Dio vero, tradotto a Roma dai suoi apostoli dall'Oriente. (2009: 123)

(In what sense does Roman imperial Christianity represent a real chapter in the history of Eurocentrism? I would say that it really and truly inaugurates the Eurocentric mentality, combining the sign of the Roman Empire [...] with a religion which claims to be 'universal' and to descend from the one true God, brought to Rome by its apostles from the East.)

This 'uni-versal' conception of the Mediterranean space, opposing the principles of reciprocity and openness which pre-Platonic philosophy had already elaborated through Anaximander's thought – conversely based on the notions of *apeiron*, infinity and multitude – were reinforced in the centuries that followed by a sort of re-actualization of the myth of antiquity diffused by the culture, thought and aesthetics of the Italian Renaissance. Playing a part in idealizing and reinterpreting the past splendours on a cultural and aesthetic level, the fortune of Platonic philosophy favoured crystallization of the Mediterranean space. Until the historical and cultural revision brought about by the so-called postcolonial age and literature, the Mediterranean will mainly be regarded as a closed space in Western Christian culture, which is dominant and 'uni-versal', ready to impose its cultural and identity model on any civilization that it encounters on its path of conquest.

The modern age: The Mediterranean space as the 'frontier-periphery' of the world

The pressure of Asian populations located in the eastern Mediterranean and of the Arabic countries of the southern coasts made the Europeans – who in the meantime had become aware of living in the 'western corner' of the Asian continent – go beyond the western boundaries of the known world. It was the age of the major geographical discoveries which ushered in the modern age. It was also the beginning of the long and very painful colonization process which started with the occupation of northern and Latin America by the European naval powers (Britain, Spain and Portugal). From the fifteenth to the sixteenth century, the Mediterranean lost its geopolitical 'centrality', while maintaining its cultural prestige based on the past splendour of its history and culture.

If, from an economic point of view, the Atlantic Ocean replaced the hegemonic role that the Mediterranean had long possessed, from a cultural point of view, Eurocentrism continued, progressively transforming itself into a mentality and a reality expressed through the conquest of the western part of the world and the colonial experience legitimated by the capitalist philosophy of the dominant European cultures. Australia – the world's fifth continent – the Orient (from India to China up to Indochina), a great number of territories in the Pacific, including the small islands and the Polynesian archipelago up to Japan, and, finally, Africa all shared the same destiny.

The modern age thus started with the discovery of the New World, achieved thanks to Christopher Columbus and Ferdinand Magellan, among others. The new and fertile lands on the other side of the Atlantic fuelled the 'American dream' in the Europeans: they occupied, colonized and imposed their mentality and their identity on the natives. From this moment on, Eurocentrism became not only a mentality but, through capitalist colonialism, also a powerful reality.

From the eighteenth to nineteenth century, the Mediterranean Sea progressively lost its central position in favour of the Atlantic Ocean, located between the two new economic world powers: the United States and Britain. Armando Gnisci masterfully explains the historical and cultural passage which had consequences not only on Europe but also on other populations of the planet:

> Nel XVIII e nel XIX secolo la coppia continentale atlantica che forma il centro e il comando del mondo si concentra a nord del pianeta e diventa quella Inghilterra-USA: nel 1876 la regina Vittoria accetta la proposta del primo ministro conservatore Disraeli di assumere il titolo di "Imperatrice delle Indie"; nel 1884 una Conferenza internazionale di astronomi a Washington stabilisce che il meridiano passante per Greenwich-Londra diventi il meridiano base a 0° di longitudine, sul quale fondare anche il calcolo delle variazioni degli orari nelle varie parti del pianeta. Così la terra estrema e insulare, England, e quindi non-continentale dell'occidente atlantico europeo, diventa la misura dello spazio e del tempo del pianeta e di tutte le genti. (2009: 129–30)

(In the eighteenth and nineteenth centuries, the Atlantic continental pair that formed the centre, and the command, of the world were concentrated in the northern hemisphere and became England and the USA: in 1876, Queen Victoria accepted the proposal of the Conservative prime minister Disraeli to assume the title of 'Empress of the Indies'; in 1884, an international conference of astronomers in Washington established that the meridian passing through Greenwich, London should become the prime meridian at zero degrees, which was to be used as a reference for the calculation of time variations in the various parts of the world. Thus the extreme, insular – and therefore non-continental – land in the European Atlantic West, England, becomes the measure of space and time of the world and of all its people.)

Nevertheless, Western Europe remained the real centre of the world throughout the twentieth century: the two world wars occurred on the old continent; the great capitalist powers continued their colonization in a certain number of African countries, while in the Caribbean a new Creole culture developed, based on a complex network of relations between different populations who happened to live in the same limited geographical area. According to José Martì, it was the constitution of 'Nuestra América mestiza' composed of White, Black, Native, Indian and mixed-raced people.[3] Based on the principle of interculturality, and on a mutable and *in progress* identity model, this pluralist culture of Creole origin questioned the idea of a fixed and immutable identity spread by the Europeans, who in turn realized the risk of becoming a 'central province' with fossilized Mediterranean culture, tradition and heritage.

The crisis of the Mediterranean space: The critique of Eurocentrism

The critique of Eurocentrism has mainly been made by various authors and scholars from the Caribbean, such as Aimé Césaire, Edouard Glissant, Frantz Fanon, Derek Walcott and Alejo Carpentier, as well as by Gandhi, Agostinho Neto and Nelson Mandela, who confronted Europeans with the hidden aspect of Eurocentrism, the one that has produced centuries of oppression, violence and slavery.[4]

By putting itself 'in the middle' of these different worlds (and not at the 'centre') and devaluing the concepts of centre and periphery, the geographical, cultural, identity space of the Caribbean imposed itself at the same time as a 'place' open to the world and in close relationship with the sea. Thanks to the spread of this new cultural perspective, Europeans

---

[3] For an in-depth analysis of the Cuban scholar José Martì, see Retamar (1975).
[4] In his work 'L'Europe est indéfendable', Aimé Césaire writes : 'Le fait est que la civilisation dite "européenne", la civilisation "occidentale", telle que l'ont façonnée deux siècles de régime bourgeois, est incapable de résoudre les deux problèmes majeurs auxquels son existence a donné naissance : le problème du prolétariat et le problème colonial ; que, déférée à la barre de la "raison" comme à la barre de la "conscience", cette Europe-là est impuissante à se justifier : et que, de plus en plus, elle se réfugie dans une hypocrisie d'autant plus odieuse qu'elle a de moins en moins chance de tromper.' ('The fact is that the so-called "European" civilization, the "Western" civilization, as it has been shaped in two centuries of bourgeois rule, is incapable of solving the two major problems to which its existence has given rise: the problem of the proletariat and the colonial problem; that, subjected to "reason" as well as "conscience", this Europe is unable to justify itself: and that, more and more, it takes refuge in a hypocrisy that is all the more hateful because it has less and less chance of deceiving.') (1955 : 7–8). In this regard, see also Fanon (1961).

could now reconsider the function and meaning of their culture, thought and, above all, their single-rooted identity model based on the traditional trinomial language-culture-nation. This process of historical and cultural revision placed Europe in a different position in a 'contemporary world' which demanded to know and discover the Other and Elsewhere through a sort of 'relationship poetry' capable of denying the desire for power and force within the different cultures. This 'relationship poetry', which Glissant often refers to, enabled Europeans to decolonize their mind and, as a result, open the Mediterranean space up more freely to otherness. This process also favoured the circulation of ideas and knowledge through the different languages and cultures that have previously contributed to creating the richness and geopolitical complexity of Mediterranean civilization.[5] As Maria Gabriella Pasqualini writes:

> Il Mediterraneo non è certo più, ai giorni nostri, il centro del mondo, ma è sempre una sorta di modello primario di una notevole complessità geopolitica. È ancora uno degli spazi principali, nei quali, volontariamente o non, il mondo cosiddetto occidentale mette in gioco il proprio ruolo di potenza mondiale. [...] Il Mediterraneo è dunque una frontiera geografica e geologica e uno spazio di civilizzazioni, costituendo essa stessa uno spazio dalle molteplici componenti. La geografia è, in prima battuta, la causa fondamentale di quello che oggi il Mediterraneo rappresenta: in nessuna altra parte del mondo forse il concetto di geopolitica ha un senso così evidente. (2000: 14)

> (Nowadays, the Mediterranean is certainly no longer the centre of the world, but it is still a sort of primary model of considerable geopolitical complexity. It is still one of the main spaces in which, voluntarily or not, the so-called Western world brings into play its role as a world power. [...] The Mediterranean is therefore a geographical and geological border, a space of civilizations which constitutes a space of multiple components in itself. Geography is, primarily, the fundamental cause of what the Mediterranean represents today: in no other part of the world does the concept of geopolitics have such a clear meaning.)

The increasing mobility of the populations from one Mediterranean coast to the other nowadays constitutes an endless source of exchanges that can

---

[5] It is important to note that one of the most influential intellectuals of Mediterranean culture and history, Fernand Braudel, wrote that around this sea different landscapes, seas and civilizations have lived. He clarifies that travelling in the Mediterranean means deploying the Roman world in Lebanon, finding prehistoric traces in Sardinia, Greek towns in Sicily, Arabic traces in Spain, Turkish Islamism in the Balkans. For an in-depth analysis, see Braudel (1977, 1978).

write a new page in European history. Situating the Mediterranean space of the third millennium in the middle of the worlds, this 'political poetry' of reciprocity somehow forces Europeans to confront themselves with the numerous populations, cultures, languages and histories that have developed around the Mediterranean since at least the 1970s and 1980s. Placing oneself in an intercultural perspective today means being ready to create a shared foundation, a unique horizon where differences can find their place in relation to specific features. In other words, the Mediterranean space, including its different cultures and identities, has to accept being 'translated' into other languages, other cultural, social and political perspectives by the Other. This 'translation' process also implies rewriting the meaning of the division between the different civilizations so that each might find in the Other the difference needed to reinvent, communicate, change and evolve.

This reciprocal encounter, achieved by an act of 'translation' of the one into the other, becomes the fundamental issue which enables each culture and identity to be aware that we all belong to a common human species.[6] Explaining that the main role of the Mediterranean should today be to put any limit and notion of frontier at its 'core', Franco Cassano revisits the idea of a Mediterranean space which he regards as a connection place capable of creating a real intercultural dialogue:

> L'espressione latina *mare nostrum*, odiosa per il suo senso proprietario, oggi può essere pronunziata solo se si accetta uno slittamento del suo significato. Il soggetto proprietario di quell'aggettivo non è, non deve essere, un popolo imperiale, che si espande risucchiando l'altro al suo interno, ma il "noi" mediterraneo. [...] Oggi Mediterraneo vuol dire mettere al centro il confine, la linea di divisione e di contatto tra gli uomini e le civiltà. Esso non illustra la nostalgia di una vecchia gioventù, di una "grandezza", che produce sempre, come ci ha insegnato Simone Weil, esiti tragici, ma il compimento della maturità, il momento in cui si acquista compiutamente coscienza della finitezza. ([1996] 2005: xxiii–xxiv)

---

[6] Reconsidering the Caribbean cultural and identity model, Armando Gnisci writes: 'La via caraibica sembra la più pratica e fruttifera: essa induce a credere che stare *in mezzo al mondo* non signifchi starne al centro né al capo, ma voglia dire stare ovunque, nel flusso della corrente, in mezzo al mondo che non ha centro né periferie, né avanguardie e stati-maggiori, e che ha, invece, paludi e lagune, stagni e pozzanghere. Sono portato a pensare che stare in mezzo al mondo signifchi andare insieme nel Caos-Mondo verso il futuro Tutto-Mondo, *in mezzo alle correnti*.' ('The Caribbean way seems the most practical and fruitful: it leads one to believe that being in the middle of the world does not mean being at the centre or at the head of it, but it means being everywhere, in the flow of the current, in the middle of the world that has no centre or peripheries, no vanguards or major states, and that has, instead, swamps and lagoons, ponds and puddles. I am inclined to think that being in the midst of the world means to go together in the Chaos-World towards the future All-World, in the midst of the currents.') (2009: 15).

(The Latin expression *mare nostrum*, which is odious because of its proprietary meaning, can only be uttered today if we accept a shift in its meaning. The subject related to this adjective does not and must not be an imperial population, which expands by sucking the other within itself, but the Mediterranean 'we'. [...] Today, Mediterranean means to place the border at the centre, the line of division and contact between men and civilizations. It does not illustrate the longing for an old youth, for a 'greatness', which always produces, as Simone Weil taught us, tragic results, but the fulfilment of maturity, the moment in which we become fully aware of our finiteness.)

The most recent waves of migration, favouring the elaboration of a new identity and cultural *koinè* through the act of 'translation' carried out by the experience of wandering peoples, also help to trace the profile of a 'different us' produced by the encounter-collision with 'multiple-others'.

Rewriting the meaning of the divisions between different world cultures, following the West Indian or Indian example today implies an additional effort:[7] the desire to replace the dialectical principles of coexistence and juxtaposition (on which Western European knowledge is based) with the flowing and circular notion of 'translation'. This new sense of 'measure', calling into question the relationship dynamics between two or more cultures on the basis of a bipolar dialectical system, establishes its fulcrum in the awareness of the multiple and *in fieri* feature of cultural forms whose peculiar value derives from the feeling of finiteness in relation to identity, experience and the culture of a 'different we'. Refusing dialectical, dichotomous and Manichean knowledge, this new relationship system is built on knowledge, which in turn is based on the force of the oxymoron, where any identity process can only affirm itself through its provisionary and evolving forms and expressions.

Rewriting and translating the Mediterranean space: Italian migration poetry

In this rewriting and 'translation' process of the 'us' into a 'different us', literature plays a fundamental role as it greatly contributes to developing

---

[7] The principle of interculturality is based on the deep conviction that any identity model cannot be the only element of comparison between cultures but, conversely, it has to express itself and function as a 'transitional place' where the various identities can be defined as in a subtle and complex mirror. In this system, the hierarchy of values is replaced by the slow and patient process of learning, welcoming and, above all, mutual knowledge.

profound reflection on language, identity and culture, as Gnisci states in his work 'Traducendo il mondo':

> La letteratura *lavora* l'immaginario, la lingua, la mente del lettore, la storia delle culture e delle civiltà. Il lavoro letterario, *l'opera, traduce* il mondo *presso* ognuno di noi-tutti in una forma linguistica che lo riassuma in una narrazione o nell'"altra lingua' letteraria: entrambe le vie traduttive producono senso in più rispetto al mondo che ci appare non averne, e rispetto a tutte le altre forme sociali di comunicazione umana, eccetto le altre arti, che sono governate totalmente dal mercato dell'immaginario. (2009: 83)

> (Literature *works* on the reader's imagination, language, mind, on the history of cultures and civilizations. The literary work *translates* the world for each and every one of us into a linguistic form that summarizes it into a narrative or into another literary language: both ways of translating give the world more meaning compared to the one it appears to have, and compared to all other social forms of human communication, except other artistic forms, which are governed entirely by the market of the imaginary.)

When he speaks of 'another language', Gnisci alludes to poetic language which, by nature, places itself in a nonconformist position compared to any other type of language (see also on this topic Sinopoli 2009).

Poetry, by affecting individual and collective imagination and translating reality, enriches the world with 'another meaning' which can transform the concept of frontier into an act of creation, resulting in a space of reciprocal insight. In other words, imposing itself as a language device and favouring the flowing circulation of creative forms, poetry traces an invisible (and always *in fieri*) path which develops a sense of mental, geographical dispossession and dislocation in each individual's inner world. This double-fold emotion leads to considering otherness as a mirror in which the multiple images of the 'I' and the 'other' are reflected until they trace a common horizon that is the awareness that we all belong to the same human community.

One must recall that the etymology of the word 'translation', which implies the action of leading someone or something from one place to another, or from one time to another, also implies the ability to enter and leave a place, a universe or an experience and, at the same time, the feeling of being 'between two' meanings, frontiers, limits. This perspective enables us to conceive the act of writing as a permanent form of translation as it (and especially poetry) allows us to enter and abandon any meaning and any pre-established representation thanks to a text which acts as a sort of translation, of 'trans-position'. Therefore, it is no longer possible to consider an encounter with diversity as a 'shock' between different world civilizations but, conversely, as the possibility for transforming the concept of frontier into a permeable space which opposes the constraining sacralization of the 'I', due to the fear of accepting the feeling of diversity.[8] Affirming itself as a cultural melting pot,[9] this process of getting to know the other, on the one hand, encourages a meeting between the languages, cultures and civilizations that form the 'different us' and, on the other, challenges any form of language, cultural, mental homologation and standardization.

Thus, imposing itself as a 'common home' where the word tends to migrate from one meaning to the other, from one representation to the other, the poetic text trains us, on a critical and aesthetic level, to read and interpret within a shared space the different meanings of the contemporary world. This flowing and circular translation succeeds in acting in a nonconformist manner compared to the fixed, immutable and stereotyped image which prejudices give us, not only of ourselves but also of the other and the elsewhere.

Poetry more strenuously becomes a place of nonconformity and elaboration of intercultural identity when we consider the literary production of migration writers. They are very often men and women who have left their countries to settle in one of the Western European countries. Beyond their peculiar features resulting from their different cultures and languages, they share the experience of colonization, wandering, voyage, exile and, above all, the awareness of being between two or more cultures, languages and civilizations.

Unlike other Western European countries, Italy has only known the migration phenomenon since the 1980s.[10] Mainly based on the concepts of wandering, 'between two' and plurilingualism, and by translating the experience of passing from one world to the other in the language(s) of the host country (or countries), migration poetry is capable of depicting the Mediterranean space from other perspectives for the native populations, recreating not only their existences but also their individual and collective imagination.

---

[8] For an in-depth analysis of the concepts of 'barbarism' and 'civilization', of 'culture' and 'collective identity' as well as the feeling of fear present in the Western world when facing each other, see Todorov (2008).

[9] On the 'cultural melting pot', Silvia Albertazzi writes: 'Caratteristica fondamentale del meticciato delle culture è, al contrario, il contagio culturale, non più accumulo o collezione di nozioni disparate recuperate alla luce di una prospettiva (occidentale e eurocentrica) unificante, ma energia compartecipe e condivisa, come la stessa etimologia del termine (con + tangere = entrare in contatto) suggerisce.' ('On the contrary, the fundamental characteristic of the interbreeding of cultures is cultural contagion, no longer an accumulation or collection of disparate notions recovered in the light of a unifying (Western and Eurocentric) perspective, but shared energy, as the very etymology of the term (con + tangere = to come into contact) suggests.') (2000: 15).

[10] For a definition of 'Italian migration literature' and the different stages leading to the spread of this type of literary production in Italy, see Pisanelli (2008).

In this often painful and complex transition from one language to another, one discourse to another, one representation to another, the migration poet questions the single-rooted European identity principle which – as already mentioned – is based on the trinomial language-culture-nation. Finding themselves in a world which fails to exist and one which is slowly developing, migration writers elaborate, through their writing process, a sort of plural and composite identity capable of simultaneously and continuously transforming itself into the mutable space of the 'between two', and offering Europeans a sort of 'translation', both personal and pluralist, of the Mediterranean space they have just moved to:

> Cette poétique de l'interculturalité et de l'"entre-deux', proposant une identité, une culture et une langue qui changent et se métamorphosent en permanence et s'appuyant sur l'expérience de l'errance, accélère les processus de créolisation et de métissage culturel. La notion de créolisation, reposant sur l'idée d'une identité constamment *in fieri* et sur la rencontre entre la langue maternelle et une ou plusieurs langues d'usage, conçoit l'image d'un espace géographique et mental où la périphérie et le centre réduisent leur distance et favorise à la fois la représentation d'un temps synchronique où le passé, le présent et le futur convergent sur la notion de 'frontière-charnière' qui assure la rencontre-collision et, par conséquent, le sentiment de dépossession et de dislocation. (Pisanelli 2009: 489–90)

> (This poetics of interculturality and the 'in-between', by proposing an identity, a culture and a language that are constantly changing and metamorphosing, and by relying on the experience of the wanderer, accelerates the process of creolization and cultural interbreeding. The notion of creolization, based on the idea of an identity that is constantly *in fieri* and on the encounter between the mother tongue and one or more used languages, conceives the image of a geographical and mental space where the periphery and the centre reduce their distance and at the same time favours the representation of a synchronic time where past, present and future converge on the notion of a 'border-connection' that ensures the encounter-collision and, consequently, the feeling of dispossession and dislocation.)

---

[11] Silvia Albertazzi reconsiders the impact of migration poetry on the customary representation of the Mediterranean space by Europeans: 'Elemento destabilizzante, l'immigrato forza l'occidentale a ridisegnare la mappa delle differenze culturali, a prendere coscienza, in altre parole, dell'alterità periferica come complementare al centro metropolitano, della presenza in seno alla propria nazione di identità diasporiche accanto a quelle locali.' ('As a destabilizing element, the immigrant forces the Westerner to redesign the map of cultural differences, to become aware, in other words, of peripheral otherness as complementary to the metropolitan centre, of the presence within their own nation of diasporic identities alongside local ones.') (2000: 133).

The poetic and existential condition of the 'between two' reinforces, transforms and enriches the representation of a given geographical and mental space.[11] Youssef Wakkas, an author from the eastern Mediterranean coast (Syria), who has been living in Italy for many years, states in the preface to his work *Terra mobile: Racconti* that he always thinks in Arabic and writes in Italian, in a sort of process that forces him to 'move on while translating' through the cultures and languages that form his biographical and creative universe. Assia Djebar, an author from the southern Mediterranean coast (Algeria), explains that being between two languages means finding herself in the querulous and irritating, painful and mysterious space of each language and culture (1999).

Italian migration poetry plays a considerable role in rethinking the contemporary Mediterranean space and, above all, gives Europeans the possibility to mentally and culturally 'decolonize' themselves from the unequivocal image they have elaborated of their 'identity space': a centripetal and Eurocentric image which has conditioned the European point of view on extra-European cultures and civilizations, throughout the centuries.

Using words as true musical notes, the Romanian poet Mihai Mircea Butcovan, who has lived near Milan for many years, translates and transposes the different features of his existential and historical universe on to the background of a Mediterranean sun which he depicts in an apparent immobility, deaf to any episode, memory or future:

Una stagione come tante altre / La stessa ma più bella / Forse perché l'ultima / Sole mediterraneo / Processi di beatificazione al traguardo / E feste nazionali / Bilancio inopportuno di / Una coscienza in manette / Un prigioniero del proprio passato / Uno schiavo ribelle, rivoluzionario / Controcorrente, negativo / Recalcitrante, comunista / Cristiano, eccetera. // Eccetera vuol dire che ho fatto di tutto / Per non essere questo o quello / E quando non facevo questo ero quello / Così la mia mente si chiede dove / È morto nessuno in me / Sono vivo ma sogno / Meglio un morto sveglio / [...] (Mihai Mircea Butcovan, 'Primavera italiana', in Lecomte 2006: 56)

(A season like so many others / The same but more beautiful / Perhaps because it's the last / Mediterranean sunshine / Beatification processes at the finishing line / And national holidays / Inopportune evaluation of / A conscience in handcuffs / A prisoner of one's own past / A rebel, revolutionary slave / Counter-current, negative / Recalcitrant, communist / Christian, etcetera. // Etcetera means that I've done everything / Not to be this or that / And when I wasn't doing this I was that / So my mind wonders where / Nobody has died in me / I'm alive but I'm dreaming / Better a wake up dead man / [...])

In the time-space paralysis and through subtle humour which tends to disorientate the reader, the poet decides to rebuild the unity of an identity and of a memory dislocated between the 'here' and 'elsewhere', between dream and reality, between one or more moments in time – the ones of death and regeneration – which coexist and build a new possible identity.

The poet Gëzim Hajdari also reconsiders the idea of a homeland which is situated between life and death, here and elsewhere. It is a 'utopian' place which does not belong to any geographical area but which can be named 'poetic writing'. Poetry thus becomes the only homeland where one can live freely without any spatial or mental boundary:

> Ogni giorno creo una nuova patria / in cui muoio e rinasco / una patria senza mappe né bandiere / celebrata dai tuoi occhi profondi / che mi inseguono per tutto il tempo / nel viaggio verso cieli fragili / in tutte le terre io dormo innamorato / in tutte le dimore mi sveglio bambino / la mia chiave può aprire ogni confine / e le porte di ogni prigione nera / ritorni e partenze eterne il mio essere / da fuoco a fuoco da acqua a acqua / l'inno delle mie patrie il canto del merlo / che io canto in ogni stagione di luna calante / sorta dalla tua fronte di buio e di stelle / con la volontà eterna del sole. (Gëzim Hajdari, 'Ogni giorno creo una nuova patria', in Lecomte 2006: 97)

> (Every day I create a new homeland / in which I die and am reborn / a homeland without maps or flags / celebrated by your deep eyes / that chase me all the time / in the journey towards fragile skies / in every land I sleep in love / in every dwelling I wake up as a child / my key can open every border / and the doors of every black prison / eternal returns and departures my being / from fire to fire from water to water / the hymn of my homelands the song of the blackbird / that I sing in every season of the waning moon / rising from your forehead of darkness and stars / with the eternal will of the sun.)

Hajdari's poetry expresses and translates the 'plural I' from one meaning to another, one word to another, one world to another, focusing on an ambiguous and polysemic otherness – the beloved woman, the maternal image, the absence of a relative or more vaguely the 'Other-than-me' – capable of breaking the geographical idea of boundary and linking the identity principle to the translinguistic notion of 'song'.

Italy's Po Valley, and in particular the Bologna region, is surprisingly and strongly present in the young Iranian poet Nader Ghazvinizadeh's poetic verse. He arrived in Italy with his family in the early 1980s for a short holiday and remained there because of the revolution and, later, the war which has marked everyday life in his home country. Through his poetry, Ghazvinizadeh outlines a precise portrait of the Bologna province which, on the one hand, shows the slow integration process in a different social and political context and, on the other, a sort of vis-à-vis detachment from a world the poet observes and depicts through a filter which always reminds him of his wanderer's experience and the impossibility of thoroughly possessing this new host land:

> Sono uscito con il gozzo sporco dell'acqua di porto / ho lasciato la città di pietra / il mare prosegue l'idea di pianura / nessuno vuol capire / lo stesso discorso che faccio mille volte sul legno / e mi cucino, mentre tutto trema / e già il silenzio mi cambia l'accento / arriverò fino dall'altra parte, nei bar di legno / a capire se fanno come da questa riva / lambendo le città battute dal vento / barcaioli, legno sulla pianura d'acqua alle otto. (Nader Ghazvinizadeh, in Lecomte 2006: 83)

> (I went out with the boat dirty with the water of the port / I left the city of stone / the sea continues the idea of the plain / nobody wants to understand / the same speech that I make a thousand times on the wood / and I cook for myself, while everything trembles / and already the silence changes my accent / I'll reach the other side, in the wooden bars / to understand if they do as they do on this shore / lapping the windswept cities / boatmen, wood on the plain of water at eight o'clock.)

While passing from one Mediterranean coast to the other, homeland and hostland landscapes tend to overlap as if one were the continuation of the other. The poetic word imposes itself as the conjunction which eliminates the breach of which the reader cannot even find trace. Nevertheless, the sea which separates progressively transforms itself into welcoming plains: the two Mediterranean coasts find themselves connected by an existence, the poet's, which nevertheless remains divided, split and expressed through the poetry of the 'between two' which characterizes all migration poetry.

Through a choral, anonymous composition close to orality and elicited by a memory which makes the individual a stranger to his own personal life, the poet Ubax Cristina Ali Farah evokes people, places and landscapes which seem to live and act in an elsewhere that alludes to the distance dividing the poet from her two cultures, Italian and Somalian. Thus the poet cannot help referring to memories and images that constitute the same and unique personal cultural heritage:

> Nel gruppo di donne. / Sono di madre europea, / questo mi distingue. // Un'adolescente snodata. / Sulla sabbia, in mezzo alle coetanee, / cado giù in spaccata. / Attenta che ti strappi! / Goccerai sangue. Ceeb. / [...] Ci laviamo con le altre donne. / I miei figli sono i loro figli. / Voglio tenere insieme tutti i pezzi. / Indossare l'abito con le altre. / Senza di loro, vecchie ed adolescenti, / storpie e bellissime, bianche e nere, / io non esisto. / Sono una donna finché loro esistono. (Ubax Cristina Ali Farah, 'Strappo', in Lecomte 2006: 30–1)

(In the group of women. / I'm from a European mother, / this distinguishes me. // A teenager elastic body. / On the sand, among the peers, / I fall down in a split. / Watch out, you'll tear! / You'll drip blood. Ceeb. / [...] We wash with the other women. / My children are their children. / I want to hold all the pieces together. / Wear the dress with the others. / Without them, old and adolescent, / crippled and beautiful, black and white, / I don't exist. / I am a woman as long as they exist.)

The Iraqi poet Thea Laitef, who died in Rome at the age of forty-one, often dealt with the idea of connecting distances, of differences that made exchanges and sharing possible, and with the experience of living on the border by translating it. In her poem 'Fiori', she wrote:

O navi di questa mattina / come affondaste in quel pomeriggio / nel fango dei nostri giorni, / i fiori che seguivano il giro / dell'annaffiare / improvvisamente s'alzavano / tra i nostri panni / le vecchie case e l'estate / preoccupavano quel vento. / O navi di questa mattina / che hanno dato al mare / ciò che univa le due estremità. (Thea Laitef, 'Fiori', in Lecomte 2006: 110)

(O shipsof this morning / as you sank in that afternoon / in the mud of our days, / the flowers that followed the turn / of watering / suddenly rose / between our clothes / the old houses and the summer / worried that wind. / O ships of this morning / that gave the sea / what joined the two ends.)

The voyage and movement are mainly metaphors for the concept of initiation and a new process which rarely leads to a precise destination. The 'translation' made by the poetic text is never definitive: the aim of the voyage is the voyage itself and its duration, where opposing principles recognize themselves as being similar and decide to coexist. Movement thus remains the only device making it possible to go beyond the border, transforming it into a common space where all differences can be asserted, renewed and 'translated' into all possible forms. In Laitef's poetry, the Mediterranean coasts crisscross and establish their provisional centre within poetry that tends towards the precious and refined style of Eastern traditional lyrics and those, more concise, of the past century's traditional Western poetry:

Ho una preghiera sulla strada / da percorrere / in una lunga serata, / la mia speranza è l'alba / dei nostri prossimi giorni. / Il mio passo è sviato dal temporale / nella sosta ho messo i finimenti ai cavalli / e d'un grido ho riempito la mia gola. (Thea Laitef, 'Passeggiata', in Lecomte 2006: 110)

(I have a prayer on the road / to travel / in a long evening, / my hope is the dawn / of our next days. / My step is diverted by the storm / in the break I have harnessed the horses / and with a cry I have filled my throat.)

In some of the migration poets' texts that we have analysed and that were written in Italian, the cultural and identity differences between the eastern and western coasts of the Mediterranean basin, just like the northern and southern coasts, find new horizons of permeability in poetry. In this way, the various Albanian, Bosnian, Romanian and Polish poets, as well as the Iranian, Iraqi, Senegalese, Somali or Cameroonian ones, who live and write in the Italian language, become true 'culture transmitters', capable of rewriting and re-depicting the profile of an ever-changing and *in fieri* Mediterranean culture and identity. The result is an image of a composite, mixed-raced, plural, geographical and cultural space which also expects to be received and translated by Europeans through new perspectives and dimensions open to intercultural and global poetry.

In this dynamic of reciprocal and incessant writing, thanks to migration literature, the Mediterranean space has the opportunity to regenerate and renew itself, starting from its 'inhabited frontiers' which seem ready to welcome the 'finiteness' of each culture and language, and in harmony make 'communication' possible among the different realities of a world which has continuously been constructed and deconstructed over the centuries.

References

Albertazzi, S. (2000), *Lo sguardo dell'altro: Le letterature postcoloniali*, Rome: Carocci.
Braudel, F. (ed.) (1977), *La Méditerranée: L'espace et les hommes*, Paris: Arts et métiers graphiques.
Braudel, F. (ed.) (1978), *La Méditerranée: Les hommes et l'héritage*, Paris: Arts et métiers graphiques.
Cassano, F. ([1996] 2005), *Il pensiero meridiano*, Rome: Laterza.
Cassano, F. (2012), *Southern Thought and Other Essays on the Mediterranean*, trans. N. Bouchard and V. Ferme, New York: Fordham University Press.
Césaire, A. (1955), *Discours sur le colonialisme*, Paris: Présence Africaine.
Djebar, A. (1999), *Ces voix qui m'assiègent*, Paris: Albin Michel.
Fanon, F. (1961), *Les damnés de la terre*, Paris: F. Maspero.
Glissant, E. (1996), *Introduction à une poétique du divers*, Paris: Gallimard.
Gnisci, A. (2009), *L'educazione del te*, Rome: Sinnos editrice.
Lecomte, M. (ed.) (2006), *Ai confini del verso: Poesia della migrazione in italiano*, Florence: Le Lettere.
Pasqualini, M. G. (2000), *Sicilia, Tunisia e la poesia di Mario Scalesi*, in S. Mugno (ed.), *Sicilia, Tunisia e la poesia di Mario Scalesi*, 13–18, Palermo: ISSPE.

Pisanelli, F. (2008), 'Pour une écriture plurielle: la littérature italienne de la migration', *Textes & Contexte*, 2.

Pisanelli, F. (2009), 'La frontière invisible: la poésie italienne de la migration entre diglossie et "dislocation", identité(s) et dépossession', *Italies*, 13: 487–507.

Retamar, R. F. (1975), *Para una teoría de la literatura hispanoamericana y otras aproximaciones*, La Habana: Casa de las Américas.

Sinopoli, F. (2009), *La dimensione europea nello studio letterario*, Milan: Bruno Mondadori.

Todorov, T. (2008), *La peur des barbares. Au-delà du choc des civilisations*, Paris: Robert Laffont.

8

Naples and Europe, past and future: The *Sud* review – a link between the Mediterranean and Europe

Cathryn Baril

> *A Napoli, la diversità sta nella resistenza al cambiamento, la volontà di rimanere una tribù a parte, refrattaria al moderno, ma anche alle massificazioni.*
>
> *(In Naples, diversity lies in the resistance to change, in the will to remain a separate tribe, refractory to the modern, but also to massification.)*
>
> PIER PAOLO PASOLINI, 'LA NAPOLETANITÀ', IN PASOLINI (1999: 230)

Throughout the centuries, Naples has always been seen as a crossroads, a pivotal place for both national and European cultural trends. However, following the creation of the Italian State and the resulting political demise of the Kingdom of the Two Sicilies, it suffered not only the loss of its role as a European capital but also serious economic, artistic and social impoverishment. This impoverishment, which affected all sectors, was due, on the one hand, to the contradictions among the Neapolitan intellectuals who hesitated between tradition and openness towards the new, towards modernity (and this in different forms of expression, whether it be art, poetry or literature), and, on the other, to the bourgeoisie who, having lost all sense of liberalism, proved its inability to move forward politically and especially to change the cultural physiognomy of the city. These facts may have been considered explanation enough from 1860 until the present day, but that can no longer be the case. Indeed, 150 years later, revisionism of pre- and post-unitary history brings to light some rather incredible factors:[1] if the request to reopen the Risorgimento historical archives is successful (at present they are still classified as State secrets), it could totally change the negative vision that the south has always been given and could provide us with a new interpretation that differs considerably from today's official version.

By looking at the failure of the literary journal *Sud*, which was created immediately after the war, we shall consider here why the Parthenopean city did not manage to recover its European cultural dimension at the time of the reconstruction. The study thus begins in 1945 in Naples. But the examination of the context, with multiple legacies outlining a very particular ideological configuration, leads us to skim over half a century, the intention being to capture the mindsets available, consequences of a historiographic past, largely influenced by the thinking of Benedetto Croce.

> I have never doubted the European dimension of Neapolitan culture, it is the culture which allowed Vico to converse with Descartes, by opposing Imagination against Reason; Basile to precede Perrault and Grimm, by supplying the West with great stories; Giannone to revolt against the power of the Church, by reaffirming in his Storia civile the priority of the secular state; Genovesi to speak of economics with the same authority as Keynes; Filangieri to describe institutions for good government with Montesquieuan skill and Galiani to charm the Parisian salons with the art of conversation and intellectual brilliance.[2]

In fact, Naples has never stopped being a *world-city*. In order to be able to assume this title, a city must have, right in its heart, a variety of intermingling cultures; Naples has effectively always been a place of fruitful meetings between cultures. Bruno Arpaia expresses very well this idea of a synthesis of cultures through a metaphor: 'Siamo oggi un gran calderone in cui è difficile distinguere ciò che è greco da ciò che è romano, gli elementi normanni, svevi, angioini, aragonesi, da quelli strettamente spagnoli,

---

[1] Let us remember it was only in 1861 that Italy was established and not until 1918 immediately after the First World War (which thus became the Fourth War of Italian Independence) that Unification was totally completed.

[2] Extract from the interview with Raffaele La Capria (July 2011) during my PhD research which was entitled 'Naples et l'Europe. Entre mémoire et futur: La revue Sud (1945–7)'. See also on this topic La Capria (1994: 83) and La Capria (2009: 311).

austriaci, francesi, tedeschi, americani' ('We are in a great melting pot where it is difficult to distinguish what is Greek from what elements are Roman, Norman, Swabian, Aragonese or from Angers, or that are merely Spanish, Austrian, French, German or American') (Arpaia 1994: 11).

If, for example, we go back to antiquity, Romans, Samnites and Greeks all lived together. In the Middle Ages, each succeeded the other: Latin heredity, Byzantine Hellenism, and Germanism from the North with the Lombards, Francs, Normans and Swabians. The Angevins formed an alliance with the Hungarians. The advantage of Spanish domination, despite its seriously damaging consequences, was that it introduced many Neapolitan artists and men of culture into the Austro-Spanish Empire. In the eighteenth century, Naples had an Italian and European vocation, thanks to the economic and legal school of thought of Genovesi, Filangieri and Giannone. In the nineteenth century, it was the first Italian city to discover the modernity of Hegel's school of thought, thanks to Bertrand Spaventa, Ottavio Colecchi and Francesco de Sanctis, while Italian philosophy was still with Rosmini and Gallupi. And finally, at the beginning of the twentieth century, the Parthenopean city was the capital of Italian neo-Hegelism thanks to Benedetto Croce and Adolfo Omodeo, along with the Florence of Giovanni Gentile.

The concept of 'Europe' was therefore firmly anchored in the 'Kingdom of Naples' and in its culture. This culture has always been reflected in the city itself, contained its destinies, represented the will of Naples to become once again a European capital. Only three centuries ago, Naples was a 'Philosophical city', a cultural centre which rivalled those of Florence and Rome. Naples embraced the philosophy of the Enlightenment, which seemed extraordinary in the eighteenth century, through its innovations in the fields of culture, science and technology; a city permeated with 'mitteleuropa' culture, making Mezzogiorno a 'luogo elettivo della differenza meridiana' ('selected place of southern difference') compared to the civilization of northern Italy. Cultural life in Naples was therefore exuberant, dynamic and privileged, first by its climate and landscapes but equally by a varied and eclectic social life which attracted travellers from all over the world. And the multiple journeys on the peninsula, which became a favourite destination on the Grand Tour, from the seventeenth century onwards, with an obligatory stopover for great minds in the Parthenopean city, contributed to the diffusion of ideas and the cosmopolitan mind, which have since become part of the great Neapolitan tradition.[3]

---

[3] From the sixteenth century, the journey to Italy seemed to become a European-wide fashion. Especially in the seventeenth century when Italy and Naples, in particular, became a major destination on the Grand Tour, an educational journey which completed the young aristocracy's and the upper bourgeoisie's training.

However, according to Raffaele La Capria, all that came to an end after the Bourbon Repression of 1799 and with the advent of the Restoration. Naples then entered 'a period during which Neapolitan culture withdrew into itself and its dialect, as if seeking refuge from the disorder of the world and to worship its own feelings and particularity, exercising a pathetic local populism, void of perspectives and ideologies' (La Capria 1986: 35). Literary tastes increasingly adapted to this state of affairs, which deteriorated still further after Unification, with the frustrations of a Naples stripped of its role as capital.

After Unification, the city's high level of illiteracy combined with the lack of structures for diffusing culture show how the cultural life there suffered both from isolation with regard to European thinking and from a worrying degree of provincialism.[4] However, it would appear that, after 1860, the 'North' had the schools in the south shut for fifteen years, with the intention of effacing the memory and culture of an ancient civilization.

The same was true for journalism in the early twentieth century, which Benedetto Croce qualified as 'narrow-minded and provincial'. Federigo Verdinois, in one of his works dedicated to Naples culture, invited Neapolitan journalism to embrace scientific and literary arguments, particularly wishing Naples to stop closing in on itself in a milieu of politics and tittle-tattle, all with a local bent, depriving the city of a European breath of fresh air (see Croce 1947). All this was an attempt to reduce the damage caused by isolation, which threatened Neapolitan cultural life and led a great many talented people to leave the city to find work in other Italian cities or abroad. Federigo Verdinois, through his work as a translator, was frequently in contact with the world of European literature and accused Neapolitan society of ignorance and unawareness of this world:

> Noi siamo parchi di lode pel valore indigeno e modesto. Epperò siamo i primi a stupire, e in perfetta buona fede, quando ci accade di udir decantare all'estero un ingegno di casa nostra. Ed è così, lo si può affermare senza esagerazione, che ci si è accorti, dopo le consacrazioni francesi, tedesche, russe, perfino americane, che Napoli ha dato al romanzo Matilde Serao, alla lirica Gabriele D'Annunzio, agli studi sociali e giuridici Raffaele Garofalo, al teatro Achille Torelli, Roberto Bracco, Salvatore di Giacomo, alla poesia popolare lo stesso di Giacomo e Ferdinando Russo, al giornalismo Peppino Turco, e alla storia, all'archeologia, alla linguistica, alle scienze esatte, agli studi politici tutta una falange di cultori insigni, la cui azione civilizzatrice è più efficace che non si creda e il cui valore tanto

---

[4] P. Ricci(typescript) (s.d.), Archivio di Stato di Napoli (ASNA), Archivio Paolo Ricci, Parte Generale, 2/115.

meno si può disconoscere quanto più volentieri lasciamo agli stranieri la cura di esaltarlo. (Picone 2005: 61)

(We have scant praise for indigenous, modest values. However, we are the first to be surprised, in perfect good faith, when we hear that a talent from our land is lauded abroad. In this way (and we can say it without exaggeration) after French, German, Russian and even American consecrations, we realize that Naples gave to the novel Matilde Serao, to the poem Gabriele D'Annunzio, to social and law studies Raffaele Garofalo, to theatre Achille Torelli, to popular poetry Roberto Bracco and Salvatore di Giacomo, Di Giacomo again and Ferdinando Russo to journalism, Peppino Turco to history, and to archaeology, linguistics and exact sciences a multitude of distinguished scholars whose civilizing action is more important than we could believe, and whose value, the more we ignore it, the more we willingly let foreign people celebrate it.)

During this period, which was nevertheless intense in other areas – theatre, music, song – men such as Settembrini, Spaventa, De Sanctis, Labriola and Benedetto Croce did not give in to '*napoletanità*' culture and continued to weave together Neapolitan and European culture. Without the writings of these 'secular priests' – Croce, Dorso, Salvemini, Fortunato, Nitti, Villari, Amendola – as Michele Prisco (1994: 124) called them, the southern Italian problem would have been, in Neapolitan literature, a problem of colour and humour, a problem of myths and representations. On the death of Francesco De Sanctis, it was mostly Benedetto Croce who presided over the Society of Ideas and took on this responsibility not simply for the young editors of the review *Sud* but also for those who had come before. He was appreciated by all Neapolitan intellectuals for his equally reassuring and polemic ways, his rigorous methods, his paternalist role and his unswerving passion. He thought on a European level, and he engaged in a dialogue with the great minds of the time, criticized Marx and corrected Hegel.

Very rapidly, he affirmed that history needed to be in the service of political efficacy, and he therefore put this point at the centre of his philosophical reflections. During the Fascist period, he wrote: 'History, that of Naples, placing it into that of Italy which in turn was placed in that of Europe. They were therefore all contained in one matrix, in one place. Naples thus found its place in History' (Croce quoted in La Capria 1994: 83).

For the young editors of *Sud*, Croce was a figure of reference, a crossroads of ideas and a point of reference; and for the Neapolitans he was above all a guarantee: 'Look, he speaks European. We, too, then, are Europeans and Naples is still a great European capital' (La Capria 1994: 84).

This is what they told themselves. One only need look at *La Critica*, a review founded by Le Maître in 1903, which allowed culture to go beyond its frontiers, thus becoming the only surviving mirror of European conscience during the fascist years. For them, to speak of Croce meant a reference to *Napoli Nobilissima*, a magazine of which they were so proud and of which they dreamt. Croce seemed 'to make this dream possible by his presence and the vivacity of his enlightened mind, in a city of slumberers. Sent to sleep by the *'napoletanità'* (La Capria 1994: 84). However, although Croce tried to broaden Parthenopean and Italian culture in order to embrace wider European culture, it is also true that some of his attempts remained isolated, or indeed unrealized, because the time was not ripe and later generations fairly quickly spotted the limits of 'Croce' teachings.

Let us now look at the reviews that appeared after the war, for example; mostly literary, they reveal considerable flexibility, which allowed them to include pages on philosophy and politics, a policy that was contrary to the philosopher's instructions regarding the identity of reviews.[5] He would have preferred them to be a kind of specialized and sectorial questionnaire, and above all totally free of political and economic differences of opinion, and this with the intention of experimenting with concrete strategies of reconstruction.

As Croce was also doubtless too preoccupied with writing 'his' novel about Naples,[6] he was absent from the literary scene during Giolitti's time, when the Italian novel transformed; consequently, he did not become aware of certain great questions regarding the novel as a literary genre but also at the irresolute core of literature in Naples. He therefore understood little of the twentieth century, which is why he was obliged (despite being competent at everything) to leave literary tradition behind and hence the future of literature. Because of his training and his tastes, he showed little interest in a great number of twentieth-century authors (such as Sartre, Camus, Kafka, Isherwood, Auden, Joyce, Hemingway, Fitzgerald and Faulkner) who, on the other hand, proved important for the generation of Prunas and his companions, La Capria, Ghirelli, Scognamiglio, Compagnone, among others.

But for the *Ragazzi di Monte di Dio*, this was of no importance. They discovered this literature and its authors by themselves. However, none of this would ever have been possible if Croce had not prepared and trained them, if he had not been an incomparable master and guide for them during

---

[5] 'Le riviste e i giornali letterari debbono tenersi estranei ai pratici contrasti politici ed economici, e la loro sola ulteriore partizione sarà tra quelli specialistici e quelli di cultura e d'interesse generale' ('The reviews and literary journals should be kept far from specific, political and economic conflicts, and their only subdivision will be between specialized ones and cultural and general interest ones') (Croce 1945: 112).

[6] He was the first true creator of the 'great Naples novel' which Matilde Serao wanted to write but which was ultimately written by Croce; in it, he wrote about the history of Naples, its theatres, its legends and its intellectual heroes, with the indefatigable prose of a historian, philosopher and novelist.

the Fascist period. He made it possible for them, at a time when people could no longer distinguish good from evil, to understand morals, ethics and aesthetics. He was, as Marinetti writes in his novel *L'Alcova d'Acciaio*, the father of all their freedoms. He was the only one to manage to teach them what the word 'freedom' really meant. And for them that meant 'parlare europeo' ('speaking European').

It is also interesting to note that, despite Mussolini's endeavours, the dominant culture was that of the bourgeoisie which had made Italy and had only temporarily delegated to Fascism the right to halt the Communist attempt at subversion after the war. This culture, for the young people aged between ten and twenty-five, mixed elements of great morals with the remnants of a world vision that had by then become obsolete. High-quality institutes, such as the Umberto I college, acted as an ideal place to train and transform them, insofar as the teachers guided them towards maturity using their strict competence. The teachers' intransigence above all helped them to realize, over time, the limitations of their message and particularly the limitations of the model founded on class struggle, to which the group was linked. In other words, they helped them to face reality, without it being masked by the principles upon which their education was based. Thus, each one, without exception, discovered the flip side of the coin, namely 'the immoral compromise made between the local and national bourgeoisie and fascism, the conformism and looseness of their morals, the approximation of its culture still linked, on the one hand, to the typical style of D'Annunzio and, on the other, to folkloric sentimentalism' (Ghirelli 1998: 12).

They also discovered that the snobbism of the ruling class held a certain disdain for the plebeians and that the misery of the people and increasing poverty of the middle class left them totally indifferent. In short, the ruling class had neither the ability nor the will to put into place a recovery plan designed to halt the decline of the city. Already in 1923, Benedetto Croce had understood the situation and, in his work *Il dovere della borghesia nelle province napoletane*, he sent out a message of national liberalism:

> È necessario che nella borghesia delle nostre province si diffonda o si radichi, più che finora non sia accaduto, il sentimento che il migliore pregio della vita, la maggior soddisfazione che in essa possa provarsi, è data non dalle fortune materiali, non dagli arricchimenti, non dai gradi conseguiti, non dagli onori, ma dal produrre qualcosa di obiettivo e di universale, dal promuovere un nuovo e più alto costume, una nuova e più alta disposizione negli animi e nelle volontà, dal modificare in meglio la società in mezzo a cui si vive, godendo di quest'opera, come un artista della sua pittura o della sua statua, e un poeta della sua poesia [...]. In questa creazione del bene comune, si apre il più bel campo dell'uomo [...]. Ma il punto essenziale così nella vita di un individuo come in quella di un popolo, il punto che decide dell'efficacia di ogni

riforma, e di ogni programma e di ogni metodo, il punto a cui, in ultima analisi, si è ricondotti, è poi sempre questo: se vi sia o non vi sia l'anelito all'universale, la disposizione a considerare e a trattare noi stessi come strumenti di un'opera che va oltre di noi, il pungolo interiore del dovere, lo scrupolo di coscienza che ci chiede conto del modo in cui adoperiamo il nostro tempo e ci fa arrossire quando lo spendiamo, in vili pensieri e vili azioni, o quando lo guardiamo scorrere davanti a noi come se non fosse nostro. (Croce 1955: 313)

(It is necessary that among the bourgeoisie of our provinces spreads out and takes root the feeling that the best value of life, the greatest satisfaction that we can feel in it, is not given by material wealth, by enrichment, by degrees or honours acquired, but by producing something objective and universal, by promoting a new, higher custom, a new, higher attitude of the soul and the will, by improving the society we live in, enjoying this work, as an artist does his painting or statue, and a poet his poems. In this creation of common good, the best field of human beings opens up [...] But the essential point in the life of either an individual or a nation, the point that decides the efficacy of any reform, in every program or method, the ultimate point to which we are led is always this: whether or not there is aspiration for the universal, the attitude to consider and to treat ourselves as the tools of a work that goes beyond us, the inner goal, the scruple of the conscience that calls us to account our way of using time and makes us blush when we spend it in vile thoughts and actions, or when we see it flowing as if it was not ours.)

As the Fascist regime was consolidating its alliance with the Nazis and invading the private lives of inhabitants, there was an increase in criticism and doubt. These young people began to feel the suffocating absurdity of Fascist censorship, all the more so as their desire for contacts, exchanges, new experiences and intellectual and sexual freedom was growing. Indeed, the more official culture became autonomous and shut in on itself, the more these young people became anarchic and internationalist. The frontiers of the cultural Italian sphere were most definitely closed but the young editors of *Sud* fought against them wholeheartedly. The more Fascism boasted of being nationalist and conditioned them into becoming nationalists, the more they began to become distrustful and even hostile towards their own nation, going as far as to look elsewhere, beyond their frontiers, for an ideal homeland as they did not have the strength within themselves (and only regained it at the time of the Resistance) to help them distinguish and separate forever the healthy roots of their country from the corrupt roots of the sick plant of Fascism. Their anti-Fascism, before becoming political, was in fact cultural: their first gestures of freedom were to read prohibited works. It was not just school and Benedetto Croce who stimulated these desires; it was also the authors that they had discovered (Mastriani, Viviani, Joyce, etc.) and those they were in the process of discovering (Sartre, Elbot, etc.), but equally American, French, Soviet films which invaded Italian screens in the cine-clubs and in the GUF (Gruppi Universitari Fascisti) and which managed to slip through the Ministry of Popular Culture's net.

These future young editors developed in the Neapolitan GUF, in the 'littori di Largo Ferrandina', a kind of free zone during the Fascist years; years during which this 'generation without Masters' had their first literary, artistic and political experiences from English, French, American and Russian cultures.[7] At the heart of this GUF, people discussed class struggle, anti-Fascism and Marx while others read Baudelaire, Rimbaud and Verlaine. All or most of them gained experience in a time that was influenced by the so-called 'fascism of the left': Prunas in the review *Gioventù in Marcia*, of which he even became chief editor; and Luigi Compagnone, Antonio Ghirelli, Tommaso Giglio, Raffaele La Capria and Gianni Scognamiglio, all of whom contributed to the review *IX Maggio*.[8]

It was in the latter that trends and ideas, inaugurated in *Belvedere* (a different GUF review), were able to develop and reach a conclusion, while historical events were becoming more and more troubling. As Sergio Riccio writes, during this period one felt the need for pure and revolutionary fascism mixed with the concept of 'uninterrupted revolution' which had developed in the heart of the *Littoriales*' experiences and which had, in the literary world, led to the defence of hermeticism and the discovery of the Americans and French (Riccio and Percopo 1977). The review *IX Maggio* can thus be seen as the first true vehicle for experimentation for the young Neapolitan intellectual generation. The experience of GUF was, for these young intellectuals, almost a required rite of passage, with the purpose of gaining an identity and of existing as an individual distinguished from others. All, or most of them, believed in improving Fascism from within, changing its direction rather than fighting against it. However, it is important to be cautious regarding these young intellectuals' position concerning Fascism within these reviews.

Thus, using the teaching of Croce and the social analysis of southerners, La Capria and his companions refused a tradition which for them had become sickening and attempted to introduce into their vocabulary and writings a catalyst for thinking and criticizing, 'which would have helped them to see their city and the vast world in a less narrow and limited way and especially less provincial, and if possible, beyond the *piccolo-borghesi* parameters of the *napoletanità*' (La Capria 1994: 88). According to Tortora: 'The town is to be conceived and re-invented, not only represented following

---

[7] Quotes from the author's interview with Raffaele La Capria (July 2011).
[8] *IX Maggio* was the bimonthly of GUF and the University of Naples.

the usual and easy game of photography of facts and the oleography of myth' (Tortora 1994: 143).

The writer Raffaele La Capria is an interesting character because he always felt his literary career was determined by the need to rediscover, through his writing, the link between Naples and Europe. And it was indeed this idea that guided him and his companions, in the aftermath of the war, when they founded in Naples a review, or rather a 'literary journal', while all around them was nothing but ruins caused by the bombing. The liberation of Naples was a huge upheaval, as Raffaele La Capria describes:

> Quando arrivarono gli americani accade alla città ciò che accade a una pentola quando salta il coperchio. Anni e anni di compressione sotto il coperchio del regime, della guerra, dei bombardamenti quotidiani, della paura, della fame, dell'isolamento. E all'improvviso, dopo questa lunga costrizione arrivano gli americani [...] e salta il coperchio [...]. Tutto divenne possibile, che il povero diventasse ricco (con la rapina o il contrabbando),[...] che il bene e il male si confondessero e ogni valore fosse rovesciato in un rimescolio di razze, di mentalità, di lingue. (2003: 1023)

> (When the Americans arrived, the same thing happened to the city as to a pressure cooker when the lid pops off. Long years were spent bubbling away beneath the lid of the regime, the war, daily bombardments, fear, hunger, isolation. And suddenly, after all that pressure, the Americans arrived [...] and the lid blew off [...]. Everything became possible, the poor could become rich (with robbery or smuggling) [...] good and evil melted together, and every value could be overturned in a shuffling of races, mentalities and languages.)

The arrival of the American liberators put them immediately in contact with a new world, and Naples, which had become confusedly cosmopolitan, 'agreed to meet' the people and writers who until then had been read clandestinely. Once the war was over, it thus became normal to express a non-provincial idea of culture, and this generation in particular felt the need to embrace what lay beyond Naples in their writing, thinking, creations and comedies. For them, therefore, if Naples had something to rediscover and regain, it was its European vocation. And thus everyone wanted to reconnect with Europe, after the interruption caused by the war. To create a review was, in their opinion, a means of participating in 'the spiritual renaissance of the South in general, and of Naples in particular'. What followed was thus an explosion of political and 'politico-literary' reviews in Naples, which generally appeared and disappeared rapidly, confirming the close link between the urgency for change and the need for the birth of new periodicals. There was a constant arrival of new reviews which replaced those that had disappeared; their aim was to traverse this long transitional phase in an incisive manner.

Sud was thus not an isolated initiative, even if the concept was totally new. In 1945, publications such as Adolfo Omodeo's *L'Acropoli*, Francesco Flora's *Aretusa* and Palmiro Togliatti's *Rinascita* enlivened the post-war cultural panorama. And two years preceding the birth of *Sud*, it was already possible to witness an atmosphere of cultural and civil mobilization, with representatives at the forefront of a generation who had cultivated a critical conscience and a desire for revenge during the period of Fascism.

Shortly before the birth of *Sud*, on 4 October 1943, *Il Risorgimento* came into being.[9] The alternating versions of this review, which swung from libertarian and republican tendencies in its first years to the heavy intervention of Achille Lauro in the last three years of its existence (1947–50),[10] are revelatory of the complexity of the Neapolitan political situation which saw, relatively quickly, the old positions of Fascist power resurge and consolidate their gains at the heart of the new democratic coalitions.

Hence, in this context the review went far beyond the idea of being merely an intellectual and political practice vehicle for research. For everyone, the experience offered the opportunity to reinforce their presence and become well-known. For Prunas and Scognamiglio, the plan was more ambitious still: they wanted to create a research facility that would be the headquarters for thorough, theoretical debate and systematic practical confrontation. Their meeting was determined by cultural challenges, the will to find themselves and identify themselves with a group, and the same desire to act on a cultural level; all this fed by the same intellectual curiosity.

According to the critic Gianni Invitto, at the heart of the review a rich work of reflection was taking place, between experiences and periods rather than social classes and man. 'The final result is destined for readers selected by certain filters, the first naturally being linguistic. The concentration on language, while on the one hand confirming the sociological definition of the periodical formula, on the other it shows the insoluble dichotomy between trainer-discloser behaviour and elitist behaviour with a closed destination' (Invitto 1980: 20). It was not by chance that, in 1944, Francesco Flora, introducing the *Aretusa* project, steered the 'theoretical energies relative to the project towards function of the *logos* and the stabilising action of Form, and broadened the literary domain of the periodical (narrative, poetry, criticism) in part-historical and part-disciplinary directions, intending to group heterogenous topics and subjects together' (Striano 2006: 148).

---

[9] Edited by La Società Editrice Meridionale, this newspaper regrouped under its title various Neapolitan daily papers which were unable to be published due to lack of funds. The directors were Paolo Scarfoglio for *Il Mattino* and Emilio Scaglione for *Il Roma*.
[10] See Note 19.

The reviews seem to have appeared out of nowhere; in other words, as Invitto emphasizes, they seemed to have had the certitude of 'constructing new moments of human and cultural development by means of multiple changes in the typographic and editorial structure, the aim of which was to desacralize graphic and structural stereotypes' (1980: 28).

The future editors of *Sud* had been waiting for change for a long time; these scholars had anticipated the need to retain the human value which they, above all, recognized within themselves. In addition, they felt with an ever-increasing force, the need to give birth to a periodical which was 'equidistant from the opposing concepts of Marx and Croce, aiming to regain room for autonomy where artistic experience could be both shared and ethical, while civil assumptions could be satisfied' (Striano 2006: 148).

The founder, Pasquale Prunas, was extraordinarily skilled at channelling these requirements into a cultural project of secular humanism and this against the propagation of irrationalism and passions. Prunas, in the first ever edition of *Avviso*, wanted a totally different status from that of the previous review, *Aretusa*; he believed that 'to make literature meant fulfilling a social and political duty' (1945: 1), to accomplish an educational action, to highlight the humanist roots of literature above and beyond social classification: 'Quando noi diciamo letteratura e letterato noi diciamo uomo. Dire uomo significa operaio, contadino, borghese ed aristocratico' ('When we say literature and writer, we say man. To say man, means worker, farmer, bourgeois and aristocrat').[11]

From these first statements, their ambitions seemed modest and the review's scope appeared to have leant to the left, both in comparison with Francesco Flora's review and in the vague and subjective horizon of *Latitudine*. On top of that, Prunas attached great importance to the graphic presentation of the journal, which he considered a means of modern communication, a counterpoint to the text and no longer simply serving as decoration or filler. In the editorial, Prunas described the formation of the periodical, which, born from a spiritual need, had an ambition: to be 'a voice, a marker in the times and of the times, a creature as living as the idea of this periodical which has accompanied us through the years in our pain' (1945: 1).

Ruggiero Guarini, who witnessed the performance of Pasquale Prunas and his comrades, defined the review as the 'first serious attack on the song and postcard myth of the old and convectional *napoletanità*'. The tone was thus set. But the revolution invoked by *Sud* was merely spiritual, as La Capria liked to clarify, with a unique and fundamental objective, the liberation of Man. In this review, various essays and translations were

---

[11] Prunas (1945: 1). The anastatic reprint of all the seven issues of the review *Sud* was edited by Giuseppe di Costanzo (1994). The review was trying to reclaim southern intellectuals, while Vittorini's *Le Politecnico* targeted a broader, popular public.

published which disseminated ideas of poets and writers such as Kafka, Eliot, Faulkner, Auden, Isherwood, Dylan Thomas, Sartre and Camus; they spoke of existentialism, of American narrative and dramatic trends and of so many other authors who perfectly represented the spirit of the time. These southern intellectuals did not simply define themselves by their ability to represent the city; they were duty-bound to be Europeans above all else.

The spirit which drove these young editors – Prunas, Ortese, Compagnone, Ghirelli, Giglio, Scognamiglio, Patroni Griffi, Rosi and others – was first to banish clichés[12] and to extricate themselves from the narrow local literary milieu of napoletanità;[13] but the goal was particularly to renew links with interwar European and American literature such as that of Proust, Joyce, Hemingway and Mann, who had been judged decadent and officially kept at arm's length during the twenty years of Fascism (in other words, during their entire adolescence). Moreover, Prunas, in his very first editorial, fully intended to remove any ambiguity concerning the name of the review: 'Sud non ha il significato di una geografia politica né tantomeno culturale; il Sud ha per noi il significato di Italia, Europa, Mondo. Sentendoci meridionali, ci sentiamo europei' ('Sud does not identify with any political or even cultural geography; Sud means for us Italy, Europe, the World. As much as we feel southern, we feel European'; 1945: 1).

Added to this, after the arrival of the American liberators, Naples had become a city of transition where many fleeing intellectuals and writers would stop: in this way, Soldati, Longanesi and Malaparte stopped off and Radio Napoli, directed by Ugo Stille, transmitted both culture and propaganda. This visit inspired Malaparte who, shortly after, published *La Pelle*. Culturally, in 1944 Naples was therefore a dynamic and interesting city. A wind of change was thus finally blowing after the cultural isolation of Fascism. In Naples, too, this brief season was enthusiastically embraced, with this group of intellectuals enjoying breaking down limits and frontiers by establishing a network of connected vessels with the most active and creative foreign outposts of intellectuality. As La Capria recalls, they believed that, in order to become true Europeans, they had to change their usual lexicon, not totally rejecting it but making it less self-contemplative, more analytical, detailed and, above all, more distant. Some of them even dreamt of finding new forms of expression, even in the novel, to show they could employ the techniques used by the authors of the European '*grande-borghese*' novel – secretly obtained and read.

They thus bestowed on the cultural overview of southern Italy an openness to European ideas and literary techniques, leaving behind the

---

[12] 'This landscape for tourists', 'the postcard with pines and smoking Vesuvius' (Prunas 1945: 2).

[13] Namely, the fact of not wanting to understand the actual reality of the city, of sticking to and feeding its myth and of later feeding off that myth.

naturalistic and paternalistic influence of the Neapolitan writers stuck in their formalism. In one of Scognamiglio's articles taking stock of Italian and Neapolitan culture, one can quickly sense the desire to break with the national tradition of Italian and European culture: 'Credo sia ormai pacifico che proprio con Croce la cultura napoletana abbia raggiunto il suo culmine e insieme che con Croce sia giunta ad un vero e proprio arresto: ad una fermata nel tempo rispetto alla linea della cultura non soltanto europea ma anche italiana' ('I believe it is now self-evident that with Croce, Neapolitan culture had reached its summit and, at the same time, with Croce it arrived at a real stop, at a halt in time regarding not only European but also Italian cultural lines').

For them, breaking with the formal rules and earlier paternalistic naturalism of the southern novel (for example Serao), so dear to the lower bourgeoisie, meant 'dissociating from the latter, even morally, depriving it of that solidarity which had conditioned them since birth. And it is only by resisting its charms of seduction, that they could understand it and be able to describe its physiognomy' (La Capria 1994: 88–9). It is for this reason that La Capria, explaining his intentions, wrote:

> Come avrei potuto tenermi fuori dal punto di vista della piccola borghesia (napoletana), come avrei potuto mostrarla quale veramente è e non quale presume di essere, se poi avessi adottato il suo stesso linguaggio e la sua stessa idea (appagante) della forma? (pp. 88–9)

> (How could I keep myself outside of the (Neapolitan) lower bourgeoisie's view, how could I have shown things as they really were, and not as they claimed to be, if I had adopted its own language and its own (rewarding) idea of form?)

Looking closely at the protagonists, we note that the dynamics of their commitment and their relationship with politics, power and society followed the fluctuations imposed by the periods of history. This other language was that of a Neapolitan bourgeoisie, who felt like 'a discontented European' (taking the term used by Francesco Compagna in an article in *Sud*), wanting to look at reality in a critical and non-emotional way, capable of irony and detachment. In order to acquire this, according to La Capria, one needed 'to go back to Neapolitan culture's greatest tradition, in other words, to the essay rather than to literature, because the latter was steeped in '*napoletanità*' (1994: 88–9). This was indeed what the young editors of Sud believed.

---

[14] Ghirelli (2005: 1); see Striano (2006: 155).

This was the revolution that had to take place, in a suddenly enlarged European and international context, with an eagerness to participate on the world stage: the Fascist prison had suffocated them because it had excluded them not only from the real world but especially from the great and hard debate between the democratic bourgeoisie and Bolshevism. Their objective was not to be afraid of facing reality head-on, of recognizing it and changing it with this knowledge of modern culture.[14] This conviction had led them to adopt an unequivocally ethical line of behaviour within which they modified their intellectual engagement.

This modern way of thinking, disposed to 'contamination', had found an absolutely extraordinary cultural infrastructure in Naples, marked by incessant exchanges between the young Neapolitan intellectuals and the cultured American and British soldiers.[15] Closer to Europe than any other Italian city, Naples was at this time a laboratory of ideas whose protagonists felt capable of breaking all ties with tradition by preparing a new literary creation, reflecting its times but also incisive and constructive.

However, it was just a temporary honeymoon period, a brief interruption in the silence of reason, in this succession of periods marked by difficult confrontations with reality. On 26 August 1947, shortly before the end of *Sud*, Prunas bitterly explained the tragedy of marginalized intellectuals in a letter: 'In Naples, the intellectual is always isolated from us, at least the intellectual who does not aspire to follow the path of dialect. Here, the intellectual is forced to become inadvertently a man full of resentment, toward himself and others, closed in on himself and lost.' The last issue of *Sud* was dated July–September 1947. Then, La Capria explained:

> *Sud* died from lack of air, not just money, the lack of a true answer that is always the problem in Naples, we felt isolated, left to our own devices, and this has always been the attitude of a city which seems to be suspicious of every intellectual initiative.[16]

Sud was a review with great ambitions but with meagre financial resources – and no political backing. It therefore did not have the financial

---

[15] Let us take William Bill Weaver as an example, a stretcher-bearer during the war who became friends with R. La Capria and with whom he discussed literature and what young Americans were reading.

[16] Interview with Raffaele La Capria (July 2011).

[17] The political engagement (which was neither political sectarianism nor defence of the interests of just one party), which encouraged them to publish with conviction the last *Lettera al fratello* by Giaime Pintor, was the catalyst. Consequently, the review became unsettling for everyone, for the 'official', reactionary culture but also for the Communist Party with whom a distant and somewhat conflictual relationship was established. This first provoked Prunas to refuse financial backing from the Party and the support of Elio Vittorini in 1947, on the occasion of the infamous polemic with the PCI which ended with the latter's departure.

strength to resist. But the reasons for this failure and isolation were more of a political and cultural nature than due to finances. Prunas, who was not a member of the Communist Party (PCI) and showed no interest in the Soviets, believed that the communist concept of culture was a *piccolo-borghese* axiom and that Marxism should recognize, in its dialectic nature, the impossibility of affirming itself as a new religion with dogmas and articles of faith.[17]

Dialogue with the Party was no longer considered possible, and the decline of *Sud* was therefore announced, partly due to Prunas, who preferred to bring an end to the periodical rather than renounce his anarchic brand. The start of the review's decline can be traced back to a meeting held at the headquarters of *La Voce*, in the presence of Emilio Sereni, Mario Alicata, Luigi Amadesi, Alberto Iacoviello, Maria Antonietta Macciocchi, Paolo Ricci and Michele Pelicani, where financial backing for *Sud* by the Communist Party was considered. Alicata stated that he would support the proposition only if *Sud* took a strong political stance. Prunas refused, so as not to deform the free and experimental nature of his creation and not to betray the work of his friends, who, fascinated by contemporary foreign literature and new philosophical trends, had extracted their ideological orientation and literary parameters from them.

Other more profound reasons for the review's failure must also be taken into account. On the one hand, the Parthenopean city did not want – or was not able to take up – the challenge of attaining Italian, European and world values without any geographical connotation or tendency towards a local sense of identity – a refusal that flew in the face of history and which Pier Paolo Pasolini was to later qualify as 'fatal' (quoted in Ghirelli 1976). Naples thus found itself incapable of responding to the onslaught of modernity without taking it in, accepting it in order to adapt and refashion it, in ways that were respectful of the past but in keeping with future demands.

Thus, after an involuntary revolution of its own urban and anthropological physiognomy, after the fight for peace, Naples preferred to turn in on itself, giving in to an immobility that remains with the city today, congested, degraded and abandoned, which, as La Capria emphasizes, is the most obvious sign, the symbol (La Capria 2003). On the other hand, no ruling class of the time was able to benefit from the potential within Neapolitan culture. The educated classes, in a manner of speaking, enclosed themselves in the *autoreferenzialità* circle (see La Capria 2002), with memories of Naples' *Nobilissima* and Benedetto Croce's philosophy; for them, it was a reassuring but particularly regressive way of closing themselves in on their own identity to avoid confronting, through literature, the ocean of modernity, in other words the future and the changing of our time.

---

[18] Most people were landed gentry – living off their income – and for whom industrial culture did not exist.

In practice, highly cultured people – such as Croce – had received the humanist culture that was no longer suited to modernity. In short, technical, scientific and industrial culture were ignored by Neapolitan philosophers or the upper bourgeoisie.[18] Another defect was perceptible; between the creator and the consumer of culture, there was a huge gulf: contact was intermittent and there were few interests in common. Cultural initiatives rarely managed to get beneath the 'skin' of the city. No intellectual from the immediate post-war period was able to establish true dialogue with civilian society. There are two main reasons why 'making culture' was made difficult: first, discord between the city and its intellectuals; second, an innate weakness in the cultural industry. Over the centuries, an untraversable gulf had arisen between the utopian vision of intellectuals and artists on the one hand and the real city on the other, always happy to concede to the worship of song and Piedigrotta festivals. Concerning the former, it is interesting to note Iaia Caputo's definition; according to her, the relationship between Naples and its intellectuals is 'lo stesso di quello che la città ha con i bambini, ne produce a caterve, li ama visceralmente, riserva ad entrambi la retorica dei buoni sentimenti, poi li abbandona, precocemente, al loro destino' ('just like the link between the city and its children, it produces many, it loves them viscerally, and for both it reserves the rhetoric of good feelings, before abandoning them early to their own destiny') (quoted in Zanardi 1994: 24). This brings us to the second point, more worrying than the first. The same writer wondered how it was that the post-war writers were published by non-Neapolitan editors. In her opinion, it was simply the consequence of giving up: they went looking for a welcome elsewhere, wherever they could find it.

In conclusion, the problem also arose from the passage between old and new situations which was more difficult than it seemed. The desire for renewal collided with an objective 'cultural power', still held and managed by the old guard artists and intellectuals. This ultimately led to the end of the review in 1947 and plunged Naples back into a deep sleep, 'The silence of reason'. The consequence was not long in coming: a curse which has affected Neapolitan and southern culture continuously right up to the present day and which has forced its young intellectuals to leave Naples and to create the Neapolitan diaspora. Already in its first issue, *Sud* had the visionary title '*Essi se ne vanno da Napoli*' (*They leave Naples*) (Compagnone 1945: 1).

The consciousness of a predestined fate was underway, entailing in a prophetic manner not just individuals but the city as a whole. Among the review's editors, Gianni Scognamiglio was certainly the most tormented and misunderstood. His life experience, far from Naples, plunged him into a deep despair. The curse of the exile can be seen in the verses of a poem published by *Sud* in June 1946:

Io non voglio più credere all'uomo in questa città
ove l'amore e l'odio non sono più rivali fecondi

ma giacciono divisi per sempre su un arido suolo
e il timore di non essere più vivi è già certo
Io me ne vado per sempre da questa città
nel suo tiepido sole non dà frutto alcun seme
nei suoi ruscelli non si è mai spenta la sete dell'uomo
e i suoi sguardi non sanno qual è la nostra attesa

(I no longer want to believe in the men in this city
Where love and hatred are no longer fruitful rivals
But lie separated forever on arid ground
And the fear of no longer being alive is certain
I am leaving this city forever
In its lukewarm sun, the seeds give no fruit
In its rivers, man never slakes his thirst
And its sights know not of our waiting)
(Scognamiglio in Di Costanzo 1994: VI, 80)

Once the review had been disbanded, the tragedy of the forced flight affected the best minds of a city and of the whole south for decades. Thereafter, 'laurism'[19] and cronyism, the *trasformismo* (political powershift), conformism and the blindness of the ruling classes expelled all those whose tenacity to reason was not enough to resist the centrifugal force which was dispersing intellectual resources in Italy and elsewhere, resources which could, on the contrary, have provided the force needed for change. The weakest left the city, ending their lives: Francesca Spada, Renato Cacciopoli and Luigi Incoronato were among those who suffered from the strain of this evil darkness.

The strongest, on the other hand, did not allow themselves to be trapped by this comforting and consolatory call, 'one must stay, as the south asks us to'. They achieved success in other cities and other countries which would have been unthinkable if they had not cut the umbilical cord which ran the risk of suffocating them. This ability to escape the land which 'sends you to sleep or inflicts deadly wounds on you', to quote La Capria, prevented the slow decaying of minds, which elsewhere were able to produce science, economic activitiy and art.

Having begun with one of La Capria's answers, it is therefore logical to conclude with one of his reflections on the European dimension of Neapolitan literature. According to him:

---

[19] Achille Lauro inherited his first ships in 1912 and built up a substantial fleet of freighters before the Second World War. During the 1950s, Achille Lauro became a very rich person, known as the 'King of Naples', and owner of a fleet of fifty ships.

there is therefore no book and no Neapolitan author, as Ortese said, who managed to breach the walls of certain European experiences, to conquer this universality which makes a book great. We are dissatisfied Europeans, but at least we have tried. I don't believe it is possible to make a cultural leap of this magnitude in one go, even if nothing is impossible for a true artist, but in short, I should like to say that henceforth the conditions are right, and it is the authors of my generation and their ambitions, whether they are correct or not, which made this possible. Good luck to those who follow us! (La Capria quoted in Tortora 1994: 55)

References

Arpaia, B. (1994), 'Andare via, restare', in G. Tortora (ed.), *Il risveglio della ragione: Quarant'anni di narrativa a Napoli, 1953–1993*, 9–16, Cava dei Tirreni: Avagliano.
Compagnone, L. (1945), 'Essi se ne vanno da Napoli', *Sud*, 1: 1.
Croce, B. (1945), 'Postille. Dell'arte delle riviste e delle riviste letterarie odierne', *Quaderni della Critica*, 1.
Croce, B. (1947), 'La vita letteraria a Napoli dal 1860 al 1900', in *La letteratura della nuova Italia*, vol. 4, Bari: Laterza.
Croce, B. (1955), *Cultura e vita morale*, Bari: Laterza.
D'Ajello, G. (1998), *L'Umberto: tradizioni militari e scolastiche*, Naples: Istituto grafico editoriale.
Di Costanzo, G. (1994), *Sud: Giornale di cultura: 1945–1947*, Bari: Palomar.
Ghirelli, A. (1976), *La Napoletanità: Un saggio-inchiesta*, Naples: Società Editrice Napoletana.
Ghirelli, A. (1998), 'Prefazione', in G. D'Ajello, *L'Umberto: tradizioni militari e scolastiche*, 8–24, Naples: Istituto grafico editoriale.
Ghirelli, A. (2005), 'Un atto semplice', *Sud – Rivista Europea*, 6: 1.
Invitto, G. (ed.) (1980), *La mediazione culturale. Riviste italiane del Novecento*, Lecce: Milella.
La Capria, R. (1986), *L'armonia perduta*, Milan: Mondadori.
La Capria, R. (1994), 'Il cuore a Napoli', in G. Tortora (ed.), *Il risveglio della ragione: Quarant'anni di narrativa a Napoli, 1953–1993*, 83–91, Cava dei Tirreni: Avagliano.
La Capria, R. (2002), *Cinquant'anni di false partenze ovvero l'apprendista scrittore*, Rome: Edizioni Minimum Fax.
La Capria, R. (2003), 'L'occhio di Napoli, Taccuino (1992–1993)', in *Opere*, intro. and ed. S. Perrella, 905–1119, Milan: Mondadori.
La Capria, R. (2009), *Napolitan Graffiti* in *Napoli*, Milan: Mondadori.
Marinetti, F. T. (1921), *L'Alcova d'Acciaio*, Milan: Vitigliano.
Pasolini, P. P. (1999), *Saggi sulla politica e sulla società*, ed. W. Siti and S. De Laude, vol. 1, Milan: Mondadori.

Picone, G. (2005), *I Napoletani*, Bari: Laterza.
Prisco, M. (1994), 'Una generazione senza eredi?', in G. Tortora (ed.), *Il risveglio della ragione. Quarant'anni di narrativa a Napoli. 1953–1993*, 123–30, Cava dei Tirreni: Avagliano.
Prunas, R. (1945), 'Avviso', *Sud*, 1: 1–2.
Riccio, S. and Percopo, G. (eds) (1977), *La Campania dal fascismo alla Repubblica: società, politica e cultura*, vol. 2, Naples: Regione Campania.
Striano, A. (2006), *Le riviste letterarie a Napoli, 1944–1959*, Naples: Libreria Dante & Descartes.
Tortora, G. (ed.) (1994), *Il risveglio della ragione: Quarant'anni di narrativa a Napoli, 1953–1993*, Cava dei Tirreni: Avagliano.
Zanardi, M. (ed.) (1994), *Le lingue di Napoli*, Naples: Edizioni Cronopio.

9

The Mediterranean town in question

Raffaele Cattedra

Introduction: A deconstruction of the model

This chapter offers a reflection on the paradigm of 'the Mediterranean town'.[1] The approach suggested does not attempt to define 'the' Mediterranean town as such, by attributing it a status with scientific credentials. Rather, this is a paradigm that is both foundational and vulnerable, the latter being durable, in a dialectic which expresses multidisciplinary thinking on the urbanism and scientific invention of the Mediterranean. Many works on this topic nevertheless attempt to *describe* this type of model, to *justify* it in an *a priori* 'positive' approach that assumes the reality of the *object*, without elucidating other than in ideological terms the theoretical foundations of its objectification, formalization and *actuality* (if we adopt Foucault's terminology).[2] It is therefore a matter of questioning the *genealogy*[3] and

---

[1] I use the word 'paradigm' here borrowing at least two meanings proposed by T. S. Kuhn (1970): on the one hand as a founding myth of a scientific community, on the other as an element constituting a disciplinary matrix – as such, it conveys a scientific imagination capable of assuming a teleological configuration: the belief in the 'realization of a promise' (Dematteis [1985] 1994: 102; see also Bernard 2003).

[2] In other words, according to Foucault (1969), the manner in which an 'event' goes through a process in which discourse, practices, ideologies and actions are contextualized both historically and socially concurs so much that it finds its 'conditions of appearance' in the present.

[3] Regarding these two notions of Foucault's vocabulary, the first is used explicitly in the titles of three works until the beginning of the 1970s; the second poses the question of dispersion as opposed to linear or continuous appearance of objects in history and their 'actualization' in the present crossing several fields: historical ontology, power, ethics; see Revel (2002); Foucault (1969: 80–4).

the affirmation of this paradigm, and of proving its limits, the avatars, even the mythological dimension, beyond the facts which seem to shape today's generation and validity.

My hypothesis is that to interpret the 'success' of this paradigm, it is essential to place it in relation to a dual system of references: on the one hand, in relation to evolution in urban studies, in their relationships with knowledge of diverse subject matter (from social sciences to orientalism); and on the other, in relation to the process which has gradually led, since halfway through the nineteenth century, to the edification of a scientific object, which constitutes the substantial referent: the Mediterranean. The Mediterranean town is thus said to have emerged as a *regional urban category* from an 'artificial' geographical object, that of the Mediterranean. In this chapter, I shall address the first of these two aspects. As for the second, it is enough to remember here that the Mediterranean must be taken in the way that it was 'invented' and has gradually become established (Sinarellis 1998; Deprest 2002; Cattedra 2005, 2008, 2009) – beyond its status as an inner sea – as a 'geographical region' or 'cultural zone' that is autonomous in different ways (climate, vegetation, cultures, lifestyles, etc.). These criteria have led to identifying the Mediterranean as a 'value' (positive and shared) and above all to seeing it as a 'political project'.

But when one looks closely, it is clear it is not a monolithic paradigm. I advance the theory that the latter develops according to three key figures: a *unitary figure*, based on the matrix of historicity and on the principles of shared heritage and civilizing values which engage, in turn, Mediterranean universalism; a *figure of divergence*, which tends to oppose – at the ideological level as well as the morphological level – diverse representations related to Mediterranean towns; and a *figure of recomposition*, which takes up certain elements of the previous figures and offers an actualized version of them in an approach which could be considered postmodern. The fact is that these figures can appear in succession, in opposition and even concomitantly. In the end, they can present themselves in a configuration of *dispersion* (still according to Foucault's vocabulary; Foucault 1969: 80).

Evidence and paradoxes: The aporias of urban taxonomy

Before dealing with these three figures, let us focus on some evidence and one paradox. Scientific production on the theme of the 'Mediterranean town' is abundant, at the risk of over-publication. Turning in particular to geographical literature in French, and without claiming to have exhausted this area, several works published since the 1970s can easily illustrate this point.⁴ Let us not forget either that, since 1995, the Barcelona Process and then the project for the 'Union for the Mediterranean' have created a rather favourable climate for such publications.⁵

However, despite this accumulation of scientific production, if one looks closely at certain generalist works and manuals on the subject of the town published in the last forty years, one can clearly see that there is no reference to the category 'Mediterranean town' or even 'towns of the Mediterranean'. Whether the approach is based on Weber's thoughts, aimed at the comparison of ideal-types of structures and political functions (Rossi 1987); whether it is anthropological and focusing on urban 'civilization' (Roncayolo and Paquot 1992; Turri 1994); whether it is historical and ideal (Mumford 1961); whether it takes into account 'a kind of regional study of large towns in the world' (Pelletier and Delfante [1989] 1993); whether it adopts 'geographical' categorization criteria to question the 'specific characteristics' (Bruyelle 2000); whether it presents 'urban panoramas' (Biget and Hervé 1995; Paquot 1996); whether it studies 'the towns and economy in history' and states even the points of departure and arrival of a historical journey: 'from Jericho to Mexico' (Sica 1970) or 'from Babylon to Tokyo' (Moriconi-Ebrard 2000), the fact remains that none of these works presents either a chapter or an article by a well-known author dedicated specifically to the 'Mediterranean town'.

And yet, if we follow Predrag Matvejević ([1987] 1999: 22), we note that just about everything has been said about Mediterranean towns: 'about the *polis* and politics, plans and cadastres, about buildings and their styles, about stone and stonemasonry, sculpture and architecture, temples and ceremonies, private dwellings and public buildings, walls and fortresses, squares and fountains, about the street and street life in the Mediterranean'. And how can one not agree with Matvejević, writes Alberto Clementi: 'Never

---

⁴ Muscarà (1978); *Villes en parallèle* (1978); Lefebvre and Régulier (1986); Leontidou (1990, 1993); Serra (1993); Clementi (1995); Doumenc (1995, 1997); Miossec (1997); Troin (1997); Vallat (1998); Corna Pellegrini (1998a, 1998b); Voiron-Canicio (1999); Béthemont (2001); Nicolet, Deapule and Ilbert (2000); Moriconi-Ebrard (2000); Escallier (2001, 2002); Chaline (2001); Carrière (2002); Froment (2002). I have not kept here works pertaining to just 'one part' of the Mediterranean zone and which attempt to analyse specific towns or urban phenomena of such and such subregion (European Mediterranean, Maghreb, the Near East, Balkans, etc.), nor the numerous monographic issues of reviews and periodicals more or less specializing in the Mediterranean. For example: *Méditerranée: Revue géographique des pays méditerranéens*; *Cahiers de la Méditerranée*; *Rives nord-méditerranéennes*; *Espaces et territoires*; *Bulletin de la société languedocienne de géographie*; *Peuples Méditerranéens*; *Villes en parallèle*; *Confluence Méditerranée*; *Nord e Sud*; *Africa e Mediterraneo*; *Afriche e Orienti*; *Civiltà del Mediterraneo*; *Méditerranéennes/Mediterraneans*; *La pensée de midi*.

⁵ The René-Seydoux Foundation listed in 1999, in its 'Répertoire méditerranéen', 800 centres or organizations covering more than 80 fields of human, social and applied science; among them, some 150 actively devoted to architecture and urbanization, to town and country planning and human geography in 43 countries.

has the sayable been all said (like in the case of Mediterranean towns); even the imaginary is henceforth saturated with representations so widely shared that common places become familiar and superficial' (1995: 267). But as soon as one has got rid of these pre-formatted images and clichés, doubts and questions appear: 'Does a Mediterranean town really exist?' (p. 267). Is it possible to propose a synthetic and coherent model for towns, admittedly open to the same sea, but belonging to three different continents? Or would it be better to say that this idea is the fruit of an 'intentional construction' and of a 'symbolic investment' which seeks to 'bend the elusive multiplicity of situations' and Mediterranean forms of human agglomeration? (p. 267).

Beyond the paradoxical absence of the 'Mediterranean town', the category that we have been looking at, there is the more general question of logic and the theoretical grounds of categorization which must be addressed. The 'classification logic' as Lorenza Mondada (2000a, 2000b) puts it – and this is the identification with a geographical, historical, morphological, economic or cultural characteristic, categories of towns or types of urban phenomena – in addition to reducing the complexity of reality and establishing protocols of priority, translates just as well a *matching* effect in the categorization system proposed for methods of recognition of the world at a given time. If one follows Denis Retaillé, this kind of operation of 'meaning [...] consists in treating appearances as scientific objects, in order to simply delineate, state its properties, by establishing that which can only be transitory as the capture of reality' (Retaillé 2000: 278). And this snapshot is elucidated synchronically in relation to the historical contexts of their presentation and, chronologically, in relation to a horizon of knowledge to which the authors subscribe or in relation to their discourses and cartography (Quaini 2005).

To try and understand the appearance of an urban model or typology with reference to the Mediterranean, it is worth observing the evolution in taxonomic categories, stated under their diverse registers (historical, cultural, geographical, etc.). This fact will play a part in the process of configuration and scientific legitimation of a paradigm of the Mediterranean town. It will be representative of one of the *instances of demarcation and specification of the system*, as Foucault (1969: 57–9) would say.

The founding and unifying figure: The universalism of the Mediterranean town

It must be agreed that it is the reference to history, heritage and patrimony that constitutes one of the matrices structuring the paradigm of the Mediterranean town. These instances seem to me to represent its common denominator, either from a genealogical point of view or because they have attributed to the town (in the absolute sense) a generative unifying function of the model.

However – another paradox – for a long time, as far as the Mediterranean was concerned, the urban universe played only a minor role. In his analysis of French Mediterranean geographical studies, Paul Claval pointed out that, although the vision of Vidal de la Blache, the recognized founder of French geographical academia, did not suggest the use of monography, on the contrary it is 'the regional approach which takes its revenge on the 1940s and 50s' (1988: 400). And this will not be in a position to produce a 'collective vision and a coherent interpretation of Mediterranean realities'. According to Claval, these writings on the Mediterranean produced during the first half of the twentieth century 'let go of the urban and industrial world' (p. 400). In any case, for geographers who describe *the* Mediterranean, the town is not a worthy subject. In fact, it is studied or evoked only very occasionally.

Of the earliest geographers to concern themselves with the Mediterranean, Elisée Reclus is of note. The Mediterranean is present in this author's works from the very first pages of his *Nouvelle Géographie Universelle* (1875–94). Although he covers it in several of his volumes,[6] it is in the first, dedicated to Southern Europe, that one chapter is entirely devoted to it.[7] This is, in itself, a novel and founding act for the geographical and scientific establishment of the Mediterranean, as other authors have already highlighted (Ruel 1991; Liauzu 1994; Fabre 2000; Deprest 2002). According to Anne Ruel (1991), with Reclus, the Mediterranean became a 'subject of civilization', a geographical space which transforms itself into 'value'.

Claval, however, forgets that Elisée Reclus wrote a text in 1895 entitled 'The Evolutions of Cities' and that, returning to this theme, he devoted an entire chapter to towns in l'*Homme et la Terre*, entitled 'Répartition des hommes' (Reclus 1905–8: vol. 5, bk 4, 335–76). Although some works were set in motion regarding Reclus's contribution to urban analysis (Roncayolo and Paquot 1992; Boino 1999; Pelletier 1999; Steele 1999), I shall evoke briefly certain avenues concerning the interpretation he proposed of an urban Mediterranean world, according to what he called 'the logical study of towns' (Reclus 1905–8: vol. 5, bk 4, 354).

It is first useful to highlight his organicist inspiration for the town. This can be seen through pretty evocative formulas: 'like all developing organisms, the town tends to die' (Reclus 1895: 246). For him, towns 'will

---

[6] *L'Europe Méridionale* (vol. 1, 1875), *La France* (vol. 2, 1877), *L'Asie Antérieure* (vol. 9, 1884), *L'Afrique septentrionale* (vols 10–11, 1885–6), as well as in chapters of his previous work *La Terre* (1868–70).

[7] See chap. 3, 'La Méditerranée' (Reclus 1875: vol. 1, 33–52). This chapter is made up of twenty pages and is in three parts: Part I – 'Formation and the waters of the basin'; Part II – 'Fauna, fishing and salt marshes'; Part III – 'Commerce and navigation'.

be able to become organic bodies perfectly healthy and beautiful' (Reclus 1905–8: vol. 5, bk 4, 379); and that 'movement between the cities [...] can be compared to the ebb and flow of blood in the human body' (p. 379). Such a vision still, however, remains somewhat ambiguous.[8] If, as far as Mediterranean towns are concerned, no true model appears clearly, nor formulas for the 'Mediterranean town', four points seem to be salient to me (Cattedra 2009), namely: (1) analysis of the origin and the situation of port towns; (2) the onset of coastal development;[9] (3) emphasis on the cosmopolitan nature of certain Mediterranean cities;[10] and (4) identification of a heritage dimension of universal value. These elements play a part to a certain extent in the configuration of a paradigm of the Mediterranean town which has developed since the last quarter of the twentieth century.

But to return more explicitly to the archetypal figure of the paradigm analysed here, and which one could identify as the *first part of heritage*, this is recognizable through at least three aspects: historical continuity, the morphological and spatial dimension, and cosmopolitanism and universalism.

Continuity

Continuity is the expression of a long historical duration. It is the key thread of the founding figure and expresses the presupposed particularity of the Mediterranean urban dimension. It develops along with the idea of the transmission of the past and of heritage. And the culturalist stereotype of this historical dimension is ever present, for example, with the epigones of Vidal de la Blache, such as Max Sorre and Jules Sion in the 1930s:

---

[8] The organicist works of Reclus, while integrating an evolutionist interpretation 'from the village to the town, to the city' but – one must note – which was related to the 'class war', was adopted in an ambivalent way, both as a metaphoric figure of the discourse and as a paradigm of the analysis. Organicist vision or language influenced urban vocabulary throughout the twentieth century, adopting the anthropomorphic comparison of the town where its districts are sectioned into cells, frames, organs (heart, lungs, etc.) but also physiological (traffic, flux) and pathological (macrocephaly, physical and moral degradation, spreading cancer, etc.).

[9] This phenomenon – already mentioned in Reclus's (1869: vol. 2, 656) work *La Terre*, about the descent of the hilly Sicilian or Spanish villages towards the coast – is evoked in these terms in *L'Homme et la Terre:* 'The call of commerce and the repression of piracy changed the situation of many towns built on the rocky coastline of the Mediterranean. Formerly they were perched on steep hills encircled by thick walls for defense against warlords and Corsairs, now they have descended from their rocks and spread along the breadth of the coastline: everywhere the "borgo" has become the "marina", Piraeus replaces the Acropolis' (1905–8: vol. 5, bk 4, 336).

[10] Notably Istanbul, Salonica, La Valette, Venice, Marseilles, Tangier, Cairo and Jerusalem.

> The Mediterranean regions are all impregnated with history. The past is engraved on their ground by the ruins, the conquest or abandonment of the land, the position of localities; it perpetuates itself in often archaic human activities. A German has difficulty imagining how the ancient Germans lived; a Greek sees every day in the fields and the ports scenes which could lead him to believe he is a contemporary of Homer. (Sorre and Sion 1934: 52)

Continuity is an essential referent for Fernand Braudel:

> Without a doubt, the Inner sea is modelled with historical resurgences, tele-histories, lights which come to it from apparently dead worlds but which however live on. ([1977] 1985: 163)

The idea of continuity is also taken up in these terms by Maurice Aymard:

> Each civilization has thus left its urban heritage and has helped define the framework where men continue to live, even today, in the midst of constraints from the past, even though the conditions which guided its creation no longer exist. ([1977] 1985: 198)

To sum up, this concept was prevalent for twentieth-century authors and one has to conclude that history and heritage are understood as being the identity and formal matrix of the Mediterranean town. The register of this same figure of temporal continuity is also deployed in another dimension, like a structural co-matrix: it is the idea of the historical force, even the permanency, of the urban Mediterranean network, of which Braudel made it one of the key points of his discourse, even though he himself recognized that he owed this thought to an intuition of Lucien Febvre.

> Human unity, in the Mediterranean, is at once this road space and this urban space, these lines and these centers of force. Towns and roads, roads and towns are but one and the same human spatial device. Whatever its form, its architecture, the civilization which enlightens it, the Mediterranean town is a road creator and at the same time is created by them. (Braudel [1949] 1990: 254)[11]

One must, however, remember that this representation had already been expressed by Reclus in 1876, in other words well before the publication

---

[11] Braudel continued this theme in other essays: 'The Mediterranean is land and sea routes linked together, routes, in fact one should say just as well towns, modest sized, average sized, and the largest all holding hands' ([1977] 1985: 76).

of Braudel's thesis. This approach, also present throughout the twentieth century, consists in analysing, in the long term, the specificity of Mediterranean human establishments according to the structured network of antique maritime routes, Roman roads, up to the networks of new international migrations and immaterial flows, with towns as the relays and terminals – a network which also allows towns to go beyond the strict limits of the Mediterranean.[12] In brief, in such a perception of things, as Braudel writes, 'the road and urban order is, by excellence, the *human order of the Mediterranean*' ([1949] 1990: 225).[13]

Spatial localization and the form of the town

Continuity, incidentally, comes with a series of elements which simultaneously characterize the origin of the Mediterranean city, even that of the city in any part of the world, in other words, the criteria of site and localization. A pretty widespread example is that of the 'acropolis model' which is found in cities with outlooks such as Athens, Marseille, Barcelona, Nice, Sète, Genoa, Naples, Dubrovnik, Istanbul, Izmir, Algiers, Oran, Tangiers and so on. The other major element is the heritage of monumental Graeco-Roman architecture: the agora, fora, temples, arenas, circuses and grid plan are the devices for *standardizing* the model.[14] This is how Elisée Reclus described it in his last work, from 1905:

> In the Mediterranean region, it occurs that the love of the city instead of populating the countryside with outskirts, depopulates it on the contrary. The great benefit of being able to discuss public interest has, by tradition, changed everyone into city dwellers. The appeal of the agora, as in Greece, city life as in Italy, attracts the inhabitants to a central square where they

---

[12] 'One can see just how much the Mediterranean routes have expanded the space exploited by the towns and the inner sea merchants' (Braudel [1977] 1985: 79).
[13] This idea of Elisée Reclus, who is too often overlooked, was found in Maurice Aymard who expressed it in the following way: 'Far more than to the climate, the geology and the topography, the Mediterranean owes its unity to a network of towns and villages which were created in very early days and have been remarkably tenacious: it is around this that the Mediterranean space has been formed, it is what animates it and gives life to it. The countryside does not give birth to towns, but the towns to the countryside which just needs feeding' (Aymard [1977] 1985: 194).
[14] Aymard developed in 'Espaces' the idea thus: 'Modern urbanism was born in the Mediterranean, in 5th century Greece, with Hippodamos de Milet, the inventor of the checkerboard town layout. He triumphed at every occasion when cultural standardization took place where the systematic reproduction of an established model won over spontaneous development a kind of revenge: hellenistic Greece, Rome, the Renaissance and the Baroque period, our contemporary world. More than functional necessities, Haussmannian before his time, he proclaimed total transparency of the space inhabited by people: the victory of order over spirit' ([1977] 1985: 203–4).

can debate common business, more easily on the public promenades than between the sound walls of the city house. (1905–8: vol. 5, bk 4, 372)

The 'love of the town' of which Reclus spoke and which would constitute with its spatial consequences one of the morphemes of the figure of 'the compact town' in the Mediterranean expresses well – between reality, 'myth and archetype' (Farinelli 2003: 132) – all the importance and interest attributed to the Mediterranean 'city world' and to public spaces. Maximilien Sorre and Jules Sion were of a similar opinion when they wrote in 1934:

> Towns are right to protect the monuments of their past jealously because they owe to them not only the influx of tourists, but sometimes their very existence. What would have become of the decrepit Rome of the 14th century without its great souvenirs? Athens would still be the sordid Albanian village which Chateaubriand experienced without the prestige of its name. (1934: 52)

Another more 'sensitive' version invites us to read the historical and architectural sedimentation, in the way of Corboz, like a 'palimpsest'. Jean-Paul Volle saw what he called 'the environmental topic' of the Mediterranean as an expression of 'heritage'. In other words, the product of the contextualized relationship of usage and urban practice: the relationship between the stone and construction which produce certain densities; the narrowness of the plains and the mountains close to the sea, the *fractures* of the land which result in fractured forms and structures of agglomeration based on 'micro-cells' (CERTU 2006: 2–14).

Cosmopolitanism and universalism

The third dimension of the unifying figure is based on two other items linked in a relationship of reciprocity: universalism and cosmopolitanism. In the presupposed identification of a common matrix of 'the' Mediterranean town, the contribution of diverse civilizations takes a special place: the Mediterranean, like a palimpsest of domination and amalgamation. What Albert Memmi wrote about Tunis (in *La Statue de sel*) could have been written about Naples, Istanbul, Salonica, Alexandria and so many other cities, by slightly modifying the names of the people and the conquerors:

> (Tunis) When I read a little history, I got dizzy; Phoenicians, Romans, Vandals, Byzantines, Berbers, Arabs, Spaniards, Turks, Italians, French, I forget others and I must be muddled over some of them. Five hundred steps and one can change civilization. (1966: 110)

When looking closely at the first geographers, with Reclus it was Paul Vidal de la Blache who highlighted this aspect in a little-known text, his 'Leçon d'ouverture du cours d'histoire et de géographie' at the University of Nancy Arts Faculty, written in 1873, entitled *La Péninsule Européenne: L'Océan et la Méditerranée*. One of his passages helps pinpoint the emergence of the urban cosmopolitan myth of the Mediterranean at the end of the nineteenth century:

> Marseilles, Odessa, Alexandria present, despite the distance between them, a similar site: life and business everywhere you look in the open air as in the time of the agora, noisy activity and a heavy mass of cosmopolitan people where East meets West; totally diverse languages ring in your ears; amongst this Babel a sort of weird creation emerged, this arbitrary and composite jargon which has been labelled lingua franca.[15] (Vidal de la Blache 1873: 16)

So, as we shall see in the section 'Attempts at recomposition: The resurgence of a unitary figure in the postmodern matrix', cosmopolitanism will play an important role in the third figure of the Mediterranean town. Before Braudel, it was Paul Valéry who, in a text dedicated to the 'Mediterranean system', explained clearly in 1933 his idea of Mediterranean heterogeneity as a heritage and a model of reference which was of universal value:

> On the edges, large numbers of extremely different populations, large numbers of temperaments, of feelings and very diverse intellectual capacities, came into contact. Thanks to the ease of movement, already spoken of, these people had relationships of all kinds: war, commerce, voluntary or involuntary exchange of things, knowledge, methods; mixing of blood, words, legends, traditions. The number of ethnic elements present or in contrast, over the ages, customs, languages, beliefs, laws, political constitutions, has always engendered an incomparable vitality in the Mediterranean world. Competition (which is one of the most notable traits of our modern era) reached very early on in the Mediterranean an exceptional intensity: competition for trade, influence, and religion. In no other region in the world has such a variety of conditions and elements been met to such an extent, such richness been created and renewed over and over again. All the factors of European civilization are products of these circumstances, in other words local circumstances have had (recognizable) effects of interest and universal values. ([1933] 1960: 1136–7)

In short, various authors, including contemporary scientists, have been able to see, in the movement brought about by Mediterranean commerce,

---

[15] See Dakhlia (2008) for 'lingua franca' in the Mediterranean.

diasporas, military conflict and colonization, as well as by anthropological and cultural mixing, that this movement has over time been able to engender the expression of a common foundation built over time. They did this by identifying an ideal model, made from the inputs of numerous civilizations, such that, going beyond this unifying and cultural view, in the 1970s even the geographer Hildebert Isnard asserted the link between towns, their forms and their heritage:

> There are perhaps no other regions in the world where the different civilizations have influenced their urban concepts so much: in succession Greece, Rome, Islam, Western Europe have all brought their influence to bear on the lay-out of these cities. (1973: 77–8)

Now, if by looking at scientific and literary production we can easily observe the recurrence of the cliché of the Mediterranean as the birthplace of civilizations,[16] there is a point which I think is important to evoke: that of the relationship between the birth of civilization(s) and the idea of universalism. In the first instance, it would be useful to know about which civilizations we are speaking. The Mediterranean has in turn been construed as the 'cradle', the 'home', the 'melting pot' (of diverse civilizations), where all three expressions obviously do not have the same meaning.[17]

While Reclus identified three civilizations (Arians, Semites, Berbers), for Braudel the three civilizations are those of the Western Universe (based on the contributions of the Romans and Christianity), the Islam Universe (founded on the Assyrian, Carthaginian and ancient Egyptian contributions) and the Orthodox Universe (founded on a Greek template and with Constantinople having influenced the Balkans).[18] The neoclassical vision heavily emphasized the spiritual influences from the ancient Mediterranean to the supposed universal civilization: philosophy, the birth of rationalism and of law, harmony and so on.

---

[16] 'Everyone says it, everyone knows that "the first civilizations" were born in the oriental Mediterranean of the Middle East' (Braudel [1977] 1985: 83).

[17] The 'foyer' constitutes the second of the seven 'Mediterranean models' proposed by Roger Brunet (1995): (1) 'le lac', (2) 'le foyer', (3) 'le détroit', (4) 'l'isthme', (5) 'les croissants', (6) 'la barrière', (7) 'le chott'. These 'figures' represented for Brunet 'theoretical situations' which emerge from geopolitical analysis of the relationships between the territorial structures of the Mediterranean.

[18] Braudel wrote: 'civilization [...] is not only a religion, although that is the core of every cultural system, it is a way of life, a thousand ideas which repeat themselves' ([1977] 1985: 164); in his last works, he accorded an important role to the Phoenicians, following the findings of archaeological digs in the 1960s and 1970s and the works of Sabatino Moscati, highlighting the rivalry of the latter with the Greeks. Mumford (1961) also reminded us of how the idea and supposed superior role of the Greek *polis* arose during the nineteenth century at the expense of other contemporary civilizations, like that of ancient Egypt.

And it is on this subject that the universalism of Reclus seems to me again to be the precursor: he wrote about the Judo-Muslim Andalusian monuments as being 'the common property, not just of Spaniards, but also of everyone who is interested in the life of humanity, in the development of science and the arts' (Reclus 1875–94: vol. 1, 745). He thus clarified, in just a few words, the founding principles which generated the concept of 'World Heritage', introduced officially by UNESCO a century later in 1972:

> However desertlike Andalusia may be, compared to how it could be if it had access to suitable funding, it is still another Italy thanks to the glory and beauty of its towns. The names of Granada, Cordoba, Seville and Cadiz are amongst those most celebrated by poetry and which awaken in our minds the most joyous ideas. The souvenirs of history, more even than the splendour of the monuments have made these ancient moresque cities the common property, not just of Spaniards, but also of everyone who is interested in the life of humanity, in the development of science and the arts. (p. 745)

The figure of *divergence*

A first example helps to illustrate from the outset the evocative power of the Mediterranean town stereotype which develops according to the figure which I call *divergence*. All you need to do is note just how this model is presented in an uncritical and tautological way, and how the legitimation of the concept is asserted assuming – in a simplistic but efficacious way – both Mediterranean universalism (but appertaining uniquely to the Western town) and an irreducible divergence with the 'Islamic conception' of the town:

> The Mediterranean city.
> The Western concept of the town as a centre for artisanship, commerce and politics with public spaces for civilian activity and whose physical layout responds to a preconditioned strategy is practically a Mediterranean invention, appeared in Greece and developed by Rome. European towns are part of the landscape and still further are its principal orchestrators in that it is the town which governs and models the totality of the territory. Rome extended the idea of city life and of civitas – from which we get 'civil' and 'to civilize' – favouring, almost everywhere, the principles of urbs, or structural development – from which we get the term to urbanize: thus to civilize and urbanize become correlated terms.
> Beyond the noticeable effects exerted on the whole country by towns, the urban landscape of Mediterranean towns is very characteristic. In this landscape, the predominant structure is reticular or radial, in other words always in relation with a determined centre, where, from the outset, the

buildings of power are concentrated. Often in towns structured around military buildings (or castrum), the fabric articulated by perpendicular axes (cardo and decumanus) are the norm [...] Transported by the Castilian empire, this reticular concept was exported to the American colonies, where it still exists a little everywhere. In the south west, one can see the Islamic concept, with a central 'medina' devoted to commerce, a large boundary, although more confused, of residential dwellings and a large government palace which can be sited in different places. Here one cannot use the Latin term 'urban centre'. Nonetheless these historic centres only represent today a modest part, even a very modest part, of the total surface of the town. (Roque 2001: 86)

Arab-Muslim town versus Western town

Unlike in the first unifying figure, it is the opposition and contrast between models – ideological, cultural, religious, morphological – which helps this second paradigm of the Mediterranean town emerge. As Fabre wrote, 'the clash in the representations of the Mediterranean revolves around heritage, and notably around the acceptance or rejection of "the Semitic East", in other words the Arabic and Jewish contributions' (2000: 66). It is in this confrontation – which is strictly linked to political, economic and ideological (i.e. imperialist) rationales from colonialism – that a divergent interpretation of the underlying cultural elements arises to the idea of a unifying and universal model of the Mediterranean town.

It is a question of evolution that explicitly tends to lead universality once again towards the West and Europe. Leonardo Benevolo (1993) expressed this idea very clearly, with regard to the modern town, when he wrote that 'the identity linking European and modern towns has been accepted as a fact, leaving aside the enormous problems of compatibility with other urban realities and the ensuing, hybridization in Europe as on the other continents. [...] We must recognize that our model is just one of many possible models for the modern town' (Benevolo quoted in Tosi 1987: 46).

Orientalism has played a determining role in the disconnecting effects of the Mediterranean town's unifying figure, by highlighting the confrontation between two models: the European or Western town and the Arabic, Muslim or Eastern town. Historically, orientalism is built on an ideological attitude which simply formalizes a discourse based on the concept of 'cultural specificity'. Almost echoing Benevolo's discourse above, André Raymond stated that

> perhaps because too tightly enclosed in an 'orientalist' view, specialists of Muslim history and art have no doubt overly neglected the fact that an 'urban specificity' exists, of which the Islamic or Arabic town represents but one aspect: problems of structure, of urban functions which arise in

Arabic or Islamic towns can very often be clarified by a comparison with the general problems posed by towns, as well as by a reference to the sole impact of Islamic civilization on towns in Arabic territory. (Raymond 1985: 14; see also Raymond 1995)

In a previous work (Cattedra 1998), I was particularly interested in the construction of this latter model with a critique on the foundations and references belonging to diverse disciplinary areas of knowledge (orientalism, geography and social sciences) through which this ideal-type arose as a paradigm and was asserted. The hypothesis of this study suggests that the idea of an 'Arabic/Muslim/oriental town', applied most often as an original and unique model of spatial and social typology, does not represent the endogenous product of a culture *per se* and which, by its reflexivity, can be identified as 'Arabic-Muslim'. On the contrary, it appears to have come about through Western orientalism. Subsequently, this model would appear to have been adopted and appropriated by the same ideological system that orientalism created in an arbitrary way (Said 1978) and which we have come to call the 'Arabic/or Muslim world'.

In this way, a paradox is affirmed which states that this model, somewhat present in the imagination, becomes a referential paradigm of the urban concept as an expression of an endogenous culture, while it is the product of ideological fabrication formalized by an 'other' knowledge. I advanced the hypothesis that this idea founded on cultural specificity was received and appropriated by the intellectuals of the southern Mediterranean shores, on two fronts: either in parallel to the general adoption of Western values or because it supported the most ancient values of their own culture (Cattedra 1998; refer to Roussillon 1990).

This last stance was, moreover, affirmed by the symbolic but essential purge which rightly, from the beginning and right up to the Enlighteners, acted as the theme of predilection of orientalism: this purge was founded on the elimination of a continuity – and of the heritage – of Islam in relation to the classical world; Graeco-oriental, Roman and Byzantine (Concina 1990; Fantar 1993). Was this 'purge' to signify that its proponents were postulating that Islam introduced a hiatus, a rupture in the course of history? On the other hand, today, the ideology of certain 'Muslim States' seems to me to simply throw over this stance, in that they (re)build and 'stage' (to use Anderson's (1991) meaning and Nora (1986)) a (national) history which only begins in the seventh century with the birth of the propagation of Islam. It is useful to recall here the passage from a text by Maxime Rodinson in which the author examines the evolution of the vision of the East by the West during the last few centuries:

> The unconscious Eurocentrism of the 18th century, directed by the universalist ideology of this time, respected civilizations and peoples

from outside Europe, rightly took note, in their historic evolution or their contemporary structure, of universal human traits, attributing to them only, with a pre-critical naivety, the same under-lying bases as for European culture, only conceiving some kind of specificity at a far too superficial level. The conscious and theorized Eurocentrism of the 19th century made the opposite mistake. Irreducible specificity is supposed at every possible level, universal motivations and traits are denied or scorned. Contradictorily, the only possible universality is conceived as the adoption of the European model in all its aspects. ([1968] 1993: 86)

After that, the fundamental problem is understanding how the ideal model of the 'Arab-Muslim city' actually came into being. This means evaluating in what way the orientalists took up a position regarding this 'other' town *of the Orient*, making it a special object, denying in this way its universality and attributing to it – beforehand and by presupposition – distinctive characteristics. Starting from this premise, it is possible to state that it is the protocol of construction, or *invention* of the paradigm, explaining the Arab-Muslim city which needs to be discussed and called into question. In order to do this, we need to refer to the ambiguous position which superimposed, especially during the nineteenth century (but even more in the twentieth), a whole series of writings relating to 'cultures of otherness' – writings including travel literature, scientific exploration reports, archaeological documents, works on urban history, oriental rediscoveries of Arabic texts and so on – which subsequently elaborated on the differing positions and ideological or scholarly ideas of the texts' authors.

Now, this model is proposed (by interpreting various disciplinary approaches) from a certain number of elements and constant urban *dimensions*, which would appear to correspond to architectural forms, to particular urban typo-morphologies. Through such a dominant interpretation, these elements and dimensions thus become functional variables creating a (presupposed) organization of the urban society in Islam, in what is considered fundamental in the day-to-day functioning of the practical, religious, cultural, social, economic and political aspects of Muslims lives. These *ingredients* are the central mosque, the souk or the bazaar, the *hammam* (Moorish baths), the *casbah* (the military citadel) and the system of ramparts, to which must be added domestic architectural buildings, like houses with patios, the government palace, the urban layout but also specialization based on the economic production in certain quarters and differentiation for their ethnic and faith. Certain institutions necessary for the town's functioning were also identified: the organization of *habous* or *awqâf* (religious foundations corresponding in a way to religious endowments), trade guilds, administrative and legal buildings of the Ulamas, Koranic schools and magistrates (see especially Gardet 1954). I have thus been able to identify various major criteria to support (or criticize) the validity of the paradigm.

In support of the special relationship of reciprocity which was established between 'the city and Islam' came the thesis advanced by Ira P. Lapidus, according to which, the *higrah*, the migration which led Muhammad from Mecca to Medina, in other words what symbolizes the supremacy of 'The Town' par excellence (*madîna an-Nabî*': the city of the Prophet) truly corresponds to the transformation of Bedouin (or rural) life to city life. This migration would signify, in the strongest possible way, the crucial, symbolic and founding moment, that of the passage from paganism to the advent of Islam, as a new monotheist religion (Lapidus 1973: 53). Another fairly widespread theory proposes a special and almost unique relationship between 'the mosque and the town', considering the former as the fundamental element for the organization of the urban structure and of the social and economic life of the city. This was envisaged by Jacques Berque (1958, 1984) for example, but before him, it was Georges Marçais (1945, 1957) who proposed this idea, stating explicitly that 'the mosque creates the Muslim city'.

It was notably the German geographer Eugen Wirth who proposed a critical assessment of various authors who aired their thoughts on the Arab-Muslim town. Wirth thus disagreed with William Marçais (1928, 'L'islamisme et la vie urbaine') and Georges Marçais (1945, 'La conception des villes dans l'Islam') because both authors attributed to Islam an eminently city-like dimension, thus construing a model for the Muslim town. Summarizing their positions (i.e. that urban foundation appeared to be solely due to the action of a ruler; and that it was only in a city context that a Muslim could lead a life conforming to Islam), Wirth stated that from that 'Islam is seen to be closely linked to the town. But, on the other hand, one cannot conclude that there exists an archetypical Islamic town' (1982: 194).

Wirth also set about a critical assessment of various authors' ideas, remarking that

> if in such definitions of the 'Islamic town' one were to replace the word 'mosque' by 'cathedral' or 'church', the number of cited characteristics would equally apply to traditional towns of Western Europe. They therefore hardly seem apt to characterize the particular traits of Islamic towns. One can only find an answer to the problem of the 'Islamic town' if one manages to detect common characteristics between Northern African towns and Western Asian towns which one can only find here and not in Classical antiquity or medieval Europe. (p. 194)

Wirth believed that the specificity was to be found at other levels: the author thus advanced the theory that 'for a geographer, the *sûq* (*market*) is probably the only determining factor of a Middle Eastern town which can be considered as a cultural heritage of Islam' (pp. 197–8).

It should, however, be noted that even Wirth did not escape from the idea of having to find and identify – *a fortiori* – the distinctive characteristics of the 'oriental town', or the 'Arabic town', thus recognizing the urban specificity of this cultural area, although his vision tended to secularize the town in Islam.

On the urban and morphological front, it must be noted that most classical interpretations of the Muslim town have highlighted another salient point: the 'anarchy' of the urban make-up. Dead-end alleyways, cul-de-sacs and tortuous layouts are most often seen as evidence of an incomprehensible 'disorder' of the medinas and ancient town centres. This disorder appears to be totally opposed to an alleged Mediterranean model of order originating from Graeco-Latin antiquity, of which the so-called European and Western town (which itself emanates from a Mediterranean matrix) would be a perfect example, and compared to which the Muslim town is considered different. Disorder therefore became a recurrent element of what can be considered the *figure of divergence* of the Mediterranean town. It is not only the prerogative of orientalists but tends to marry well with a meta-historical presentation of 'Muslim towns'.

Many researchers have strongly contested this fact and have tried to demystify, not without difficulty or academic obstacles, these preconceived and often accredited opinions.

The corollary of urban disorder between Muslim towns and Third World towns

It must be recognized, despite the efforts of many researchers to demystify the preconceived idea of spatial anarchy as one of the specific characteristics of the Arabic-Muslim town,[19] that this idea has established itself as a pertinent variable and has been considered as 'objective' in a whole field of scientific literature. It can be found in a huge number of descriptions and urban analyses, including Lavedan ([1936] 1959), Birot and Dresch (1953), De Planhol (1957, 1968), among others.

However, there is an overrun. During the 1960s, even among the progressive geographers such as Michel Drain, the cliché of the 'irregular lay-out called to mind (by) the lay-out of Muslim towns with numerous dead-ends' was adopted to describe the ancient treasures of southern Spain in Andalusia (Seville, Granada, Cordoba), while in the case of Barcelona and Madrid, this layout is understood as 'reflecting an expansion through

---

[19] In the late 1970s, Dominique Chevallier was still attempting to convince that 'a true urban organization exists in Arab countries; imposed by society and its life' (Chevallier 1979: 8; see also Chevallier 1972).

burgeoning outskirts which a new enclosure subsequently envelops' (Blanc, Drain and Kayser 1967: 47). We can therefore see the persistence of this stereotype which can even be found in the work of Maria-Angels Roque (2001) in *L'espace méditerranéen latin*, quoted in the beginning of the section 'The figure of *divergence*'. And besides, a whole series of works discussing urban phenomena in the world (still) continue to refer to the 'specificity' of this model and its constituent anarchy.

The corollary of urban disorder, according to all morphological, economic and social versions, is inherently linked to the emergence of another urban taxonomy which is that of 'the town of the Third World' (or even the 'developing' town and/or 'of the South') (Cattedra 2008).

Following Pierre George's example, between the mid-1950s and the 1980s, many geographers, in turn, in a regionalist and functional approach, did not hesitate to class agglomerations on the northern coastline of the Mediterranean, such as Barcelona, Naples and Athens, as belonging to (or at least partially belonging, depending on certain characteristics) the category of underdeveloped or Third World cities, despite being situated on European soil.

This classificatory, statistically based reason has contributed to, if not founded but nonetheless nourished, the institution and reproduction of the division of the world from which this last model has emerged. Beyond this, it must nevertheless be noted that the system in which (and by which) is produced the emergence and institution of a field and an identifiable category of 'Mediterranean town' reposes on another order of criteria and discourse, despite, from the 1960s to the 1970s, registering the Third World question as an underlying element of the figure we have defined as '*divergence*'.[20]

However, from a political point of view, the underlying debate of the figure of *divergence* pertains more explicitly to the relationship between town and State. I will point out two aspects: on the one hand, the fact that many authors

---

[20] As an example we can cite the debates which animated the first symposium devoted to 'Capitals and Mediterranean metropolises', whose proceedings were edited by the review *Villes en parallèle* (1978), and which saw the participation of numerous well-known geographers and urbanists. It is useful to note, apart from the reference to economic theories 'center versus outskirts', Guy Burgel's lecture which highlighted the idea of 'analogies' between the types of growth 'of the capitals of the Northern Mediterranean' and those of 'less-developed countries'. This relationship thus posed the question of the 'filiation' and of the reciprocity of the questions between the Third World and the Mediterranean World – the latter often being referred to as 'basin' during debates. Next, the question of the 'model', evoked on several occasions, had to be addressed. Therefore, at the end of the symposium Pierre George concluded that, as far as he was concerned, the set of 'characteristics' noted during the meeting (the weakness of urban networks, slow investment, the weakness of industrialization, the ruling classes' real estate origins, the fluidity of the middle classes and of reproduction of the under classes) 'evoke unequivocally the structural problems of the towns of Latin America' (George in Burgel 1978: 255).

have highlighted the conflictual dimension which, in the long term, creates the relationships between town and State. In the Mediterranean, towns often came into being before States. And Mediterranean port towns have thus been seen as the reproduction of the Greek model of the city-state. As Antonio Tosi stated in a comparative study, 'the analysis of the relationship between the town and the state becomes that of the opposition between urban autonomy and the formation of the modern state' (Tosi 1987: 40). On the other hand, the political form of the commune and of medieval and modern European municipalities was adopted as an element of comparison to show the specificity or the delay, notably in the Mediterranean, of the 'Muslim city' compared to the European town (for a critique of this idea, see Abu-Lughod 1987).

Attempts at recomposition: The resurgence of a unitary figure in the postmodern matrix

Rather than explicitly attributing it to geographical knowledge, in my opinion, it is in the domain of history and using a cultural approach that it is best to inscribe the archetypal and favoured field of the emergence of the paradigm of the Mediterranean town. Then, caught in a tropism opposing diverse modes of categorization and of division of the world – the 'European town' or 'Western', against 'the Arabic-Muslim or oriental town' and then 'the Third World town', 'underdeveloped' ('developing' or 'town of the South') – the supposed unitary matrix of the model of the Mediterranean town has tended to unravel. But from this second effigy, based on the figures of divergence and fracture, resurges again the idea of a common Mediterranean model, which several authors consider to be postmodern.

The latter, inspired by a somewhat mythological ideality, seduced one could say by the 'romantic fantasy of the Mediterranean' (Vieille 1986), is similar on the one hand to Mediterranean historical cosmopolitanism and, on the other, underlines the values of informality of all kinds: from the black market to the informal economy, from a mix of social groups to an ethnic melting pot, musical and culinary interbreeding, from the animation of public spaces to urban disorder, by ending in the fragmentation of the fabric of the towns. In a word, these last instances are no longer seen as negative and stigmatized clichés but, on the contrary, as creative and positive resources. One example among others is the recognition of the territorial effects of migratory movements in the Mediterranean. Thus, this third figure restores life and breath to the primitive matrix, but based on other ideological and use values.

If we follow Robert Escallier's (2001) analysis on the mechanism of the informal sphere in Mediterranean towns, one notices an articulation between the systems of social organization and the transition towards a post-Fordist system of the organization of work. This point seems to return me to two interpretations still relevant today on the model of the Mediterranean town. On the one hand, it refers us to the question of underdevelopment, and therefore to the founding criteria of the category of Third World or town of the South, which establishes a syntactical link between the Mediterranean and underdevelopment; and on the other hand, to a postmodern view of the Mediterranean, proposed particularly by Lila Leontidou (1993).

It is therefore a question of postmodernity founded on a very wide spectrum of manifestations of the informal, as aforementioned: from certain artistic expressions to ordinary and 'spontaneous' informal production related to the urban habitat; from architectural practices not coded by modernity (contrary to the regularity, the continuity, the order and the norm of the Modern town) to the diaspora caused by migration mentioned in the section 'The founding and unifying figure: The universalism of the Mediterranean town' and its 'ethnic' effects on towns; and also to the so-called informal economy. This would suggest that the informal was not a sign of pre-modernity: by following this reasoning, Mediterranean towns appear to have anticipated to a certain extent the supple paradigm of postmodernity rather than to have been subject to it by outside influences.

To resume, Mediterranean urban postmodernity seems to depend on a dual vision: either it is linked directly to a *pre-modern* universe because Mediterranean towns, bar a few exceptions, do not seem to have experienced modernity;[21] or the informal would not appear to be a pre-modern form of production but to have anticipated the post-Fordist transition in the Mediterranean, rather than being a result of it. Indeed, the informal would characterize the system of Mediterranean towns in that they oppose the figure of ordered continuity, by an 'anti-planning' practice which can be seen in the 'spontaneity' of the production of the habitat, in the *disorder* of the landscape but also in artistic, architectural, cultural and musical production.[22] This debate is still very topical.

---

[21] This idea, often proffered to explain the lateness or the absence of industrialization or even the underdevelopment of Mediterranean towns (in the figure of divergence), must be qualified, as several of them during the period between the end of the nineteenth and the beginning of the twentieth century experienced transformations and important experimental and modern urban operations, as seen in several works on Cairo (Arnaud 1998), Naples (Parisi 1998), Barcelona (Cerdà and Soria y Puig 1999), Marseilles and Alexandria (Ilbert 1996) and Algiers and Casablanca (Cattedra 1990).

[22] These theses, notably the second, were proposed by authors such as Leontidou (1990, 1993) and Minca (2004, 2005); see also Coppola (1996); Porcaro (2005: 118–21); Lamberti (2004); Borghi (2008); and Chambers (2007). More recently, they are included in approaches to postcolonial studies through an English-speaking matrix.

The expression of this postmodernity would appear to be a definitive return or 'the rediscovered emancipation' of a (Mediterranean) culture considered as subordinate or alternative (Leontidou 1993). Such an interpretation attributing positive and creative value to informality seems to agree with the figure of a unifying and universalizing model of the Mediterranean town.[23] It should be noted, however, that behind the expression of a unifying figure a plethora of definitions and categories is hidden which continue to compose and recompose ideal and material figures of what I define as a *fundamental and vulnerable paradigm*.

In the end, as Foucault says, 'if unity exists [here the unity of the paradigm of the Mediterranean town], it is definitely not in the visible and horizontal coherence of the formed elements; it is to be found far below, in the system which creates and governs them' (1969: 95). If one accepts – according to Foucault – 'the principle of multiplicity and dispersion', one would therefore be admitting that

one of the elements or several of them [i.e. the Third World town, the town of the South, the town of Mediterranean Europe, The North African town, the Eastern town, the Arabic town, the Muslim town, etc.] – can remain identical (retain the same shape, characteristics, structures), but belong to different systems of dispersion [the Western town, the town of the South and so, finally, the Mediterranean town] and be subject to distinct laws of formation. (1969: 226)

Roland Courtot, when presenting an assessment on works carried out in towns in 2001, in an article entitled 'Méditerranée et les villes de la Méditerranée' in the journal *Méditerranée,* for a special edition of '40 years of Mediterranean geography', wrote the following:

Does the study of all these pages written about Mediterranean towns provide the answer to the question of whether or not a model or archetype for 'Mediterranean towns' exists, in the sense it exists in urban geography manuals, 'European' towns, 'American', 'Chinese'? What is more, no-one amongst the geographers has as yet risked it, even if sufficient specific characteristics have pointed to the existence of 'the' Mediterranean town, at least in the collective imagination. (2001: 37)

---

[23] One can cite as examples – a by no means comprehensive list – the diverse ideas of Muscarà (1978); Lefebvre and Régulier (1986); Clementi (1995); Kayser (1996); Troin (1997); Corna Pellegrini (1998b); Nicolet, Depaule and Ilbert (2000); Escallier (2001); Chaline (2001); Carrière (2002); Crozat, Viala and Volle (2006); Viganoni (2007).

References

Abu-Lughod, J. (1987), 'The Islamic City: Historic Myth, Islamic Essence, and Contemporary Relevance', *Journal of Middle East Studies*, 19: 155–76.
Anderson, B. (1991), *Imagined Communities*, New York: Verso.
Arnaud, J.-L. (1998), *Le Caire, mise en place d'une ville moderne*, Paris: Sindbad-Actes Sud.
Aymard, M. ([1977] 1985), 'Espaces', in F. Braudel (ed.), *La Méditerranée: L'espace et l'histoire*, 191–223, Paris: Flammarion.
Benevolo, L. (1993), *La ville dans l'histoire européenne*, Paris: Seuil.
Bernard, A. J.-M. (2003), 'Paradigme', in J. Lévy and M. Lussault (eds), *Dictionnaire de la géographie et de l'espace des sociétés*, 683–6, Paris: Belin.
Berque, J. (1958), 'Médinas, villeneuves et bidonvilles', *Cahiers de Tunisie*, 21–2: 5–42.
Berque, J. (1984), 'Une héliopolis de l'Islam', in J. Berque (ed.), *L'Islam au temps du monde*, 195–225, Paris: Sindbad.
Béthemont, J. (2001), *Géographie de la Méditerranée: du mythe unitaire à l'espace fragmenté*, Paris: A. Colin.
Biget, J.-L. and Hervé, J.-C. (eds) (1995), *Panoramas urbains: Situation de l'Histoire des Villes*, Paris: ENS Éditions/Fontenay-Saint-Cloud.
Birot, P. and Dresch, J. (1953), *La Méditerranée et le Moyen-Orient*, Paris: PUF.
Blanc, A., Drain, M. and Kayser, B. (1967), *L'Europe méditerranéenne*, Paris: PUF.
Boino, P. (1999), 'Plaidoyer pour une géographie réclusienne', *Réfraction*, 4: 25–37.
Borghi, R. (2008), *Geografia, postcolonialismo e costruzione delle identità: Una lettura dello spazio urbano di Marrakech*, Milan: Unicopli.
Braudel, F. ([1949] 1990), *La Méditerranée et le monde méditerranéen à l'époque de Philippe II*, 9th edn, Paris: Colin.
Braudel, F. (ed.) ([1977] 1985), *La Méditerranée: L'espace et l'histoire*, Paris: Flammarion.
Brunet, R. (1995), 'Modèles de méditerranées', *L'Espace géographique*, 3: 200–2.
Bruyelle, P. (ed.) (2000), *Les très grandes concentrations urbaines*, Paris: SEDES.
Burgel, G. (1978), 'Montée des classes moyennes urbaines et modifications de l'espace social dans la région urbaine, capitale ou métropole', *Bulletin de l'Association des Géographes Français*, 454: 247–55.
Carrière, J.-P. (ed.) (2002), *Villes et projets urbains en Méditerranée*, Tours: Maison des Sciences de l'Homme.
Cattedra, R. (1990), 'Nascita e primi sviluppi di una città coloniale. Casablanca, 1907–1930', *Storia urbana*, 53: 127–80.
Cattedra, R. (1998), 'Il paradosso orientalista: Mitologie e patrimonialità della *città arabo-islamica*', in E. Casti and A. Turco (eds), *Culture dell'alterità: Il territorio africano e le sue rappresentazioni*, 467–92, Milan: Unicopli.
Cattedra, R. (2005), 'L'invenzione del Mediterraneo Territori e culture nelle reti di un mare alla ricerca di un progetto comune', in U. Grimaldi and P. De Luca (eds), *Mediterraneo: Scuola e incontro tra culture*, 62–93, Ercolano: Council of Europe, Italian Ministry of Education and Tilgher College.
Cattedra, R. (2008), 'Città del Terzo Mondo, città in sviluppo, città del Sud: Categorizzazione urbana e rappresentazioni del mondo', in F. Boggio, G.

Dematteis and M. Memoli (eds), *Geografia dello sviluppo: Spazi, economie e culture tra ventesimo secolo e terzo millennio*, 270–2, Turin: Utet-Libreria.
Cattedra, R. (2009), 'Reclus et la Méditerranée', in J.-P. Bord, R. Cattedra, R. Creagh, J.-M. Miossec and G. Roques (eds), *Autour de 1905: Elisée Reclus – Paul Vidal de la Blache. Le géographe, la Cité et le monde, hier et aujourd'hui*, 69–112, Paris: L'Harmattan.
Cerdà, I. and Soria y Puig, A. (1999), *Cerdá: The Five Bases of the General Theory of Urbanization*, Madrid: Electa.
CERTU (2006), *Attractivité et urbanité des territoires: Échanges Euro-Méditerranéens*, Actes de la 10ème université d'été du Conseil Français des urbanistes, Montpellier: CFDU-CERTU.
Chaline, C. (2001), *L'urbanisation et la gestion des villes dans les pays méditerranéens: Évaluation et perspectives d'un développement urbain durable*, Marseilles: Commission Méd. du Développement durable/Plan Bleu.
Chambers, I. (2007), *Le molte voci del Mediterraneo*, Milan: Cortina.
Chevallier, D. (1972), 'Les villes arabes depuis le XIXème siècle: Structures, Visions, Transformations', *Revue de Travaux de l'Académie des Sciences Morales et Politiques*, 1st semester: 117–28.
Chevallier, D. (1979), 'La ville arabe: Notre vision historique', in D. Chevallier (ed.), *L'espace social de la ville arabe*, 7–26, Paris: Maisonneuve & Larose.
Claval, P. (1988), 'Les géographes français et le monde méditerranéen', *Annales de Géographie*, 542: 385–403.
Clementi, A. (1995), 'Città mediterranee', in L. Bellicini (ed.), *Mediterraneo: Città territorio, economie alle soglie del XXI secolo*, 207–67, Rome: CRESME.
Concina, E. (1990), 'Origini: idee e forme nell'architettura araba', in Y. Rubiera and M. J. Mata (eds), *L'immaginario e l'architettura nella letteratura araba medievale*, 9–55, Genoa: Marietti.
Coppola, P. (1996), 'L'integrazione povera', *Terra d'Africa*, 5: 9–15.
Corna Pellegrini, G. (1998a), 'Mediterranean Cities', in S. Conti and A. Segre (eds), *Mediterranean Geographies*, 61–88, Rome: Società Geografica Italiana.
Corna Pelligrini, G. (1998b), 'An attemptable classification of the Mediterranean Cities', in C. Vallat (ed.), *Petites et grandes villes du bassin méditerranéen: Études autour de l'œuvre d'Etienne Dalmasso*, 563–75, Rome: Ecole Française de Rome.
Courtot, R. (2001), 'Méditerranée et les villes de la Méditerranée', *Méditerranée*, 3–4: 33–8.
Crozat, D., Viala, L. and Volle J.-P. (eds) (2006), *Villes méditerranéennes d'Europe et leurs périphéries: Mutations territoriales, innovations sociales*, Montpellier: PULM.
Dakhlia, J. (2008), *Lingua franca: Histoire d'une langue métisse en Méditerranée*, Arles: Actes Sud.
De Planhol, X. (1957), *Le monde islamique: Essai de géographie religieuse*, Paris: PUF.
De Planhol, X. (1968), *Les fondements géographiques de l'histoire de l'Islam*, Paris: Flammarion.
Dematteis, G. ([1985] 1994), *Le metafore della Terra: La geografia umana tra mito e scienza*, Milan: Feltrinelli.
Deprest, F. (2002), 'L'invention géographique de la Méditerranée: Éléments de réflexion', *L'Espace géographique*, 1: 73–92.

Doumenc, L. (ed.) (1995), *Les identités de la ville méditerranéenne*, Montpellier: éd. de l'Espérou & École d'architecture Languedoc-Roussillon.

Doumenc, L. (ed.) (1997), *L'espace public dans la ville méditerranéenne*, 2 vols, Montpellier: éd. de l'Espérou & École d'architecture Languedoc-Roussillon.

Escallier, R. (2001), 'La ville méditerranéenne', in J.-P. Lozato-Giotart (ed.), *La Méditerranée*, 47–113, Paris: SEDES.

Escallier, R. (ed.) (2002), 'Les enjeux de la métropolisation en Méditerranée', *Cahiers de la Méditerranée*, no. 64.

Fabre, T. (2000), 'La France et la Méditerranée: Généalogies et représentations', in T. Fabre and R. Ilbert (eds), *Les représentations de la Méditerranée*, 15–152, Paris: Maisonneuve & Larose.

Fantar, M. (1993), 'De la cité antique à la cité arabo-islamique au Maghreb', in L. Serra (ed.), *La città mediterranea: Eredità antica e apporto arabo-islamico sulle rive del Mediterraneo occidentale e in particolare nel Maghreb*, 47–70, Naples: I.U.O.

Farinelli, F. (2003), *Geografia: Un'introduzione ai modelli del mondo*, Turin: Einaudi.

Foucault, M. (1969), *L'archéologie du savoir*, Paris: Gallimard.

Froment, P. (2002), 'Des cités portuaires aux villes-panorama', in D. Borne and J. Scheibling, *La Méditerranée*, 72–94, Paris: Hachette.

Gardet, L. (1954), *La cité musulmane: Vie sociale et politique*, Paris: Vrin.

Ilbert, R. (1996), *Alexandrie 1830–1930*, Cairo: Institut Français d'Archéologie Orientale.

Isnard, H. (1973), *Pays et paysages méditerranéens*, Paris: PUF.

Kayser, B. (1996), *Méditerranée: Une géographie de la fracture*, Aix-en-Provence: Edisud.

Kuhn, T. S. (1970), *The Structure of Scientific Revolutions*, Chicago: University of Chicago Press.

Lamberti, A. (2004), 'I linguaggi della geografia urbana: Tel Aviv tra arte e sviluppo', PhD thesis, Università degli Studi di Napoli l'Orientale.

Lapidus, I. P. (1973), 'Traditional Muslim Cities: Structure and Change', in L. C. Brown (ed.), *From Madina to Metropolis*, 51–69, Princeton, NJ: Darwin Press.

Lavedan, P. ([1936] 1959), *Géographie des villes*, Paris: Gallimard.

Lefebvre, H. and Régulier C. (1986), 'Essai de rythmanalyse des villes méditerranéennes', *Peuples Méditerranéens*, 37: 5–15.

Leontidou, L. (1990), *The Mediterranean City in Transition*, Cambridge: Cambridge University Press.

Leontidou, L. (1993), 'Postmodernism and the City: The Mediterranean Versions', *Urban Studies*, 30 (6): 949–65.

Liauzu, C. (1994), 'Elisée Reclus et l'expansion européenne en Méditerranée', in M. Bruneau and C. Dory (eds), *Géographie des colonisations*, 129–36, Paris: L'Harmattan.

Marçais, G. (1945), 'La conception des villes dans l'Islam', *Revue de la Méditerranée*, 10: 517–33.

Marçais, G. (1957), 'L'urbanisme musulman', séance inaugurale du 5ème Congrès des Sociétés Savantes (Tunis, 1941), in *Mélanges d'Histoire et d'Archéologie de l'Occident Musulman*, vol. 1, 219–23, Algiers: Imprimerie officielle du Gouvernement Général de l'Algérie.

Marçais, W. (1928), 'L'islamisme et la vie urbaine', *Comptes-rendus de l'Académie des Inscriptions et Belles Lettres*, 86–100.
Matvejević, P. ([1987] 1999), *Mediterraneo: Un Nuovo breviario*, Milan: Garzanti.
Memmi, A. (1966), *La Statue de sel*, Paris: Gallimard.
Minca, C. (2004), *Orizzonte mediterraneo*, Padua: Cedam.
Minca, C. (2005), *Lo spettacolo della città*, Padua: Cedam.
Miossec, J.-M. (1997), 'Villes méditerranéennes aujourd'hui', in J. Sagnes (ed.), *La ville en France aux XIXe et XXe Siècles*, 105–33, Perpignan: Presses universitaires de Perpignan.
Mondada, L. (2000a), 'Pratiques discursives et configuration de l'espace urbain', in J. Lévy and M. Lussault (eds), *Logiques de l'espace, esprit des lieux: Géographies à Cerisy*, 165–75, Paris: Belin.
Mondada, L. (2000b), *Décrire la ville: La construction des savoirs urbains dans l'interaction et dans le texte*, Paris: Anthropos.
Moriconi-Ebrard, F. (2000), *De Babylone à Tokyo: Les grandes agglomérations du Monde*, Gap: Ophrys.
Mumford, L. (1961), *The City in History*, New York: Harcourt Brace & Jovanovich.
Muscarà, C. (ed.) (1978), *Megalopoli mediterranea*, Milan: Franco Angeli.
Nicolet, C., Depaule, J.-C. and Ilbert, R. (eds) (2000), *Mégapoles méditerranéennes: Géographie urbaine rétrospective*, Paris: Maisonneuve & Larose – MMSH – Ecole Française de Rome.
Nora, P. (ed.) (1986), *Les lieux de mémoire*, Paris: Gallimard.
Paquot, T. (ed.) (1996), *Le monde des villes: Panorama urbain de la Planète*, Paris: Complexes.
Parisi, R. (1998), *Lo spazio della produzione: Napoli: la periferia orientale*, Naples: Ed. Athena.
Pelletier, J. and Delfante, Ch. ([1989] 1993), *Villes et urbanisme dans le monde*, Paris: Masson.
Pelletier, Ph. (1999), 'La ville et la géographie urbaine chez Elisée Reclus', *Réfractions*, no. 4: 17–24.
Porcaro, G. (2005), 'Grandi eventi e internazionalizzazione delle città mediterranee: Quadri globali e strategie locali', PhD thesis, Università degli Studi Napoli L'Orientale.
Quaini, M. (2005), 'La rappresentazione del mondo fra allegoria e cartografia', in M. Tinacci Mossello, C. Capineri and F. Randelli (eds), *Conoscere il mondo: Vespucci e la modernità*, 127–46, Florence: Società Studi Geografici.
Raymond, A. (1985), *Grandes villes urbaines à l'époque ottomane*, Paris, Sindbad.
Raymond, A. (1995), 'Ville musulmane, ville arabe: mythes orientalistes et recherches récentes', in J.-L. Biget and J.-C. Hervé (eds), *Panoramas urbains: Situation de l'Histoire des Villes*, 309–35, Paris: ENS Éditions/Fontenay-Saint-Cloud.
Reclus, E. (1868–70), *La terre: Description des phénomènes de la vie du globe*, Paris: Hachette.
Reclus, E. (1875–1894), *Nouvelle Géographie Universelle* (NGU), 19 vols, Paris: Hachette.
Reclus, E. (1895), 'The Evolution of Cities', *Contemporary Review*, 350: 246–64.
Reclus, E. (1905–8), *L'Homme et la Terre*, vols 1–6, Paris: Librairie Universelle.

Retaillé, D. (2000), 'Penser le monde', in J. Lévy and M. Lussault (eds), *Logiques de l'espace, esprit des lieux: Géographies à Cerisy*, 273–86, Paris: Belin.
Revel, J. (2002), *Le vocabulaire de Foucault*, Paris: Ellipses.
Rodinson, M. ([1968] 1993), *La fascination de l'Islam*, Paris: Pocket.
Roncayolo, M. and Paquot, T. (eds) (1992), *Villes et civilisation urbaine (XVIIIe–XXe siècle)*, Paris: Larousse.
Roque, M.-A. (ed.) (2001), *L'espace méditerranéen latin*, Paris: Ed. de l'Aube.
Rossi, P. (ed.) (1987), *Modelli di città: Strutture e funzioni politiche*, Turin: Einaudi.
Roussillon, A. (1990), 'Le débat sur l'orientalisme dans le champ intellectuel arabe: L'aporie des sciences sociales', *Peuples Méditerranéens*, no. 50: 7–39.
Ruel, A. (1991), 'L'invention de la Méditerranée', *Vingtième siècle*, no. 32: 7–14.
Said, E. W. (1978), *Orientalism*, New York: Vintage.
Serra, L. (ed.) (1993), *La città mediterranea: Eredità antica e apporto arabo-islamico sulle rive del Mediterraneo occidentale e in particolare nel Maghreb*, Naples: I.U.O.
Sica, P. (1970), *L'immagine della città, da Sparta a Atene*, Bari: Laterza.
Sinarellis, M. (1998), 'Bory de Saint-Vincent et la géographie méditerranéenne', in M.-N. Bourguet, B. Lepetit, D. Nordman and M. Sinarellis (eds), *L'invention scientifique de la Méditerranée*, 299–311, Paris: Ed. EHESS.
Sorre, M. and Sion, J. (1934), *Méditerranée: Péninsules Méditerranéennes*, vol. 7, in P. Vidal de La Blache and L. Gallois (eds), *Géographie Universelle*, 15 vols, Paris: A. Colin.
Steele, T. (1999), 'Elisée Reclus et Patrick Geddes géographes de l'esprit: Les études régionales dans une perspective globale', *Réfractions* no. 4: 39–54.
Tosi, A. (1987), 'Verso un'analisi comparativa delle città', in Rossi, P. (ed.), *Modelli di città: Strutture e funzioni politiche*, 29–56, Turin: Einaudi.
Troin, J.-F. (1997), *Les métropoles de la Méditerranée*, Aix-en-Provence: Edisud.
Turri, E. (ed.) (1994), *La civiltà urbana*, vol. 3, Novara: De Agostini – Banca Popolare di Novara.
Valéry, P. ([1933] 1960), 'Le centre universitaire Méditerranéen', in *Œuvres: Vol. 2: 1128–1144*, Paris: Gallimard.
Vallat, C. (ed.) (1998), *Petites et grandes villes du bassin méditerranéen: Études autour de l'œuvre d'Étienne Dalmasso*, Rome: École Française de Rome.
Vidal, P. (1873), *La Péninsule Européenne. L'Océan et la Méditerranée*, Leçon d'ouverture du cours d'histoire et de géographie à la Faculté des Lettres de Nancy, Paris/Nancy: Berger-Levrault & Cie.
Vieille, P. (1986), 'L'urbain et le mal de modernité', *Peuples méditerranéens* no. 37: 141–54.
Viganoni, L. (ed.) (2007), *Il Mezzogiorno delle città: Tra Europa e Mediterraneo*, Milan: Franco Angeli.
Villes en parallèle (1978), 'Capitales et métropoles méditerranéennes', *Villes en parallèle*, 2.
Voiron-Canicio, C. (1999), 'Urbanisation et littoralisation sur les rives de la Méditerranée', in O. Sevin (ed.), *Les Méditerranées dans le monde*, 103–12, Artois: Presse de l'Université.
Wirth, E. (1982), 'Villes islamiques, villes arabes, villes orientales? Une problématique face au changement', in A. Bouhdiba and D. Chevallier (eds), *La ville arabe dans l'Islam*, 193–9, Tunis and Paris: CERES/CNRS.

10

Testimony: Where is Tunisia going?

Fethi Nagga

We do not yet know where Tunisia is going, nor what will happen in the future.[1] Will newly liberated Tunisia accomplish its much-desired process of democratization? Has the country entered a delicate yet simultaneously physiological transition phase, or has it entered a dangerous crisis from which no one can see a way out? What are the difficulties we encounter and that we will encounter in the long term, in order to get rid of all traces of our obscure past and its burdensome legacy? These are the questions every single citizen and all intellectual and political activists are asking themselves, as they watch and 'experience' the new Tunisia as it takes uncertain, unsteady steps.

Parties, syndicates, intellectuals and other social figures are in evident difficulty in this new reality, caused by last month's rapid revolution, brought forward by young foreigners with no involvement in political activism and deliberately with no political engagement. Only one terrible motivation has driven them to demonstrate: the exasperation of hearing incessant, useless, evidently not credible promises, and of enduring daily examples of oppression, whether minor or major.

A young man like them passed them the torch: he rebelled against the umpteenth humiliation by setting himself on fire. In record time, and without any warning, we were liberated from a dictatorship from which we had no idea how to free ourselves (or perhaps we were not able to, or did

---

[1] This chapter was written during the Jasmine Revolution (2011) in Tunisia.

not want to), not when we were young – in the time of Bourguiba – and not as adults – during the twenty years of Ben Ali's regime. Here we are, finally, free: young people have offered us a freedom no one expected, and they have entrusted it to us (while remaining vigilant about their achievements); but we are struggling to deal with it.

Representatives of certain political parties, proposed as the protectors of this revolution, joined the first provisional government in which different representatives of the old regime were also included: people – with once again the young at the front – rebelled again, while certain intellectuals – for different reasons – supported it. Once again, the people got the best of it and there was a government reshuffle proposing a new formation which also did not meet the general consensus. On the other hand, we have a temporary government composed of mostly unknown figures who made no hesitation to make promises – mostly objectively unfeasible – to the people and on behalf of the people: How can we not blame those who were the most sceptical?

The people – who were always silent – are now screaming out their rage, along with their large, small, legitimate or honestly absurd demands. Meanwhile, in workplaces and administrations, the 'manhunt' has started against the hated manager, the harsh boss who must be sent away immediately, after a summary trial. An emblematic example can be found in our institute (the Higher Institute of Social Science in Tunis).

The directors of all institutes have always been nominated by the government and they are members of the party of the regime. After the suspension of exams and courses during the most dramatic weeks of the revolution, on 24 January 2011, the director summoned all the teachers for a meeting in which they decided on the future of the academic year and obviously on the direction of the Institute. In his speech, the director declared that he was ready to leave office, to resign, while ensuring that the transition and handover took place under the best conditions.

After a long, heated discussion during which direct or veiled accusations were made to all and sundry, and one after the other each person admitted they had been 'forced' to collaborate with the old regime for various reasons, it was agreed that the 'compromised' director should be allowed to stay in office, in part because there were only two months left in his mandate, and because, to ensure the correct functioning of the Institute, it would be more convenient to have a less traumatic change of direction. Everybody, including the labour unions, offered to guarantee and support this solution. The exams took place and some classes were resumed – though not many. However, those who offered to provide protection for a less painful change of direction were the first to organize rallies against the director and against other people in charge (the general secretary and treasurer) in order to destitute them, and their justification was that the students did not want them, when actually the students had not started their regular classes at that time. We spent a whole week discussing whether or not to remove the director, even though his mandate was due to have finished just three weeks later. The result: so far, we have not resumed teaching, nor have we understood where we are going with this Institute. In the face of all this turmoil, the dean and the State Department are looking on, immobile, and not making any decisions on the subject whatsoever.

Becoming a democracy is very difficult; first of all, it is important that we clarify what we mean by democracy. The new post-revolution television continues, as before, to produce nonsense programmes. It often invites people who scream and shout about freedom. Watching a debate is often misleading and has an impact on convictions that are already wavering. In the newspapers, many people talk about the past (under Bourguiba and Ben Ali) but only a few dare to talk about the future. They show the country's heritage and all the treasures stolen by the old dictator, and they promise to get them back without explaining to the common people just how difficult (or impossible) this operation would be. The only party which already seems organized, and which has more or less defined ideas, is of Islamic origin and scares everyone.

In the country, there is at least one peaceful demonstration every day and most of the time nobody knows who organized it. Nobody is capable of giving correct information. The synagogue in Tunis was attacked and a Polish priest has had his throat cut. Some say the Islamists were responsible, others say the extremists from the militia of the former ruling party, while others still affirm that, behind all this, there are political parties that are not officially authorized but who are keen to put the temporary government under pressure with acts of terrorism.

General confusion reigns supreme and finding the key to the problem will not be simple at all. We are looking for men of goodwill.

11

Trilingualism in Tunisia: A disturbing topic

Alfonso Campisi

For years, as a linguist and a philologist, I have studied the language spoken by my Tunisian students.[1] This is a topic that we have never been able to approach seriously and 'peacefully' because of the dictatorship we experienced for twenty-three years under Ben Ali's regime. It is a very disturbing topic for convinced pan-Arabists, but as with all disturbing topics, this one deserves a thorough and honest analysis.

The problem of language is one of the priorities of our government. But which language are we talking about? The linguistic complexity in Tunisia has a profound effect on politics, with regard to the cultural level of our youth and the countless failures of the school system. Let us assume that each nation can have one, two or even three official and/or native languages. Take, for example, Malta, Belgium, Switzerland, Luxembourg and a significant number of African nations. The mother tongue is the one we communicate with every day, spoken on the national territory and with which I express my emotions: joy, love, but also rage and sorrow. My language is the one I use daily, without any imposition, with my parents, friends, teachers, colleagues and so on. In all those circumstances, we Tunisians use our mother tongue, which is TUNISIAN. Yes, I said Tunisian, or Tunisian Arabic to please those who, while reading my chapter, will start making faces as a sign of disagreement. Tunisian is a language. Tunisian is not a dialect.

---

[1] This chapter was written during the Jasmine Revolution (2011) in Tunisia.

All the linguistic criteria are respected, because the Tunisian language possesses all the rules typical of a language with its own grammar, which many ignore or rather want to ignore. A language is the mirror of each population and each country. The language lives thanks to external inputs that create its richness. The language reflects our cultural identity and our sense of belonging to a geographic region and/or to a political regime. If we take the example of the Maghreb countries, we realize that each country has its own culture, which it considers very important, and thanks to which, each country can be distinguished from the others. This cultural difference expresses itself mainly through language.

We can take as an example Morocco or Algeria, each of which have a specific culture and a specific language that make them different from Tunisia. So why do we continue to refuse our Tunisian language and persist in considering the Arabic language as the only mother tongue? One of the many answers is without a doubt pan-Arabism and its dictatorship. The aim of this very ancient political, cultural and ideological movement was to unite the Arab people, offering itself as support for the Arab identity. But what are we talking about? Unification of the Arab people? Defence of the Arab identity? Have you ever seen the Arabs united? Have you ever seen political, cultural or ideological unity between Arab countries?

All this is false, especially after 14 January 2011, when the uprising of the Arab people, in particular the Tunisians, once again underlined this cultural and linguistic difference. Remember that our 'revolutionary watchword' was *DÉGAGE* (GET OUT OF HERE). Therefore, we expressed ourselves in our second language, which is French. Our neighbour, Libya, did not express itself in this language, and its way of fighting the dictator was not the same either. Their process of democratization was and remains completely different from our process. And yet we are neighbours!

To get back to the school system, the lack of linguistic identity is a big problem for our youth's culture and identity. This search for an identity would explain, in my opinion, the lack of linguistic skill in our students, who, once in college, still do not master Arabic, their so-called mother tongue, nor French, their second language. At any level of schooling, students have to have the possibility of expressing themselves, writing and studying in their real mother tongue, in our case Tunisian, but also French. Those are the only two languages in Tunisia; they are not static, and they evolve every day with the contribution of neologisms linked to information technology, science, medicine and so on. On the contrary, classical Arabic is static, linked to the sacred and does not respect the fundamental principle of linguistics, which is evolution.

Our school system has an urgent need to adapt to the demands of our youth, who have been forced into savage and indiscriminate Arabization, depriving them of all their knowledge and critical thinking. It is the spoliation of knowledge expressly desired by the dictatorial regime that has created a mass of qualified illiterates, bad at Arabic, bad at French and deprived of all forms of critical thinking and analysis.

I wonder how it is possible to have a good cultural and linguistic level when our students are confronted with three 'undeclared national' languages. They speak their own language, Tunisian, but that is not an official language. They are forced to write in literary Arabic, which has all the characteristics of a foreign language, and they have classes in French. This language, French, remains the language of culture, the elite, information technology, as well as the language of teaching. It is also the passport to Europe for those who wish to continue their studies on the old continent.

We are all responsible for the decrease in cultural and intellectual levels. The new government must find a solution and start working on it immediately. We scholars cannot tolerate this linguistic schizophrenia, which results in classes taught in literary Arabic in middle school, and then in French in high school. Thus, we must decide once and for all, and choose between the hypocrisy of pan-Arabism and incompetence, opting for the generalized Arabization of our system or the development of critical thinking and analysis, suitable for a democracy that involves a complete Gallicization of education and that definitively stops seeing French as the language of the colonizer. French and Tunisian must be given the status they deserve if we really want to move on in the fight against ignorance and illiteracy.

12

The Charter of Palermo: The future of a utopia

Jean Duflot

Can *Palermo Città aperta* ('Palermo Open City': Duflot 2019a),[1] which is at odds with the crisis provoked by Europe's anti-immigration policies, ultimately lead to an alternative to the identity crisis facing Mediterranean countries? Are dreams of the Mediterranean as the matrix of a politically and culturally homogeneous civilization condemned to never go beyond the mythical utopia stage? To the south of a Europe that is starting to fall apart (with the almost fascinating dissidence of the Visegrad group and Brexit in the United Kingdom),[2] the prospect of the European Union (EU) breaking up is threatening its very foundations.

For thousands of years, the land that surrounds the Mediterranean Sea has been successively and often simultaneously the athanor for fertile human alchemy and the conflictual arena of competing and contradictory interests. Today, is the EU, a union based on the Treaties of Rome and Maastricht – the two key moments in its creation – undermined by the chaotic treatment of migratory flows and the state of emergency designed as a normal paradigm for governance?[3]

---

[1] *Palerme ville ouverte*, title of the book by Jean Duflot (*Forum Civique Européen*). See also *Palerme, une charte de dissidence* (Duflot 2019b).
[2] The Visegrad group of countries (Poland, Hungary, the Czech Republic, Slovakia) refuses the directives of Europe, which are seen as being too laxist.
[3] Inherited from the policy developed by the former state secretary for the interior, Maroni, to deal with the 'invasion of Roms' from Eastern countries (seen as an epidemic), the state of emergency has now been generalized as a paradigm of governance.

It is true that for thousands of years the coastal areas, and above all Sicily, have been the landing point for incessant waves of migration, mostly military. During the 'dark ages' of antiquity which followed the prehistoric period, the island was invaded by the Sicani, the Sicels[4] from the Maghreb and the Iberian peninsula, and colonized by the Elymi of Aegean origin. These early Sicilians were replaced by an interminable succession of pretenders. Sicily, a strategic base for the greedy powers in the Mediterranean basin, was desired as the garden and breadbasket of several empires.

Palermo was founded by the Phoenicians (*Panormos*) and was thus the capital and key area for all the armed occupations during the conflicts that focused on controlling the trading posts installed on the coast of this nurturing sea. For centuries, this port city was fashioned by redundant foreign sedimentation. The Phoenicians were followed by Greeks, Carthaginians, Romans, Byzantines, Vandals, Ostrogoths and Arab-Berbers after the decolonization of Spain, Normans, Spanish, Bourbons, Hohenstaufen Swabians, French,[5] Neapolitans and Lombards, Napoleon's army and, after a short period of British administration, once again the Bourbon dynasty. This merry-go-round only came to an end in 1861 with the reunification of the Kingdoms of Italy under the aegis of King Vittorio Emanuele.

It was this historical metamorphosis that allowed Leoluca Orlando, several times mayor of the port city of Palermo, to repeat throughout his periods of office that '*Palermo cannot afford to have a short memory*'. This vibrant, active memory has above all made it possible to transmit, down through the generations, memories of the 'Partenza' (the great migration) provoked by the terrible economic depression that followed the reunification of Italy. For a century and a half of expatriation, Sicily, like the rest of Italy, was forced to disperse its inhabitants all around the world – 150 years of suffering, in which the 'Eyeties' struggled with precarity, hardship and racial persecution in the slums in the world's largest cities. There is no doubt that this long season in hell led to the empathy and solidarity that are now developing in this southern European port.

Orlando is an exceptional mayor, elected five times by an overwhelming majority to govern the city. He makes no secret of 'respecting rights above laws' and conducted his most recent electoral campaign on the theme of opening-up to immigration. The loyalty of the electors, despite an opposition that is still influenced by the Mafia, now hiding in the catacombs of the region, has allowed him to create an exemplary oasis. And all this has taken

---

[4] The name of this ethnic group provided that of Archaic Sicily. It occasionally reappears in the dialects in the south of the island.

[5] After being colonized in the north by the army of Charles I of Anjou, the authoritarian requisition and disastrous management of the domains by the nobles in his court provoked a popular uprising (the Sicilian Vespers, 1282) and the massacre of the French.

place in a social context in which the city must deal with the unemployment and poverty of its own citizens.

All one needs to do is to wander the labyrinthine streets and alleyways of the city centre, destroyed by bombings and for many years the shabby hide-out of the *Cosa Nostra*,[6] to discover the successive aggradation of the various diasporas. In freeing itself from an *nth* colonial power – a criminal organization that had put a stranglehold on the city for decades – Palermo has in a way returned to the atavistic generosity of the Sicilian people. In a certain sense, it has reversed the tradition for welcoming people against its will, and opened the gates of its ancient ramparts. One of them – with a name that is a happy coincidence, '*Porta Felice*' (Gate of Happiness) – is where those who survive the crossing of the desert and the sea first arrive after landing on the 'Four Winds Docks'.

Behind the friendly opening-up of this major metropolis were two series of events, which can be said to be both concomitant and complementary: the collapse of the Communist bloc and its satellites in the East, from Asia to Europe, and a period known as the 'Palermo Spring' when, from 1975, Orlando started his first term of office and undertook the restoration of the architectural heritage of the glory days of this city-museum.

There is no doubt that the space saved by rehabilitating the homes in the historic centre made it possible to welcome refugees, as well as economic and political immigrants. And reversing the standard urban programme of most Western cities is not the least singularity of this urban planning facelift. Today, the heart of the city, with its Babelian markets, *Ballarò* and *Vucciria*, is home to the underclasses and dozens of communities, mostly from outside of Europe. The upper classes, the historic ancient bourgeoisie and remaining aristocracy have mostly emigrated to the periphery and a ring of buildings built at a cost of billions by real estate promoters favourable to the Mafia.

In the decade 2000–2010, the installation of these refugees and immigrants was encouraged by a pragmatic city council, also comforted by the prospect of a return to the productive activities slowed down by the stagnation or disappearance of large companies. Small shops and businesses multiplied, and even significant entrepreneurship developed (often in partnership with local SMEs and SMIs), with the result that an economy in crisis was brought back to life. With people arriving from countries in crisis or at war in the Middle and Near East (Syria, Iraq, Pakistan, Sri Lanka), Egypt or North Africa (Tunisia, Algeria) and above all the Horn of Africa (Ethiopia, Somalia,

---

[6] Criminal organization of the Sicilian mafia (meaning 'our thing'). It organized pillaging of the island and Italy for many decades. In Palermo, it was often the armed branch of a corrupt administration. During the various periods of office of the mayor Leoluca Orlando, and following a major trial of the members of the Staff (*cupola*), it was decimated and pushed south, where it is now in hiding in the catacombs of the southern provinces.

Eritrea) and almost all of sub-Saharan Africa (from Senegal to Guinea-Conakry and Guinea-Bissau), this influx of humans, supported by municipal structures, has considerably increased the possibilities for autonomy and social insertion. Several statistical evaluations, such as the Arrupe Institute's report (Observatory for the Socioeconomic Evolution of Immigration) has formally refuted the common prejudice that accuses immigration of being responsible for the budgetary deficits of the Italian state and a dangerous burden on the finances of the city. In reality, even the official statistics of the associated State departments have established that the difference between the cost of immigration and the income it generates is positive.

Since 2015, with the first arrivals of refugees from the Middle East (Syria, Iraq and Turkey) and mainly the Horn of Africa (Somalia, Ethiopia and Eritrea) and the sub-Saharan countries, the city has organized a seminar for reflection: 'Io sono persona' (I am a person). This convention brings together the networks of associations, political and trade union activists, members of academia, lawyers, legal experts, practitioners from the fields of medicine and health, civil servants from the city and Prefecture, representatives of denominational organizations and several national and international NGOs (Oxfam, UN Observatory, Amnesty International, the Human Rights League, Doctors without Borders, SOS Méditerranée). The project for welcoming people that is adapted to the subsequent arrival of massive flows of migrants is the subject of a policy document: the *Carta di Palermo* (Charter of Palermo), titled *Dalla migrazione come sofferenza alla mobilità come diritto umano inalienabile* (From migration as suffering to mobility as an unalienable human right). These works resulted in a genuine manifesto of dissidence.

After a survey conducted by the European Civic Forum in 2018–19,[7] several unscheduled meetings hosted by activists from the associations network examined and assessed the feasibility of this moratorium in favour of radical anti-establishment humanism. Their analyses are evidence of a desire to broaden the charter's application to the issue of federating the countries in the Mediterranean area. Most of these countries are confronted with greater emergencies than the danger of migration; they are thus aware of the need to change the dangerously declining ethics of nations together. It increasingly seems that the authoritarian drift of the technocratic system in Brussels concerns them by maintaining them, too, in a chronic state of underdevelopment.

---

[7] Between the station and the nicer neighbourhoods of the modern periphery, in the labyrinth of narrow streets running alongside the main north–south and east–west thoroughfares (Maqueda, Roma, Vittorio Emanuele, Lincoln), and beyond, to the suburbs and *hinterland*, the various European or extra-European diasporas are found in bands, the result of several decades of immigration.

From the outset, the first measure proposed in the Charter is the abolition of the residence permit, a measure that was perceived by the participants in this debate as being an unsurmountable (at least in the short term) aporia. More than a general constitutional upheaval, this miraculous measure would bring into question the very existence of nation-states. It is difficult to imagine them agreeing to total permeability of their borders and abandoning the national boundaries that form the contours of their sovereignty and cultural heritage. From this perspective, the utopia of this moratorium remains, for the moment, a long-term dream. However, without prejudicing its future concretization, this type of policy would no doubt make possible a collective debate and raise awareness of the immediate need to share the responsibilities and burdens induced by welcoming migration. For the inner circle of Palermitan citizens, this iterative dialogue from a summit of all the Mediterranean countries would strengthen their collegial dynamics and play a part in reversing the European Union's disastrous policy. The singularity of this proactive stance would in any case form the contradictory counterpart to the negative, almost fascinating dissidence of the Visegrad group (Poland, Hungary, the Czech Republic and Slovakia), which have banded together in their categoric refusal of even the most moderate standards of the EU.

Either way, on the fringes of the summits of the cartel of major nations, a Mediterranean federation committed to welcoming migration could remind 'Enlightened Europe' of the ethical axiom in article 13 of the Universal Declaration from 1948,[8] hidden in the vaults of the dusty archives of its governance. This is without counting that this type of initiative would remind the 'government' of technocrats that they have forgotten their own treaties in defence of ethnic minorities, immigrant workers, women and children.

As it is a question of mobility – the key theme of the Charter – for any refugees who apply to normalize their status of asylum seekers, subsidiary protection or residency, a united league of countries in the South could make it possible to collectively suggest a certain number of measures to be undertaken as a matter of urgency. It would have the weight needed to impose certain drastic reforms: a review of the norms in force, and the suppression of both Dublin III and the regulatory obligation to make requests for residency in the first country of entry into the Schengen zone. It would demand the suppression of the prison structures at the check points in the ports and CPRs (twenty permanent repatriation centres) which replace the former CIEs (centres for identification and expulsion) proposed

---

[8] Excerpt from article 13: '(1) Everyone has the right to freedom of movement and residence within the borders of each state. (2) Everyone has the right to leave any country, including his own, and to return to his country.'

as a means of sorting through the 'economic and/or political' migrants. It would examine the case for abolishing the policing mandate of Frontex, the armed militia that is omnipresent at EU borders, and which both tramples the competency of States and aggravates the climate of arbitrary violence that is the keyword in the markets of its kingdom. It would intervene at the level of the departments responsible for managing the future of refugees by reviewing and speeding up eligibility procedures in the ad hoc regional commissions. It would fight for a significant increase in, and distribution of governmental and European aid indexed to national GDPs. And finally, at a no doubt more political level, a convention for a real parliament of *entente cordiale* for the welcome given by the countries in the South could demand that there be a stop to the unacceptable massacre organized between Turkey and Greece with subsidies from Europe (Ziegler 2020).[9]

With regard to the other sections, such as the right to the dignity of a regulated reception, decent accommodation, schooling, professional training preparing access to paid work, the Charter demands that they be applied rigorously. Its recommendations should provide a group of Mediterranean States with the exemplary framework for social insertion implemented in Palermo.

What has been accomplished in this welcoming city is the key to the possible clearance of all the refugees in each Mediterranean country. Furthermore, there is nothing to stop anyone organizing acceptable (between 10 and 120 people) official reception structures (CASs, CARAs, SPRAR)[10] and refusing the CPRs which aggravate the almost prison-like retention in the former CIEs – those military 'checkpoints' destined for sifting out the ineligible migrants. The innovations made in the field of accommodation (social housing, *co-housing*, identification of renovated rental accommodation buildings, families rewarded for hosting unaccompanied minors, support for private or denominational structures) can be negotiated in most urban areas in the neighbouring countries.

The insertion policy recommended by the Charter necessarily involves appropriate paths leading to *civic symbiosis, or even the promotion of active citizenship*. Once again, the Palermo model takes into account the precondition for schooling, higher education and professional training.[11]

---

[9] The essay by Jean Ziegler shows the inhuman treatment of thousands of refugees from Turkey, piled up on the island of Lesbos and how subsidies are misappropriated on both sides of the Greece–Turkey border.
[10] Regulatory reception and concentration structures for migrants: CASs (emergency reception centres), CARAs (centres for accommodation of asylum seekers), SPRAR (System of Protection for Refugees and Asylum Seekers). The latter are increasingly used for the reception of minors.
[11] Dozens of training centres for essential professions, training courses, commercial management and industrial mechanics, teaching of Italian and English in several establishments and in particular in an annex of the University, Itastra, which provides methodical learning of modern communication techniques (computers, audio-visual and digital means).

What has been achieved is not beyond the capacities of the other countries in the Mediterranean area and should be negotiated together with regard to funding from national authorities and the EU. To complete this moratorium of innovative principles, the mobility Charter details three strategic innovations of a particularly unique nature: the right to political participation and cultural contamination, and the right to be legally documented on the civil register.

The first opens the way to sharing municipal decisions by means of an actual presence on regional councils; voting by immigrants who live in the city, ultimately also extended to that of local elections, would allow them to better negotiate the decisions concerning their civil status. As for cultural contamination, in other words, transversal pooling of the reflections and associated works in permanent symbiosis, Palermo, which was the Italian capital of culture in 2018, following on from being that of youth, and more explicitly the meridional pole for international conferences, is preparing the foundations for the possibility of full civic inclusion. With this in mind, the city has created an avant-garde cultural management centre, the *Consulta Culturale* (a municipal department composed exclusively of fifteen assessors from foreign communities), which has been presided over successively by a Palestinian doctor, Adam Darawasha, and an activist from Cape Verde, Maria Delfina Nunes. This structure is responsible for co-organizing various events throughout the city in all cultural fields: annual festivities, literature, theatre, cinema, art, music and dance, as well as for coordinating the activities of several dozen community associations. This additional cultural value was clearly announced in one of the city's annual creations, 'the festival of migrant literature': 'Palermo has undertaken a journey to recover its "trans-personal soul".' The identity of a city is an intermingling of histories, architectures, urban tissue, cultures, traditions, dialects, accents, scents and sounds. Palermo is a palimpsest of signs that come from its history, and the history of Palermo is built on migrations and contaminations. At the scale of a Mediterranean basin that is divided by economic differences, this dynamic for the de-partitioning of native and non-native communities cannot be anything but beneficial for their future development.

Finally, to crown this Charter of, dare we say, libertarian inspiration, the proposal for new legislation on the rights for effective citizenship and the precondition of inclusion on the civil register would promulgate the right of birthplace (*ius soli*) that has too often been attacked by segregation from the right of blood (*ius sanguinis*). In addition to the usufruct of all social advantages (work and residence permits, social security, access to all forms of training, possibility for naturalization), this would contain the key for unlocking a new community capable of civic racial mixing, integrating all the human beings present in a common area – a utopia whose concretization would be nothing more than fanciful should its potentialities be irreversibly refused. Ultimately, this charter requires a common effort to restore radical humanism. In the 1970s, when on television to comment on his two controversial essays *Scritti Corsari* (1975) and *Lettere Luterane* (1976), the poet Pier Paolo Pasolini anticipated a political solution to the hegemonic barbarism of the day's capitalist system: 'immigrants will come to our homes to force us to relearn what democracy is', he said. In this sense, the Charter of Palermo resounds like the echo of a sentence by a prophetic Mediterranean lyric poet.

References

Duflot, J. (2019a), *Palerme ville ouverte*, La Bauche: A plus d'un titre.
Duflot, J. (2019b), *De la migration comme souffrance à la mobilité comme droit de l'homme inaliénable: Palerme une charte de dissidence*, La Bauche: A plus d'un titre.
Pasolini, P. P. (1975), *Scritti corsari*, Milan: Garzanti.
Pasolini, P. P. (1976), *Lettere luterane*, Turin: Einaudi.
Ziegler, J. (2020), *La honte de l'Europe*, Paris: Seuil.

Appendix

International Human Mobility Charter of Palermo 2015
From the migration as suffering to mobility as an inalienable human right

The right to mobility as the right of the human being. Towards citizenship. For the abolition of the residence permit

The problems related to present migration flows must and can be solved only if they are seen in the frame of mobility as a right. We need to change our approach: from migration as suffering to mobility as a right. No human being has chosen, or chooses where to be born; everyone must have recognized the right to choose where to live, live better and without dying.

The migration process is often an emergency, a dramatic emergency. But it is just the tip of the iceberg of the ineluctable ordinary displacement of millions of human beings; this phenomenon is related to globalization and to long run economic and political crises.

Coming out from the emergency, from the many emergencies, is a must. I am human

We must avoid making emergencies chronic, this is due to a structural feature: the inability to prevent millions of human beings from moving.

Then, the solution to emergencies – present all over the world and not in the Mediterranean alone – can not be separated from the vision where the recognition of the migrant as a person is the core. I am human.

Therefore, mobility must be recognized as an inalienable human right.

Everything else, including the concept of 'security,' too many times and improperly invoked, must be coherent with this approach.

Similarly each legislative, administrative, organizational and behavioral solution cannot avoid assuming we must recognize the human right to mobility to all people.

This set up has inspired the Palermo conference entitled 'IO SONO PERSONA' (I AM HUMAN). Next to the title of the Conference of Palermo there is a fingerprint: a reminder that every need, starting with safety, must be respectful of the migrant – a human being – and of mobility as a right.

Abolishing the residence permit is not a provocation, not an unrealistic slogan. It claims a choice and a value, which requires eliminating regulatory emergency and inhuman apparatuses. History is full of emergency norms inhibiting the value of safety and the respect for human beings. History is full of inhumane laws.

It's enough mentioning the death penalty, which still persists in many countries that claim to be civilized and democratic, and slavery, as provided by laws that allowed – just as example – the great Voltaire to get rich by buying and selling human beings.

An important role should and can be carried out by the European Union that can fulfill its vision making it reality and everyday life.

The European Union – too often we underestimate or distort its meaning due to an accounting, speculative and financial logic – is an extraordinary example of the will of coexistence and cohesion since it is a 'union of minorities'. In Europe no one is a majority due to reasons of identity: not the Germans or the Muslims, not the Jews nor the French. No identity is a majority. In Europe, slavery and the death penalty have been accordingly and coherently rejected.

It is time that the European Union abolishes the residence permit for all those who migrate, reaffirming the freedom of movement of people, as well as of capital and goods, in the globalized world. A strong solicitation on a global scale, not just within the Schengen area, must be sent out from Europe to recognize the mobility of all human beings as a right.

Obviously, all this would imply adequacy, method and time. It is equally clear that there's the need to act right now 'as if' mobility already were an inalienable human right.

This means, in practice and in daily life, implementing standards and organizational models radically different from the ones used today thus avoiding to consider the migrant a danger thus resigning to see migration as suffering and excusing it in name of safety, racism, selfishness, torture and colonialism as is done today, in the third millennium, according to an emergency logic.

Migration can no longer be considered as a border, cultural, religious and identity problem – a problem of social policy and access to the labor market. The emergency logic and the policies that have lasted for decades, must be left behind. Human mobility is a structural factor in our society and not a safety issue. Human mobility should be liberalized and appreciated as a resource and a value and not as an additional burden for the destination countries. In our country, it's matter of enforcing Articles 2 and 3 of the Constitution in a practical way, making the fundamental rights of the person effective and, at the same time, removing the obstacles that prevent their full realization.

It has to be noticed an increasing number of people asking international or humanitarian protection and the considerable mobility of those already living in the different countries of the Schengen area, in particular in Italy, where many migrants live with the hope of moving to those states where is still possible to find better employment opportunities and a satisfactory welfare level.

In time of crisis, the prejudice that 'foreigners' worsen the problems faced by the less affluent classes of a population spreads. Yet immigrants have not certainly chosen where to be born and often have not moved to improve their position; they only defend their right to life. In this instance, the art. 10 of the Constitution recognizing the right of asylum to all those who are forced to flee from countries where their fundamental rights are not guaranteed must be fully implemented.

Faced with defensive reactions that increasingly characterize our society, our institutional bodies must react by applying policies and practices that foster mutual understanding, equal treatment & democratic participation. These are the factors that can ensure greater safety.

The migrants' effective access to the human fundamental rights, starting with the right to residence and movement, seems an unavoidable aim to be pursued with multilevel interventions, not only at European and national levels, but also with the contribution of local authorities and non-governmental organizations thus ensuring a peaceful coexistence and the appreciation of cultural differences as a resource.

Therefore, the long-term focus is moving from migration seen as suffering to mobility seen as a human right. Current international policies hypocritically guarantee the right to emigrate but not the corresponding right to access through a specific duty to reception by the states.

We need to build a new civil society on everyday behavior and not on ideological advocacy or simple assimilation processes. The exclusionary logic of the residence permit must be overcome; this logic reduces people's existence to a mere survival conditioned by the periodic and discretionary release of a document.

This mechanism is often trapped in a bureaucratic process of unpredictable duration, during which the migrants, even if present for years in the country, are at risk of falling back into conditions of insecurity and marginalization.

Growing out the residence permit means considering migrants as people, as human beings, regardless of the document that establishes their status, it also means not seeing them as 'social burdens' or 'resource consumers': whether they be jobs, social assistance or housing, but it means seeing them as active citizens able to develop value for the community and for the place where they live.

In perspective, abolishing the residence permit is crucial to build a new citizenship based on sharing and mutual respect, on implementing policies of empowerment, autonomy, on setting up entry channels that do not allow the arrival of people tried and offended by violence suffered at the borders and in long journeys organized by criminal organizations that allow them to avoid border procedures.

The borders. The right to life. The right to asylum

The analyses and proposals here reported are addressed to Europe, and to the individual states that make it up, are a benchmark that can and should be applied to mobility on a global scale.

In today's global mobility environment, those who are forced to leave are, in the majority of cases, victims of wars, internal conflicts and violence. People are fleeing the same horrors that today feed fears throughout the world. They are refugees, asylum seekers, who have the right to be protected – not only in Europe.

Faced with this objective reality, the recent proclamations of the European Union can not be accepted: it asks to open up channels of legal entry just to 'qualified talents' and, at the same time to outsource asylum, making partnerships with same regimes from which people are fleeing.

It is necessary to clarify the processes of Rabat and Khartoum now underway.

The proposal to outsource the right to asylum to transit countries and create camps in Africa is not respectful of the right to asylum as ratified in international conventions and the European legislation.

The effective access to the right of asylum is the absolute priority, by opening routes where arrival is safeguarded, thus allowing people to safely reach the European territory where to request international protection.

The European Union has to reconsider its policy on visas by opening legal entry channels for work – at a time of crisis in which many migrants are moving towards other areas of the world, and on asylum (international protection) to counteract the action of outlaws, that today, especially for those who are forced to migration, represents the main entry channel.

The European legislation should be substantially modified

There is the need to change FRONTEX and the Dublin Regulation as well as to ensure a European lifesaving mission, such as the mission 'Mare Nostrum', which unfortunately remained only an Italian initiative.

There should be a mutual recognition of the decisions establishing the right to international protection by eliminating the procedure requirements in the country of first landing.

The right to freedom of movement of refugees in Europe must be guaranteed through an acceleration and a simplification of the procedures. All those who are readmitted in Italy from other European countries, due to the application of the Dublin Regulation, are to be faster assisted through special social and legal measures and psychological support which ensure future opportunities for mobility, the right to appeal and the right to family reunification.

The right to protection and the right to hospitality

The situation of the Italian hospitality system is already very critical. If hospitality and integration processes (e.g. language learning, psychological recovery, orientation and willingness to work) are not guaranteed, the protection system is likely to reproduce favor-seeking behaviour and become a factory of marginalization that will impinge on all of us. Both situations are deleterious not only to immigrants but to the entire community. Investing on integration and the ability of people: regardless of their status is correct because it enhances the dignity of the person and is also profitable. Furthermore, the spaces of centers SPRAR (National Service of Protection for Asylum Seekers and Refugees) are to be incremented and decent standards for the other emergency and first reception centers and for the CARA are to be guaranteed avoiding opaque management, and concentrations of people in places that defy possibility of control.

The different types of reception centers now existing in the territory should be monitored. In particular, there's the need to check the suitability between the staffing and the skills required by the standard agreements signed by the managing bodies.

In particular, transferring modes between the different centers that interrupt integration processes and lengthen the bureaucratic process of issuing a final status of stay are to be avoided.

The right to political participation and cultural contamination

Territorial immigration councils are to be activated again and opportunities for periodic comparison has to be established with foreign central police headquarters in order to speed up procedures through the cooperation of associations, municipal offices and professionals.

There is the need to return functionality to the existing bodies by increasing channels of participation. In this sense we intend to enhance and make available the experience of the Council of the Cultures of the City of Palermo -an example of the political commitment of the community and a place of exchange and intercultural contamination.

The Council of the Cultures of the City of Palermo is the practical application of a model where citizenship rights are related only to residence.

Work. The right to dignity

Over the last two decades, the production of 'irregular' migrants has gradually taken hold as the backbone of our social system since the irregularities-amnesties cycle has become the pivot point of policies of political legitimacy and of the labor market.

Concerning the former, immigrants' repression is turned into one of the major political arenas where electors' votes are contended; on the latter, the condition of illegality of migrants encourages their poorly remunerated exploitation thus allowing the permanence of businesses that otherwise could not afford to pay their workers regularly, but also meets the basic needs of Italian families since the welfare state can not adequately provide for their needs.

At the same time, a kind of creeping economic racism has spread and, starting with seeing migrants as 'resources' needed to the production system of goods and services as well as people excluded from the welfare and social security circuits, has imperceptibly led to create a social inclusion model of neo-slavery.

Breaking the link between residence permit and employment contract -in view of the elimination of the residence permit, is a necessary step among others towards a full realization of the objectives.

Forms of regular entry and actual possibilities of permanent regularization have to be established in the presence of certain and objectively confirmable requirements.

The instrument of hypocritical periodic regularization that emerged through the annual flow decrees – now suspended, should be replaced with the possibility of a permanent regularization for those who mature the requirements of stability and inclusion in Italy.

The provision on the loss of a residence permit due to the loss of work should be eliminated. It is an unjustified attribution of power to employers, who become arbiters of the fate and often of the life of human beings, feeding even more the widespread illegal market characteristic of exasperated prohibitionism.

The integration agreement that in the present praxis risks to become a differentiating selection tool should also be abolished.

All the recognition and residence permit renewal practices should be checked at the territorial level.

There should be an independent observatory on integration policies, at the regional level and, in perspective, at the national level to prevent social exclusion, detect and disseminate good practices, provide support to local governments and counter racism and discrimination.

The house. The right to housing and the enrollment registry

In Italy, the entry in the registry lists of the resident population in a municipality pertains to the constitutional right to move and live freely within the national territory (Const. art. 16) which is an essential requirement to exercise other fundamental rights. It is a precondition for any process of integration of foreigners, including the beneficiaries of international protection and asylum seekers.

All the registration procedures including the asylum seekers and refugees – guests in reception centers should be simplified. Inclusion and assistance policies ensure decent housing solutions to immigrants as to other disadvantaged groups of the native population. The housing right should be granted to people as members of a single community of persons permanently living in a given territory and should not become reason for umpteen social conflicts or other 'wars among the poor.' Processes of self improvement with the direct involvement of immigrants, also though the cooperative management of public spaces in disuse, even with the recourse to the use of confiscated property should be enhanced; the aforementioned should be addressed not only to migrants but also to the entire resident community, by also ensuring work spaces and areas for the communication to associations.

Health. Public and individual indivisible goods

Every person in need should be guaranteed, under conditions of equality between immigrants and natives; the right to free health care; simplified procedures should be established for the enrollment to the National Health Service. The effective implementation of the principles contemplated in Const. Art. 32 must be safeguarded since they do not distinguish between immigrants and citizens, instead they concern all the people anyway present on the national territory. 'The Republic protects health as a fundamental right of the individual and as a collective interest, and guarantees free medical care to the indigent.'

Special attention should be paid to people who lose the right to enroll in the municipality registry and therefore the right of access social benefits, among them there is also a growing number of Italian citizens. All the rules and practices denying the full enjoyment of the right to health to EU citizens present in Italy must be removed.

Victims of torture and inhuman or degrading treatment. Invisible wounds

Torture and inhuman and degrading treatment take place daily and are an affront to human dignity. A growing number of victims are confused and are hiding in our midst, hoping to build a new life, a new dignity, a new story not marked by violence and lack of freedom.

In this respect, A key tool is to recognize the refugee status to all those individuals who are entitled, who, in the state of origin, risk physical and mental integrity for their political and/or religious choices, for their sexual orientation or ethnic belonging. Starting from the first reception, specific and timely treatment has to be provided for the numerous foreign children arriving in Italy and bearing the physical and psychological signs of torture or other inhuman or degrading actions where promiscuity with adults should be avoided to the applicants due to other possible violence.

Every path leading to assigning a guardian and confirming residence documents even after the age of eighteen have to be eased, also when the case foresees the recognition of an international protection or humanitarian status.

In Italy, the asylum right to victims of torture is recognized almost exclusively to those who present a medical certificate. The applicant must produce 'justified' traumatic evidences showing the possibility of having experienced violence. There is the need of a broader concept of torture that takes into account the serious violence increasingly inflicted to migrants, women in particular, during their journeys in transit countries.

However, taking care of these particular patients can not be a problem of the individual worker or professional, often working in conditions of invisibility and loneliness, but it is a larger problem, which directly involves and concerns the institutions. Services should be provided for the immediate detection of victims of torture and inhuman or degrading treatment. It is necessary to activate a specialized structure that can deal with the after-effects of trauma suffered during the trip, both from a physical and a psychic point of view. Acknowledgment and support must be given to the work done over the years by competent, multidisciplinary teams who have specialized and synergistically acted and act in this field with the aim of 'healing from torture.'

The unaccompanied foreign minors. The right to future

The Italian system for the reception of unaccompanied foreign minors sees the main problems not from the regulatory framework, rather from its praxes. Situations such as those that are periodically recorded in the CPSA (reception center) of Lampedusa and other Sicilian ports, or in hosting communities, are in clear violation with international and national standards for the protection of childhood and adolescence.

Besides being damaging to the dignity of the children involved, the risk is that the mentioned minors move away from the structures where they are accommodated, thus they may be exposed to danger. Delays in appointing guardians or transferring them to adequate shelters slow down the onset of paths for social integration of the children and adolescents.

The minors' interests should prevail in every procedure concerning unaccompanied minors. This principle should guide any worker committed in the different sectors of the care, assistance and acceptance of these vulnerable people. Since this principle, to be fully realized, requires that the individual with all its peculiarities, with its individual history and its most urgent needs be considered the most important element and the final target of any endeavour. As the Italian Constitutional Court and the European Court of Human Rights have consistently reiterated, children and adolescents are primarily foreign minors and, as such, should benefit from enhanced protection that could offer them shelter from the vulnerability they face.

Guardians assignment needs to be faster ensured, thus activating processes of training and monitoring, and the procedures for the renewal of residence permits should be simplified for minors of an age that's less than eighteen.

Requiring passports issued by the country of origin shouldn't hinder the integration paths taken by children after their arrival in Italy.

A substantial change is needed on migration in the national and regional legislation. The drafting of an organic regional law on immigration can no longer be postponed. Sicily is the only Italian region that is still lacking one. Also a constant commitment is needed towards those practices applied at the administrative level that restore effectiveness to the rights and duties and that are upheld more often than not, only on paper. A particular attention has to be given to the conditions of the most vulnerable, such as asylum seekers and refugees, unaccompanied minors and victims of illegal trades.

A new law on citizenship. Citizenship rights. Paths to citizenship

Citizenship rights can be understood as the right to legal residence, protection against unlawful processes of expulsion and administrative detention, access to the labor market, access to public services, the right to live together in a family group, access to education and vocational training, the right to security and social security, freedom of assembly and association, the right to participate to the political life, the right to participate to European elections and to use the organs of Justice, the right to mobility within the country and within the different EU countries.

There is no need to disturb universal declarations or actions of other countries to carry out a radical reform of the citizenship law, always postponed for decades by the Italian Parliament. The archaic reference to jus *ius sanguinis* has to be abandoned; recognition of a fast acquisition of the right to citizenship to the 'second generations' has to be facilitated without obstructing in any way the paths to citizenship due to the so-called naturalization process and transparency, promptness and legality has to be promoted in recognising citizenship through marriage.

Time and red tape that hinder the recognition of Italian citizenship has to be reduced without leaving it to the discretion and/or the sensitivity of the local administrations. Time and cumbersome procedures should be shortened by avoiding constant transference from one office to another.

Ensuring the automatic acquisition of citizenship to those born in Italy and allowing residents the possibility to acquire citizenship and rights at the national and/or European level has become an urgent necessity.

In perspective of a full implementation of the principle of non-discrimination, the possibility of achieving Italian citizenship should be enhanced, by overcoming regulations and administrative practices that lengthen the times and make formal recognition very difficult.

PALERMO 13–15 March 2015
Cantieri Culturali alla Zisa
IO SONO PERSONA (I AM HUMAN)

'Dalla Migrazione come sofferenza alla mobilità come diritto.'
(From migration as suffering to mobility as right)

Translated by The British Institutes of Palermo

SUBJECT INDEX

acculturation 2, 86
Africa, 4, 10, 36, 45, 48n, 52, 88–90, 102–3, 115, 151n, 194
    Horn of 185–6
    North/Northern 2, 88, 185
Aegean Sea 59, 68
aesthetic(s) 3, 42, 51, 54, 87, 114, 121, 135
Albania 108
Algeria 11, 123, 180, 185
alienation 27–8, 54
alterity 44, 51
anthropological change 24, 83, 93
anthropological destruction 16
anthropological mutation 83, 94
apeiron 69, 76, 114
Arabic 48, 123, 180–1
    classical 180
    countries 114
    language 180–3
Arabization 180–1
archaic 86, 90–3, 155, 184, 200
    cultures 4, 10, 12, 47
    myth 4
    values 7
    worlds 14, 81, 90
architect(s) 67, 74–5
architecture(s) 21, 31, 63, 66, 68–71, 74–5, 77, 151, 155–6
Atlantic Ocean 114–15
Asia 4, 185

Balkans 99, 108, 117n, 151n, 159
Baroque 30, 156n
beauty 8, 84, 103, 160
becoming(s) (the) 3, 43, 62, 76–7, 136
Berlin Wall 4
biotic community 3

borders 4, 55, 93, 98, 108, 186–8, 194
bourgeois 82–3, 85, 87, 91–2, 94, 116n, 140
bureaucratization of life 18
Byzantine(s) 75, 131, 157, 162, 184

capitalist 115–16, 190
    entropy 85–6
    imaginary 16
    revolution 88
    society 11
care 46, 101, 197–9
Caribbean(s) 14, 35n, 107, 116, 118n
catastrophe 9, 18, 22, 27–9
Charter of Palermo 183, 186–91
Christianity 112–14, 159
cinema 83, 92, 106–7, 189
    cinematographic works xii, 82, 86, 89
city, cities 2, 3, 17, 21–31, 48n, 53, 59, 60, 78, 92, 104, 113n, 125, 130, 132, 134–5, 137, 141, 145–6, 153–4, 156–7, 159, 160, 164, 183–5, 188–9
    Arab-Muslim 2, 163–4, 167
    Italian 131–2, 143
citizenship xv, 5–6, 188–9, 191, 194, 196, 200
civilization(s) 5, 18, 41, 47–9, 85–8, 91, 112–14, 116n, 117, 121n, 131–2, 151, 153, 155, 157–9, 161, 183
classical world 94, 162
coasts 1, 2, 4, 13, 98–100, 102, 104, 113–14, 125–7
collective memory 46, 49–50
colonial 35–42, 51–2, 55, 90, 108, 115, 116n, 185

SUBJECT INDEX

colonialism 12, 35, 38, 43–5, 52, 55, 88, 115, 192
colonization 36–40, 87, 98, 114, 116, 121, 159
common goods 17
complexity 2, 48–9, 55–6, 112n, 117, 139, 152, 179
conflicts 1, 54, 97–8, 112n, 134n, 184, 194, 197
cosmopolitanism 154, 157–8, 167
culture(s) xiii, 1, 3, 5–6, 10, 12, 14, 36–41, 47–9, 51, 52n, 53n, 54–6, 82–8, 91–4, 98–9, 105, 107, 112, 114–23, 127, 130–7, 141–5, 150, 162–3, 169, 180–1, 189, 196
cultural
    differences 47, 88, 3n 122n, 193
    diversity 5, 45, 54, 83, 101
    models 3, 12
    mutation 85–6, 90, 93–4
    offensive 17
    particularism 3, 43–4
    worlds 3, 5, 7, 12, 14, 81–2
Creole(s) 41, 43, 46–7, 49–50, 53–6, 105, 107, 116
    literature 53, 106
Creolization 14, 35, 43, 48, 50, 54, 105–7, 122
Creoleness 35, 43, 47–8, 54, 56
crisis xiv, 4, 26, 43, 71, 91, 116, 175, 183, 185, 193–4
Cyprus 99

decolonization 36, 38, 42, 107–8, 184
    decolonized 5, 17, 117, 123
degrowth 10, 17
democracy 89–90, 177, 181, 190
depersonalization 27
development 2, 9, 11–12, 12, 24, 49, 82, 88, 100–1, 112–13, 140, 154, 156n, 160, 168, 181, 189
dignity 41–2, 109, 188, 195–6, 198–9
disenchantment of the world 9, 12, 23, 27
disorder 2, 10, 132, 165–7
dispersion 149n, 150, 169

divergence 150, 160, 165–8
diversity 3, 15, 35, 41, 47, 54–5, 74, 97, 121, 129
dwelling(s) 6, 60–3, 65–6, 68, 70, 72–5, 92, 124, 151, 161

earth xiii–iv, 3, 5, 7, 10–3, 52, 59–62, 67–78, 85, 92–4, 104
East (the) 71, 99, 114, 158, 161–2, 185
ecology xii–iv, 5n, 16, 18
    of creation 7, 12
ecological
    crisis 4, 5
    thought 16
ecosystems xv, 3
Egypt 8, 159, 185
elsewhere 31, 41, 59, 77, 88, 105, 117, 121, 124–5, 145
emergency, emergencies 16, 183, 186, 188n, 191–3, 195
emptiness 66, 70, 75
environment 3, 9, 16–7, 38, 62, 65–6, 71, 74, 93, 157, 194
ethic(s) 65, 84, 135, 149n, 186
    global ethics xv, 6
Eurocentrism, Eurocentric 35, 38, 50, 112–16, 121n, 123, 162–3
European Civic Forum 186
Europe 2–5, 10, 12, 18–19, 37, 44, 98–9, 102–3, 106, 108–9, 113, 115–17, 129, 131, 133, 138, 141, 143, 153, 159, 161, 163–4, 169, 181, 183, 185–8, 192–5, 200
European Union 183, 187, 192, 194
European identity 112–3, 122
exchanges 1–2, 55, 60, 62, 87, 98, 112, 117, 126, 136, 143
experience 3, 9, 61, 68, 70, 75, 77, 82–3, 87, 101, 103, 105, 115, 119, 120–2, 125–6, 132, 140
exploitation 12, 98, 196
    of natural resources 8, 10

Fascism 29n, 135–7, 139, 141
feeling(s) 27, 29, 42, 60, 76–7, 84, 86, 90, 100, 102, 120–1, 132, 145, 158

SUBJECT INDEX

film(s) 10–1, 73, 83, 86, 88, 90–3, 95, 106, 137
First World War 21, 27, 42, 130n
fragility 5, 14
France xiii, 7, 10, 64, 66, 106, 153
frontier 41, 99, 93, 104, 11–14, 117–18, 120–2, 127, 133, 136, 141
futurists 21, 24–7, 29, 31–2

geopolitics, geopolitical 1, 4, 5, 14, 36, 112, 114, 117, 159n
Germany 28n, 106
ghettoization 85, 107
globalization 4, 13, 51, 83, 112n, 191
globalized semiotic matrix 87
Greece 10, 23, 30, 62, 88, 90–1, 100, 105, 156, 159–60, 188
Greek
  democracy 89
  hero, heroes 8, 11
  myth, mythology 89, 91, 94
  thought 8
  tragedy 89–90
Greeks (the) 7–8, 62, 112, 131, 159n, 184

Hagia, Sophia 75
heterotopia 70
cultural history 38, 44, 55
homogenization 18
hospitality 2, 5, 61–2, 195
hubris 8, 18
human right(s) 5, 186, 191–3, 199
humanism 65, 140, 186, 190
  anti-humanism 3
hybridization 161

identity, identities xiv, 2–3, 18, 31, 35, 39–40, 42–3, 47–50, 54–6, 67, 70, 72, 78, 99, 102, 112–24, 127, 134, 137, 144, 155, 161, 180, 183, 189, 192
  cultural 14, 40, 43
ideology 39, 72, 89, 162
  nation-centred 50
imaginary 5, 16, 49, 54, 78, 98, 120, 152

imagination 3, 9, 10, 17, 41–2, 76, 81, 112, 120–1, 130, 149n, 161, 169
immanence 68–70
  immanent freedom 68
  immanent relationship 3, 70
imperialism 36n, 55
  Western 50
in-between (the) 72–3, 122
India 10, 14, 37, 84, 87–9, 115
inhabiting (ways of) xiii, 3, 5, 23, 59–79
inner vision 5
interculturality 112, 116, 119n, 122
Iraq 185–6
Iran 74–5
Islam 113, 159, 162–5
Italian (language) 14, 37, 40n, 45, 53, 56, 108, 123, 127
Italians (the) 13, 41, 51n, 83, 157
Italian
  culture(s) xv, 6, 82, 88, 134
  migration poetry 111–28
  society 14, 83, 87–8
  writers 4, 11, 91, 103
Italy 10, 13–14, 16, 29n, 36, 37n, 38, 41, 51n, 53n, 55, 59, 81, 84, 86, 92, 102–3, 105, 121, 123–4, 130n, 131n, 133, 135, 141, 146, 156, 160, 184–5, 193, 195–200
  Southern, south of 10, 13, 88, 102, 141
interbreeding 4, 107, 121n, 122, 167

Japan 70, 115
Jasmine Revolution 175n, 181n
Judaism 113
justice xv, 8, 69, 90, 112, 200

koinè 119

landscape 22–3, 49, 66, 68–70, 73–6, 81, 86–7, 92–3, 104, 117n, 125, 131, 141n, 160, 168
language(s) 3–4, 14, 39, 43, 45, 48–9, 51n, 52n, 53, 56, 82–3, 97–8, 101, 105, 107–8, 117–18,

SUBJECT INDEX

120–3, 127, 138–9, 142, 158, 179–81, 195
Latin America 16, 114, 166n
Lebanon 99, 117n
limen 112
limit 5, 8, 17, 67, 111, 113n, 118, 120, 141, 156
literature 5n, 7, 13–4, 22, 35–9, 44–7, 50n, 53, 55–6, 100–2, 104–9, 112, 114, 119–20, 121n, 127, 130, 132–4, 140–4, 146, 150, 163, 189
living beings 9, 10, 12, 17–18
Libya 8, 36, 180

Maghreb 99, 108, 151n, 180, 184
Malta 179
marginality 39, 44
mare nostrum xiii, 1–2, 11, 2–33, 118–9
Mediterranean
  area xiv, 2, 21, 107, 186, 189
  authors 3, 5, 11
  basin 18, 60, 75, 88, 98, 100, 103, 112–13, 127, 184, 189
  city(ies) 1, 2, 154, 156, 160
  coast(s) 68, 102, 113, 117, 123, 125–6
  countries 84, 183, 187
  culture(s) xiii, 8, 11, 88, 116–17, 127, 169
  Eastern 2, 114, 123
  Northern 166n
  region(s) 17, 155–6
  Sea v, xiii, 93, 112, 115, 183
  Southern xiii, 1, 113, 123, 162
  spaces 3, 91, 111–23, 127
  town(s) 149–173
  utopia 6, 10
melting pot (the) 2, 112, 121, 131, 159, 167
metropolis(es) 25, 27–8, 166n, 185
Mezzogiorno 37, 131
Middle Ages 2, 27, 131
Middle East 2, 88–9, 91, 103, 159, 186
migrant(s) xiv, 2, 4, 60, 100, 105–9, 186, 188, 193–4, 196–7
  author-migrants 100, 106

immigrant(s) 15, 99, 104, 185, 189–90, 193, 196–7
migration xiii–iv, 2, 4–5, 36, 98–9, 101, 105–6, 108–9, 119, 121–3, 127, 156, 164, 168, 184, 186–7, 191–201
migratory flow 36, 98, 102, 183
migratory phenomenon 100, 102, 105
milieu (geog.) 65, 69, 72–5
minorities 2, 38, 50, 187, 192
modern age 27, 31, 114–15
modernity 7, 21–3, 25, 27–8, 82, 90, 129, 131, 144–5, 168
Morocco 92, 180
monolingualism 45
multiplicity (the) 71, 73, 169
myth(s) 3–4, 11, 18, 27, 30, 62, 72, 81, 89–90, 92, 94, 114, 133, 138, 140, 141n, 149n, 157–8

Neapolitan
  authors, writers 103, 142, 147
  culture 130, 132–3, 142, 144, 145
  intellectuals 129, 133, 137, 143
  literature 133, 146
Naples 3, 12, 91, 129–148, 156–7, 166, 168n
napoletanità 129, 133–4, 137, 140–2
narrative xv, 3, 6, 37, 40n, 41–8, 50–1, 53, 56, 77, 105, 109, 120, 139, 141
native population 121, 197
négritude 43
neoliberal utopia 3, 6
new culture 83, 85–7, 91, 109
nineteenth century 21, 24, 37n, 40n, 50, 115, 131, 158, 159n, 163, 168n
North (the) 2, 10, 88, 98–9, 102, 131–2
nostalgia 22, 23n, 30, 102, 109, 118
Novecento 36, 41, 43, 45, 47
novel 38, 41–2, 45, 100, 134, 141–2

oikos 62
openness 2, 5, 44, 54, 73–4, 100, 114, 129, 141
orality 39, 46, 49, 50, 125
  oral tradition 45, 54

orientalism 150, 161–2
otherness 3, 25, 82–3, 87, 117, 120, 122n, 124, 163

painter(s) 23–4, 29, 75–6, 86
Palermo xiv, 4, 183–90, 191–201
Palestine 98–9
paradigm 38, 67, 149–50, 152, 154, 161–4, 167–9, 183
participation 16, 86, 106, 89, 193, 196
perceptions 21, 43, 55, 60, 70, 84, 91, 93–4, 156
periphery 21, 37, 55, 114, 116, 122, 185–6
piemontizzazione 37, 40, 51
Phoenicians 49n, 157, 159n, 184
plurality of world 2, 5, 6, 15
poetic(s) 4, 39, 40n, 107, 112n, 122, 124
poetry xiii, 3, 11, 24n, 77–8, 87, 101, 104, 111–27
postcolonial 35–57, 98
    critique 38, 112
    literatures 36, 55, 114
    studies 35, 37, 38, 45, 47, 168n
postcolonialism 35–57
postmodern (matrix) 150, 158, 167–8
progress 22, 24, 28, 66, 92, 100
Puglia 68, 102

recollection 61
re-enchantment (of the world) 14, 15, 17, 71
refugees 4, 100–1, 185–8, 194–5, 197, 200
Renaissance (the) 65, 86, 114, 156n
rhythm(s) 68, 72, 75, 78
    analysis 76
Risorgimento 41, 130
    post-Risorgimento 37, 40, 50
ritornello 72–3
Roman dialect 82–3
Roman(s) (ancient) 2, 112, 117n, 131, 156–7, 159, 162, 184
    Empire 112–14

sacred (the) 3, 5, 8, 11–13, 16, 85, 89–95, 180
Sardinia xiii, 2, 35–57
Sardinian culture 35–57
Sardismo 42–3
Sardness 35–57
Schengen zone, area 187, 192–3
secularization 12, 101
short story(ies) 15, 44–7
Sicily 84, 87, 117n, 184, 200
solidarity 5, 18, 142, 184
SOS Méditerranée (NGO) 2, 186
South (the) 2, 10, 37, 88, 98–9, 100–4, 109, 130, 132, 128, 146, 166–9, 183, 187–8
Southern thought 10, 99–100
Spain 10, 52n, 105, 114, 117n, 165, 184
standardization 3, 15, 18, 26, 66, 121, 156
subaltern 37, 39, 40
Sud (review) 129–148
Syria 8, 92, 123, 185–6

techno-science 9, 15, 18
territory, territories 2, 3, 37, 40, 60, 62, 68, 71–4, 76–8, 97, 99, 115, 160, 162, 179, 194–5, 197–8
    deterritorialization 71–3
    reterritorialization 72–3
Third-World 88, 89, 94, 165–9
tragedy (theat.) 8, 12, 18, 89–90, 92
transcendence 27, 63, 69, 91
    transcendental arithmetic 63, 65
Tunisia 74, 175–7, 179–81
Tunisian(s) 8, 45
    language 4, 179–180
twentieth century 5, 21–2, 51–5, 116, 131–2, 134, 153–6, 162, 168n

unitary figure 150, 158, 167
United States 13, 115
universalism 150, 152, 154, 157, 159–60, 168
universality (the) 39, 47, 89, 147, 161, 163
    universal values 154, 158
utilitarian rationality 6

values xiv, 2, 5, 7, 17–18, 22, 26, 38–9, 42, 60, 83–6, 90, 92, 119n, 133, 144, 150, 158, 162, 167
violence 3, 10, 12–13, 15, 26, 88, 91, 94, 116, 188, 194, 198

West (the) 17, 35, 70, 99, 115, 130, 158, 162
West Indian(s) 46, 48, 53n, 54–5, 119
Western world(s) 1, 10, 18, 117, 121n
westernization 12, 16
    dewesternizing the world 19

NAMES INDEX

Abate, Carmine 4, 105
Aeschylus 88–91
Albertazzi, Silvia 121n, 122n
Ali Farah, Ubax Cristina 125
Anaximander 68–9, 114
Andromache 25, 30
Angioni, Giulio 43, 47–8, 54–5
Aprile, Pino 10
Arendt, Hannah 9
Argentina, Cosimo 4
Argonauts 30
Arpaia, Bruno 130–1
Asor Rosa, Alberto 38
Atzeni, Sergio 43, 47–9, 50n, 54–55

Balla, Giacomo 21, 29
Barnabé, Jean 35, 41, 47, 54–5
Bataille, Georges 82, 86, 91–2
Baudelaire, Charles 21–2, 24–5, 27, 30, 137
Baudrillard, Jean 83–4, 86–7
Ben Jelloun, Tahar 108
Benasayag, Miguel 5
Benevolo, Leonardo 161
Berque, Augustin 60, 70
Berque, Jacques 2, 164
Boccioni, Umberto 21, 24–5, 29–31
Botte, Anselmo 4
Braudel, Fernand 117n, 155–6, 158–9
Butcovan, Mihai Mircea 123

Caillois, Roger 94
Calabria, Esmeralda 12
Callicott, John Baird 3
Camus, Albert 5, 7–9, 11, 14, 134, 141
Carrera, Alessandro 38–9
Carravetta, Peter xiv, 14
Castoriadis, Cornelius 5, 13, 16–18

Cassano, Franco 5, 10, 18, 99–101, 113n, 118
Céline, Louis-Ferdinand 22
Césaire, Aimé 39, 116
Cézanne, Paul 75–6
Chamoiseau, Patrick 35, 41, 47–8, 50, 53n, 54–5
Clementi, Alberto 151, 170n
Compagnone, Luigi 134, 137, 141, 145
Confiant, Raphaël 35, 41, 47, 50, 54–55
Croce, Benedetto 130–5, 137, 140, 142, 144–5

D'Annunzio, Gabriele 132–3, 135
De Caldas Brito, Christiana 14–15
De Chirico, Giorgio 21, 23, 27, 30
De Luca, Erri 4, 103–4
De Martino, Ernesto 19, 37, 86
De Sanctis, Francesco 37, 131, 133
Deledda, Grazia 42, 44–8, 50, 54
Deleuze, Gilles 67, 71–3
Djebar, Assia 123
Dupuy, Jean-Pierre 5, 16

Eliade, Mircea 86, 93
Eliot, T. S. 21, 25–7, 141
Elytis, Odysseas 5, 77
Euripides 12, 93

Fanon, Frantz 116
Faulkner, William 134, 141
Flora, Francesco 139–40
Fois, Marcello 4, 43, 47, 50–5
Foucault, Michel 67, 73, 149–50, 152, 169
Fusillo, Massimo 90, 2–3

NAMES INDEX

Gandhi 116
Gassman, Vittorio 88–9
Gentile, Giovanni 131
Ghazvinizadeh, Nader 124–5
Ghirelli, Antonio 134–5, 137, 141, 142n, 144
Glissant, Édouard 14, 35, 38, 43, 46, 48, 49n, 50, 53n, 54, 107, 112, 116–17
Gnisci, Armando 5, 36–7, 55–6, 105–8, 113, 115, 118n, 120
Guattari, Félix 67, 72

Hajdari, Gëzim 124
Haenel, Yannick 77
Heidegger, Martin 24n, 67, 71, 77
Hemingway, Ernest 134, 141
Hölderlin 24n, 77

Illich, Ivan 10, 17
Invitto, Gianni 139–40
Iovino, Serenella 5

Jason 12, 92–3
Joyce, James 28, 134, 137, 141

Kafka, Franz 14, 134, 141
Kandinsky 89

La Capria, Raffaele 130, 132–4, 137–8, 140–4, 146–7
Le Corbusier 63, 65–8
Lakhous, Amara 108
Laitef, Thea 126
Lampedusa, Tomasi di 37, 39
Lao Tseu 59
Latouche, Serge 9, 112, 17–18
Leogrande, Alessandro 4
Leopardi, Giacomo 26
Levinas, Emmanuel 61–2
Lévy-Bruhl, Lucien 86
Lipovetsky, Gilles 85
Lo Bianco, Giuseppe 13
Longhi, Roberto 30

Maldiney, Henri 75
Mandela, Nelson 116
Marinetti, Filippo Tommaso 21, 29, 32, 135

Martì, José 116
Marx, Karl 133, 137, 140
Mattei, Enrico 13
Matvejević, Predrag 98–9, 151
Medea 11–12, 92–3
Meddeb, Abdelwahab 45
Merchant, Carolyn 5, 9
Mies, Maria 10, 16
Montale, Eugenio 111
Morante, Elsa 84
Moravia, Alberto 84
Morin, Edgar 5
Moura, Jean-Marc 36, 38–9
Mumford, Lewis 151, 159n
Murgia, Michela 4

Neto, Agostinho 116
Nietzsche, Friedrich 22, 25, 77

Odysseus 77
Oedipus 92
Omodeo, Adolfo 131, 139
Orestes 88–90, 92
Orlando, Francesco 39
Orlando, Leoluca xiv, 4, 184–5
Ortese, Anna Maria 141, 147

Pasolini, Pier Paolo xiv, 3, 5, 11–14, 81–95, 105, 129, 144
Pavese, Cesare 11
Pirandello, Luigi 14, 37
Plato 65, 69, 114
Ponzanesi, Sonia 36–7, 56
Prunas, Pasquale 134, 137, 139–41, 143–4
Pythagoras 65

Rabhi, Pierre 5
Ravéreau, André 68
Reclus, Elisée 153–60
Rizza, Sandra 13

Said, Edward 38, 162
Sant'Elia, Antonio 21–2
Sartre, Jean-Paul 134, 137, 141
Saviano, Roberto 12–13
Sbarbaro, Camillo 21, 25–7

Sciascia, Leonardo 37
Scognamiglio, Gianni 134, 137, 139, 141–2, 145–6
Serao, Matilde 121–3, 134n, 142
Shiva, Vandana 5, 10, 16
Simmel, Georg 92
Sironi, Mario 21, 23–4
Sorre, Maximilien 154–5, 157
Spaventa, Bertrand 131, 133
Stelarc 31–2

Thich Nhat Hanh 5
Todorov, Tzvetan 121
Tortora, Giuseppe 137–8, 147
Traoré 17

Valéry, Paul 1, 5, 98, 100–1
Verga, Giovanni 37
Vinci, Leonardo da 65
Vidal de la Blache, Paul 153–4, 158
Vidal-Naquet, Pierre 89
Virilio, Paul 18, 28, 31–2, 71
Vitruvius 65

Wadia, Laila 14
Wakkas, Youssef 123
Walcott, Derek 116
Weil, Simone 118–19

Zola, Emile 13
Zweig, Stefan 29n

www.ingramcontent.com/pod-product-compliance
Lightning Source LLC
Chambersburg PA
CBHW062222300426
44115CB00012BA/2182